Free Black Charlestonians in Debate

Free Black Charlestonians in Debate

The Complete Proceedings of the Clionian Debating Society, 1847–1858

Edited by ANGELA G. RAY

THE UNIVERSITY OF SOUTH CAROLINA PRESS

© 2025 University of South Carolina

The text of this book is licensed under a Creative Commons Attribution Non-Commercial No Derivatives 4.0 International (CC BY-NC-ND 4.0) license: https://creativecommons.org/licenses/by-nc-nd/4.0/.

Published by the University of South Carolina Press
Columbia, South Carolina 29208

uscpress.com

Printed in the United States of America

Library of Congress Cataloging-in-Publication Data
can be found at http://catalog.loc.gov/.

ISBN: 978-1-64336-579-4 (hardcover)
ISBN: 978-1-64336-557-2 (paperback)
ISBN: 978-1-64336-580-0 (ebook)
DOI: https://doi.org/10.61162/USNB3055

The inclusion of this book in the Open Carolina collection is made possible by the generous funding of the Northwestern University Department of Communication Studies, Duke University Libraries, and the University of South Carolina Libraries.

CONTENTS

List of Illustrations	vii
Acknowledgments	ix
Introduction: Performing Freedom on Slavery's Hearth	xi
Note on Transcription	xli

Proceedings of the Clionian Debating Society,
November 5, 1847-January 14, 1858

1847	3
1848	10
1849	24
1850	46
1851	66
1852	85
1853	99
1854	116
1855	125
1856	129
1857	133
1858	135

Appendix A	Members, Honorary Members, and Supporters	139
Appendix B	Debating Questions and Decisions	141
Appendix C	Orations	147
Appendix D	Publications Acquired for Society Library	149
Further Reading		153
Index		157

LIST OF ILLUSTRATIONS

Figure 1. John W. Hill, *Charleston, S.C.,* ca. 1850   xv

Figure 2. Proceedings of the Clionian Debating Society,
    Charleston Library Society   4

Figure 3. Daniel Alexander Payne (1811–1893)   7

Figure 4. The Reverend Henry Cardozo (1830–1886)   27

Figure 5. Continued Proceedings of the Clionian Debating Society,
    Duke University Library   77

ACKNOWLEDGMENTS

This scholarly edition is indebted, first, to the members of the Clionian Debating Society, who valued language and committed themselves to fostering learning, a project that extends to us today. It is to honor them that all royalties from the sales of the printed book are directsed to the Avery Research Center for African American History and Culture at the College of Charleston.

Thanks are also due to the Charleston Library Society and Duke University Library, which preserve the original proceedings and are supporting this publication. Portions of the introduction first appeared in "A Green Oasis in the History of My Life: Race and the Culture of Debating in Antebellum Charleston, South Carolina," delivered as the B. Aubrey Fisher Memorial Lecture at the University of Utah's Department of Communication in 2014. The lecture was subsequently issued as a pamphlet, and Utah's Department of Communication graciously permitted the material to be reprinted here. The Department of Communication Studies at Northwestern University, my employer, has supported my research and subsidized the open-access publication.

In this work I have also benefited from the intellectual generosity of others, particularly Nicholas Alena, Bill Balthrop, Megan Bernard, Carole Blair, Stephanie Brehm, Rebekah Bryer, Jasmine Cobb, Marissa Croft, Lauren DeLaCruz, Ruth Martin Curry, Carolyn Eastman, Ashley Ferrell, Matthew Fulle, Emma Gleave, Harold Gulley, Joshua Gunn, Cate Herscher, Robin Jensen, E. Patrick Johnson, Frances Jones, Elisabeth Kinsley, Sarah Lingo, Eric Long, J. Jefferson Looney, Robert E. Mills, Zachary Mills, Miriam Petty, Bernard Powers Jr., Allison Prasch, Isabella Procassini, Janice Radway, Angela Ripp, Elena Rodina, Ashlie Sandoval, Kimberly Singletary, Bjørn Stillion Southard, Paul Stob, Catalina Uribe Rincón, Sara VanderHaagen, Damon L. Williams Jr., Kirt Wilson, Carly Woods, Tom Wright, David Zarefsky, Mary Saracino Zboray, Ronald J. Zboray, and Zhiqiu Zhou. The oases in the history of my life sustain me.

INTRODUCTION
Performing Freedom on Slavery's Hearth

On Wednesday, September 18, 1850, a group of young free Black men convened on Beaufain Street in Charleston, South Carolina, for a busy meeting of the Clionian Debating Society. In a session that included a lively debate on the philosophical question "Are afflictions in any manner beneficial to humanity?"—followed by the president's verdict in favor of the affirmative—members also installed a new officer, heard a committee report on a letter of thanks to a supporter, selected a debating topic for a future meeting, and performed regular routines such as calling the roll and reading the previous meeting's minutes. Further, and more unusually, the society heard and endorsed a lengthy statement of appreciation to its outgoing secretary and treasurer, Simeon W. Beaird, who had served in those roles for six terms. "His actions need no commentary," the statement read, since "they are indellibly written upon the minds of each and every one, . . . as familiar as the records of the Society." Identifying his talents as "good deportment," "business activity," "timely counsel in the most requisite hour," "untiring industry," and "cheerfulness" in his labors, Beaird's fellow members praised him fulsomely and voted unanimously to inscribe their statement "upon the Journals of the Society."[1]

This ordinary event came and went, but the inscription, remarkably, has survived, permitting us to elicit a fleeting glimpse of long-ago actions, to recover an impression of the values and ambitions of these young men, to imagine their lives and their hopes. The passage is especially notable for its layered metaphors of writing: Beaird's actions were "written" upon the minds of his fellows, as well known to them as the written records in which their statement itself, first rendered orally, was about to be inscribed. The book before you proffers a new impression of those records, commending the care of the Clionian secretaries in inscription and preservation. These young men endorsed and sought "respectability, social advancement, and moral uplift," participating in what historian John Garrison Marks recently described as "the mainstream of early

xi

xii *Introduction*

nineteenth-century free black thought."[2] This book offers a window into that world, as expressed and enacted by the society's members and supporters.

"The records of the Society" eventually ran to two handwritten volumes that today reside in institutional archives, the earlier volume in Charleston and the later in Durham, North Carolina. The story of their provenance reveals the dynamics of race, region, and learning. In 1919 the Charleston Library Society in Charleston, South Carolina—one of the oldest continuously operating social libraries in the United States—acquired a handwritten volume of meeting minutes from the bookshops of Augustus William Dellquest and Grace Gruber Dellquest in Augusta, Georgia. Dellquest's New and Old Book Shops advertised longevity, "expert bibliographic and literary knowledge," and "personal acquaintance with the European book markets" and sometimes highlighted strengths in "Rare Old Books Relating to Southern States, Slavery, Civil War, Etc." The bound manuscript sold to the Charleston Library Society records the activities of the Clionian Debating Society from its inception in November 1847 until September 1851, when society secretary Henry Cardozo filled the last page of the volume. A seller's card inside the front cover indicates that the volume—as a bound blank book—had come into the hands of the Clionians via the King Street shop of Charleston bookseller and stationer John Mayne Greer.[3]

In 1930 Duke University in Durham, North Carolina, bought a different handwritten volume of debating society minutes from Dellquest's Rare Book Shop in Los Angeles. Proprietor Augustus Wilfrid Dellquest had opened the store in the early 1920s after working with his parents in Augusta. The first page of this volume announces in bold handwriting: "Continued Proceedings of the Clionian Debating Society." It extends the story of the Charleston group from September 1851 until its formal dissolution in January 1858, owing, according to the minutes, to "present *political* disadvantages." Inside the front cover of this volume is a penciled notation added at Duke, "11/19/30 / Flowers Collection / Fr. / Dellquest's / $25.00 / Boyd," indicating the activity of historian and library director William Kenneth Boyd in amassing materials for the George Washington Flowers Collection of Southern Americana. The minute book was among the earlier items added to the voluminous collection, which was established to provide a basis for research into the history and literature of the US South. Reports of acquisitions in the 1930s boasted of personal papers of white men who were southern educational, literary, political, judicial, commercial, and military leaders; plantation records; Confederate letters and accounts; local newspapers and imprints; and also materials "relating to Africa and the Negro and anti-slavery agitation." By 1939 the Flowers Collection would comprise more than

Introduction xiii

four hundred thousand items, including books, pamphlets, manuscripts, maps, broadsides, and volumes of newspapers.[4]

How and when the two handwritten volumes of Clionian Debating Society minutes got into the hands of the Dellquests and how and why the volumes were separated remain a mystery, although I can speculate about how the volumes might have wound up in Augusta. Simeon Beaird—he of "untiring industry" and "cheerfulness"—lived in Augusta during and after the Civil War.[5] As the debating society's first president, an active member throughout the group's lifespan, and a member of the dissolution committee, Beaird may well have been the one to retain the two volumes of proceedings when the society dissolved. If so, it's likely he took them with him to Georgia. Beaird then moved to Aiken, South Carolina, in the 1870s. He might have sold some items before leaving Augusta, although not directly to the Dellquests, because they were not yet there; the elder A. W. Dellquest was born in Sweden only in 1867. Or might Beaird's heirs have deaccessioned some of his belongings after his death in 1894? Aiken and Augusta are not far apart. However the manuscripts landed at Dellquest's bookshops, one further clue links Beaird and the Duke library: the Flowers Collection includes at least one published book previously owned by Beaird, with his signature and the date 1862 written on the flyleaf.[6] Items from Beaird's collection of scribal as well as print text—illuminating southern history—may have moved into the commercial arena of the rare book trade and hence into two major archival repositories. Recovery of further evidence may someday tell a different story, but based on what we know now, this one is plausible. Furthermore, Beaird's own character traits as shown throughout the debating society minutes, not only his zeal but also his historical consciousness, make the supposition credible.

In late 1847 the young men of the Clionian Debating Society embarked on a journey of collective learning and mutual improvement, using an educational approach broadly common at the time. Yet their social and political circumstances make their journey—and the fact that we have available evidence of it— unusually compelling. These free Black men—called free persons of color or FPC, free mulattos, or free brown men in the chronicles of their time—were living at the heart of the American slaveocracy, where in less than fourteen years the long-standing controversies over slavery would erupt into open warfare.[7] Restricted by South Carolina law since 1834 from learning legally from a person of color and prevented by racist custom and prejudice from learning in the schools and colleges available to their white contemporaries, these young men participated in clandestine learning that was fostered by their elders in Charleston's free Black community.[8]

xiv *Introduction*

Evidence suggests that the racial identity of the group's membership was not apparent at the two repositories for decades and, more perniciously, that racism and segregation promoted this ignorance. In the segregationist era of the 1930s, the sociologist E. Horace Fitchett, a Black scholar, was barred from the Charleston Library Society while conducting research for a study that would become his University of Chicago doctoral dissertation, "The Free Negro in Charleston, South Carolina." A library representative wrote to him in 1939 saying that "by index, we have nothing on the subject you are engaged upon." Even in 1981, when the volume at the Charleston Library Society was reproduced on microfiche, the racial identity of its producers as free Black men was not recorded in microfiche registers—and was likely unknown. In 1990 historian Edmund L. Drago would attribute the omission to a failure to imagine that anyone other than white elites was involved in intellectual activities of this sort. By the 1990s, however, the Charleston minutes and the social and racial identity of their producers were recognized and studied by historians such as Drago, exploring education among Black Charlestonians, and Bernard E. Powers Jr., studying the complex social histories of Black Charlestonians from the 1820s to the 1880s. The minutes at Duke, as a production of free Black men in the port city, received a mention in Michael O'Brien's 2004 study of southern intellectual history, and my own investigations, sparked initially by curiosity about O'Brien's reference, began to consider the two volumes as a single account, as an exemplary record of ordinary debating practice in the pre–Civil War United States, and as a critical text in American, particularly Black American, intellectual, social, and political history.[9]

Thus the book before you—whether you are turning paper pages or scrolling a digital file—represents a reuniting of sorts. Bringing the contents of the two volumes back together again and rendering into type the handcrafted text, this edition publishes the comprehensive minutes of the Clionian Debating Society for the first time, inviting you as a reader into this story and increasing the opportunity, now and in the future, for greater understanding of the histories that its pages present, imply, and occlude. These histories are southern histories, they are American histories, they are transatlantic histories. They are about religion and politics, learning and sociability, curiosity and amity. They tell complex stories of Black America, of youth and age, of young men thinking and talking together and of the men and women who encouraged them. They are intimately tied to a place and an era, and yet they range across distance and temporality, in the breadth of the questions debated and in the historical continuities that

Figure 1. John W. Hill, *Charleston, S.C.*, engraved by Wellstood and Peters (New York, ca. 1850), in the Miriam and Ira D. Wallach Division of Art, Prints and Photographs: Print Collection, New York Public Library, New York, NY, reprinted by courtesy.

they imply for their own time and for ours. They showcase, I believe, a profound desire for an intellectual life, thus demonstrating a performance of freedom.

The minutes you are about to read will, I hope, spark your imagination, catalyze questions, help you to see new complexities, and invite your own work of interpretation and analysis. My task in the remainder of this introduction is to supply provisional contexts within which we can make meaning of them together. Then my charge will be to step aside as a scholarly commentator and take up the role of transcriber and editor, to let the young men of the Clionian Debating Society speak their own truths in their own words.

Debating as Education, Debating as Practice

In the middle of the nineteenth century, Americans debated, formally and informally, in legislative halls, in reformers' meetings, in streets and marketplaces, in mansions and hovels, in religious buildings and private homes. As sectional turmoil increased, the US Congress debated the Compromise of 1850, passing a series of measures including the Fugitive Slave Act, which New York writer and activist Harriet Jacobs would describe as "the beginning of a reign of terror."[10] Outside legislatures, ordinary Americans deliberated their past and their collective future. Sometimes these deliberations occurred in local cultural institutions

xvi   *Introduction*

created for the purpose of convening and discussing, for this was a heyday of debating societies in urban centers and rural communities alike. Debating society participants—often though not always white and male—practiced their skills in debate, public speaking, and parliamentary procedure in contexts of homosocial camaraderie, and thus they learned and enacted the forms of political, social, and cultural leadership.

Pre–Civil War Americans thus participated in a national culture that recognized the popular debating society as a familiar social form. Debating had been associated with teaching and learning in the West at least since the fifth century BCE, when the Greek Sophist Protagoras of Abdera taught his students to argue two sides of each question. Eighteenth-century American colonists, drawing on classical models and British precursors alike, established clubs like Benjamin Franklin's Junto for debating and other intellectual pastimes, and young white male collegians founded literary and debating societies. College societies constituted extracurricular activity of their day: they were run by students rather than faculty, were conducted in English rather than Latin, and addressed issues from abstract questions of morals to current politics. Harvard's Spy Club was holding "disputations" in the early 1720s, and college debating societies thrived from 1750 onward. By 1770 the College of New Jersey, later Princeton University, boasted two groups, the American Whig Society and the Cliosophic Society, with the latter name signaling "praise of wisdom." Southern colleges followed suit. For example, two societies were organized at the University of North Carolina in 1795, the year it began offering classes. Both before and after the Revolution, such groups promoted the literary achievements and the speaking and argumentative skills of their members, as well as the pleasures of fraternal interaction and genial competition.[11]

Popular, noncollegiate debating received a boost in the late 1820s, when the Yale-educated scientific lecturer Josiah Holbrook began promoting the establishment of local "associations of adults for mutual education," which he called lyceums.[12] Although Holbrook envisioned lyceums as societies for cooperative scientific study, the cultural connection of education with debate was strong, and thousands of groups called lyceums were debating clubs, from Massachusetts to California.[13] Free Black Americans, men and women, especially in urban centers such as Philadelphia and New York, established associations that promoted education and racial uplift; scholar-librarian Dorothy B. Porter pioneered the study of these groups, and Elizabeth McHenry's *Forgotten Readers* recovers a detailed history.[14] When in 1847 the young men of the Clionian Debating Society acknowledged Clio, the Greek Muse of history, in their name and stated their goals as "the promotion of their connection [to each other] and

Introduction   xvii

the improvement of their intellect," they rhetorically linked themselves with other intellectual aspirants across the nation.[15]

Free Persons of Color in Pre–Civil War Charleston

If the Clionians' educational goals were conventional, their social and political condition made their group distinctive—although, it turns out, not unique. Their minutes record two concurrent debating societies among Charleston's free persons of color: the Enterpean and the Utopian Debating Societies.[16] These references to the other groups are, at present, the only available evidence about them, and the names of their members are unknown. Conversely, the Clionian minutes name fifty-four discrete individuals (fifty-two men and two women) who were regular members, honorary members, or supporters (see appendix A), and they also refer broadly, without enumeration, to audiences for special occasions.[17] The society's secretaries characterize these audiences, formulaically, as "enlightened," "delighted," "large," or "respectable," with *respectable* meaning reasonably numerous but perhaps also signaling self-conscious behavioral standards. The members and honorary members were exclusively male, but women of the community supported the group by attending the special meetings and making occasional donations of money or books.[18] Among the named individuals who can be identified through public records, extant accounts of other voluntary associations, or scholarly investigations, a few were members of the free Black communities in other cities, including honorary member Daniel Alexander Payne of Baltimore, a native of Charleston who in 1852 would be elected as the sixth bishop of the African Methodist Episcopal Church. Some people named in the minutes left Charleston during the society's lifespan, relocating to northern US cities or to Canada. Most participants, however, were free persons of color residing in Charleston throughout the period. It is highly likely that the audiences for the Clionians' special events were drawn from this tight-knit community, which frequently intermarried and established a variety of social institutions, including cooperative economic enterprises, benevolence and burial societies, and clandestine schools.[19]

Historians have provided invaluable foundations for the study of Charleston's free Black community, from its heightened color consciousness and connections to influential white citizens to its religious, occupational, and wealth-holding characteristics.[20] Women far outnumbered men. Protestant Christianity was an important basis for moral action, and free persons of color were active in the city's Episcopalian and Methodist congregations.[21] Many were skilled workers, with women working as seamstresses and mantua makers and men as carpenters and tailors, shoemakers and barbers, butchers and xviii *Introduction*

masons.[22] Several Clionian members, including Henry Cardozo and William O. Weston, would become Methodist ministers and educators, as well as Reconstruction-era public officials; both men also toiled as tailors during their working lives.[23] (Note that the Clionian minutes identify two different individuals by the name Henry Cardozo.)[24] Some among Charleston's most prosperous free persons of color owned considerable property in real estate and also in human chattel. Those associated with the Clionians who held other people in bondage included several honorary members in the generation older than the regular members, such as wood factor Richard E. Dereef, carpenter Charles H. Holloway, shoemaker John Mishaw, and tailors Benjamin T. Huger, William McKinlay, and brothers Samuel and Jacob Weston.[25] Historians such as Larry Koger and Loren Schweninger have shown that both benevolence and commercial advantage motivated slaveholding among free persons of color in South Carolina. In the face of legal prohibitions on private manumission, free persons sometimes nominally owned relatives and friends. But free persons also bought and sold enslaved people in order to exploit their labor. For some free men and women of color, as historian Amrita Chakrabarti Myers notes, their sense of what their own freedom meant included enslaving others.[26]

An alternative, and concurrent, connotation of freedom was the possession and skillful deployment of knowledge. Despite legal proscriptions against school-keeping by Black teachers, free Black adults in Charleston operated a number of private schools for their children. Sometimes the covert teachers were men and women of the community, including, in the 1850s, Clionian member Simeon W. Beaird and a supporter of the group, Frances Pinckney Bonneau, whose father, Thomas S. Bonneau, had taught Daniel A. Payne. Sometimes, more in keeping with the letter of the law, members of the community employed young white college students as teachers, like the Mood brothers: John Amos, Francis Asbury, and William.[27] Members of the Clionian Debating Society were educated in private schools like these, where readings might include histories of classical Greece and Rome as well as the liberty-filled speeches of Caleb Bingham's *Columbian Orator*.[28]

Comparative prosperity, educational attainments, and even participation in the enslavement of other people did not insulate free persons of color from virulent racism. Between 1820 and 1861 Charleston's free Black population experienced increased constraints and oppression from white supremacists, including prohibitions on travel outside the state, prohibitions on learning, discrimination in churches, threats of violence, and, in the second half of the 1850s, repeated legal and legislative efforts at widespread enslavement of all Black people regardless of their legal status.[29] These were "*political* disadvantages" indeed.

Introduction xix

The decade during which the Clionian Debating Society flourished was thus a time of increasing fear, uncertainty, and upheaval. What could such a society have meant for its members? Marks notes that "voluntary associations among free people of color" in Charleston created opportunities "to maintain social links with individuals matching their racial and economic profile, to bolster social prestige, and to establish themselves as models of freedom in a society that by and large viewed African-descended people as suited only for slavery."[30] The debating society's minutes are consonant with this view; Clionian meetings created social support and also encouraged members to represent themselves as independent thinkers, performatively confounding white racial ideologies. Members of the society created a place for learning, camaraderie, and the performance of a commitment to public life, enacting self-respect and community involvement even as external threats mounted. The Clionian Debating Society thus exemplifies the organizational form that communication scholar Catherine R. Squires labels an enclave public, a "discursive institution" separate from dominant publics—often "deployed in response to conditions of intense oppression"—that can serve as "a source of history, pride, or community connections" and can generate "ideologies of self-determination."[31] To attempt to elucidate motivations, goals, and achievements of the Clionians, I now turn briefly to the features of their activities. Members of the group established governing protocols for membership and communal action, they organized and performed debates, they prepared and delivered speeches, they established a small library through donation and purchase, and—as evident in the two proceedings volumes—they created an archive of their own history.

Self-Governance

The impression that emerges from the Clionian minutes is a profound sense of orderliness, a deep investment in the rule of law, and a commitment to language—written and read—as the foundation for appropriate action. The group adopted and signed a constitution immediately upon establishing the society, and members frequently read the constitution aloud when initiating new members or installing new officers. Although they often changed the rules, they adhered carefully to them once they were in place. They also appealed to the rules to adjudicate conflicts. For instance, one unusual meeting in 1848 erupted in turmoil that briefly turned physical, when "Mr. Jacob Green . . . shoved Mr. [William] Gailliard against the mantle peice." The society managed this crisis by recurring to the letter of its constitution, a solution that required several discussions but apparently restored harmony.[32]

xx *Introduction*

The Clionians conducted society business through officers and committees, and there was great scope for individual participation. They elected new officers about every four months in their most active years, a standing Committee of Queries proposed questions for debate, and the members appointed ad hoc committees to compose correspondence. They even dissolved the society by committee; at the last minuted meeting, a committee of five was appointed to effect termination.[33] Conrad D. Ludeke was a member of the dissolution committee. During his involvement with the Clionians, he had enjoyed a range of participatory opportunities. Ludeke joined the society in 1852, when he was about seventeen. He helped to write a letter of thanks to a donor, chaired an administrative committee, served as the society's reporter and president pro tem, and participated in multiple debates.[34]

The level of involvement in the debating society for Ludeke and his fellows contrasted sharply with their external situation. Although possessing rights to hold property, free Black men like the Clionian members were considered denizens, not citizens, of South Carolina, as historian Marina Wikramanayake has shown.[35] They thus lacked political rights, and so, for example, they could not aspire to vote in elections even when they reached the age of twenty-one. Within the debating society, however, they voted on everything: on the admission of new members, on officers and members of standing committees, on orators, and on society rules. They voted on when and how often the group would meet. Sometimes they determined to meet weekly, sometimes twice monthly or monthly. Thus they not only subscribed to the principle of the rule of law, but within the space of the society, they adopted the values and forms of democratic governance that the nation had failed to enact for them and for so many others.

Debates

Debating, the Clionian Debating Society's main activity, was thus conducted in a deliberate, formal fashion. Typically, the Committee of Queries proposed several questions for debate at a future meeting and the society chose among them; two members were appointed, often in an alphabetical rotation, to prepare the affirmative and negative cases. On the evening of the debate, the two presented their cases, other members of the society joined in, and the debate concluded at a time stipulated in advance. The society's president rendered a decision, although the minutes are ambiguous on whether the decision was made on the so-called merits of the question or the ability of the debaters to support positions; pre–Civil War debating societies rendered decisions in different ways, and there was not a widespread standard.[36] The Clionian minutes indicate the verdicts, but we should be careful not to assume that they necessarily reveal

Introduction   xxi

collective beliefs. Many verdicts are consonant with what we would expect this group to support, such as an affirmative decision on the question "Is education beneficial to society?"[37] Yet the president ruled for the negative in a debate asking "whether the United States was right in declaring her Independence," and the terms of that debate and the rationale for the decision remain a tantalizing mystery.[38] Further, the same question debated at different times could result in opposing decisions. Some members, such as Enoch G. Beaird, Simeon's brother, led the winning side in their assigned debates so often that it seems likely the decisions were responsive to the debaters' performance.

The direct sources of inspiration for the queries are likewise uncertain. Historians of Charleston have correctly observed that the questions debated by the Clionians are similar to questions debated by students in the Chrestomathic Literary Society at the College of Charleston, a group that had split off from the college's Cliosophic Literary Society in 1848, while Francis Asbury Mood was a student. Any implication that the Clionians followed the lead of the white collegians in selecting debate topics, however, is difficult to sustain when the dates of similar debates are compared, since the Clionians more often than not debated questions before the same questions were argued by the Chrestomaths.[39] Furthermore, debating questions were comparable around the country and had been so for decades, in college societies and popular groups alike. Although organizational records typically remained private, questions appeared in newspaper reports and in published books. For example, Charles Morley's pocket-sized handbook, *A Guide to Forming and Conducting Lyceums, Debating Societies, &c.*, published in New York in 1841, listed topics and questions that were already conventional, from "Are fictitious writings beneficial?" to "Did Napoleon do more hurt than good to the world?"[40] Later texts, such as Frederic Rowton's *The Debater* (1846) and James N. McElligott's *The American Debater* (1855), listed hundreds of debating questions along with advice about arguments, evidence, and resources.[41] We do not know whether members of the Clionian Debating Society owned texts like these, but the crucial point is this: the details of what counted as a good debating question and hence an appropriate focus of intellectual energy were circulated widely in pre–Civil War US culture. Transference of questions by word of mouth also helped some questions to become standard, a part of shared assumptions about what a debate was.

The minutes record the Clionians' debates on ninety-three questions (see appendix B). Usually they debated a single question in one meeting, but sometimes the debate was continued over two meetings. Like other debaters throughout the country, the Clionians argued issues of policy and value, both specific and abstract. They sometimes drew attention to current events. For instance, they

xxii   *Introduction*

debated in 1848 whether "the acquisition of California [would] be of any great use to the U.S.," and in 1854 they asked of the ongoing Crimean War whether "France & England [were] right in interfering in the present struggle between Russia & Turkey."[42]

These "devotees of old Clio" spent a great deal of time with questions of historical interpretation, especially military careers.[43] They asked whether Charlemagne and Caesar were great men, and they repeatedly rehashed Napoleon's life and career. They compared his military prowess to that of Hannibal, they debated whether "ambition . . . led Napoleon to battle," they twice debated whether the exile to St. Helena had been right, and they argued about the meaning of Wellington's victory at Waterloo.[44]

They also devoted attention to questions about learning, asking whether "Literary or Military glory" was more "desirable," whether "Ancient or Modern history" was more "interesting," and "whether success[es] in difficult Sciences are the results of Genius, or Industry and Perseverance."[45] The final query that the society adopted for debate—a question apparently never debated—turned out to be a poignant one. It was "Which is more conducive to Individual improvement—Solitude or Society?" At the group's next minuted meeting, eight months later, the members discussed "the propriety and necessity of a change in the object and purposes . . . from a *debating* to a *reading* association . . . which was thought would be more favorable to the circumstances of the members." Although a majority that evening chose to "continue as heretofore" and only to reduce the required quorum "from five to three members," the group would shortly dissolve.[46] Improvement would have to persist in solitude, whether or not that approach was conducive to success.

Some questions that were common elsewhere were not taken up by the Clionians, and we are left to elicit meaning through absence. Direct questions about slavery, emancipation, and legal issues related to sectional tension were frequent in debating societies throughout the nation.[47] During the time that the Clionians were active, for instance, the Chrestomathic Literary Society debated questions such as "Is the American Union threatened with dissolution by the Slavery Question?" "Will the revival of the Slave trade be beneficial?" "Will the Slavery question produce a dissolution in the Union?" "Is Slavery Right?" "Who derived the greatest advantage from the Slave Trade, Master or Slave?" and "Is the law prohibiting the education of slaves in Carolina just?"[48] The topic roiling the nation was common in many venues. Although it seems probable that issues of enslavement arose during the Clionians' debates on questions concerning topics such as the Mexican-American War, such details were not minuted.[49] The Clionians did not frame any debating questions directly about enslavement, and the terms *slavery, abolition, secession, emancipation,* and even *the South* never appear in their minutes. Why? Did they fear surveillance or retaliation by local white elites? Community experience taught the validity of this concern.[50] Did they wish to avoid fostering ill will among themselves, since members' families were both slaveholding and nonslaveholding? Or did they wish to use the comparatively safe enclave to practice their argumentative skills on questions that did not hit so close to home, to perform freedom *from* the ever-present culture of slavery?

Silence is suggestive but not conclusive. In addition to questions of enslavement and sectionalism, the Clionians did not debate common topics such as dueling, the political rights of women, or the value of theatrical entertainments, although they did debate the displacement of Indigenous people and capital punishment, two of the most common issues for debaters nationally.[51] If, as Drago observes, "the free black elite could ill afford to indulge in dueling or pander to its code of honor," it is also true that political participation was elusive for the men as well as the women of this community, and religious activity was more significant than entertainment to many of these young men.[52] Yet personal salience was clearly not a primary rationale for choosing debating questions, since it is difficult to imagine the direct relevance of a question like "Who was the Greatest and most virtuous General, Caesar or Pompey?"[53]

We can envision, however, the possible personal import of a question like "Emigration: does it tend, or has it ever tended to the advancement of civilization?" The Clionians debated this topic in April 1852, concluding with a negative verdict. *Emigration* was a term frequently used to describe not only Black Americans' colonization of places such as Liberia in West Africa but also the exodus of free persons of color from the slaveholding South. Two years before, a Clionian member had introduced the subject of "having Diplomas to present to members that may in time leave the State." Departures of free Black Charlestonians would become common through the later 1850s and early 1860s. Yet the 1852 debating question was framed in such general terms that it could have invited a discussion of foreign immigration to the United States, an ordinary topic among debaters at the time.[54]

Although the Clionians' extant records are reticent about rationales for the choice of questions and the development of arguments, they do provide frequent hints of the emotional dimensions of debating activities. The questions are stylistically earnest, but society secretaries inscribe an impression of the debates as characterized by youthful zeal, not deadly solemnity. Minutes refer to the "spirited," "animated," or "heated" nature of the debates, or they claim that only the onslaught of time prompted debates to end. For example, the xxiv *Introduction*

secretary William O. Weston in 1853 recorded, "The sands of time had slipped from under us & we could plead no more."[55] Whereas stringent local curfews imposed on the Black population made clock-watching vital for these young men, society secretaries tended to reframe the fact of legal restrictions into a commentary on the members' passion for debating. Contrary evidence appears rarely, as when in 1848 a society president beseeched "earnestly that every member would study his debate thoroughly before every meeting."[56] Far more often, the minutes portray the members as devoted and enthusiastic.

Orations

Whereas debating was the primary, titular focus of the Clionian Debating Society, the group also provided opportunities for public speaking in officers' addresses and in formal orations. The Clionians practiced the oratorical art as epideictic, naming and celebrating shared values and stabilizing the community through regular rituals. At the ceremony of officers' installation, new officers spoke to the membership, with presidents typically returning thanks, endorsing the society's perseverance toward intellectual improvement, and offering encouragement. Subordinate officers indicated their commitment to the tasks before them, promising to do their best. These inaugural occasions ritually reconstituted the society, reaffirming the relationships among society members and their elected leaders.[57] The occasions of formal orations also stressed the society's goals and, sometimes, its links to the larger community of supporters.

Formal orations were of two types (see appendix C): first, members periodically delivered short prepared speeches to other members. These were called "quarterly," "semi-annual," "regular," or "private" orations. Second, at yearly anniversary occasions, annual orators spoke to members and guests. Five of the young men who delivered quarterly orations—Enoch G. Beaird, Simeon W. Beaird, Henry Cardozo, William Gailliard, and William O. Weston—were later elected annual orator. All annual orators except the first one were regular members of the society; on January 1, 1849, honorary member Job G. Bass delivered the first annual oration.

The texts of the Clionian orations do not survive, but the minutes provide brief descriptions. Topics emphasized the importance of well-directed learning for the individual and society at large. In orations before the members, for example, Enoch G. Beaird spoke on "good and careful reading," both Simeon W. Beaird and Augustus L. Horry lauded the virtue of "perseverance," and J. M. F. Dereef promoted "the advantages of reading standard works."[58] Annual orations had similar topics, with Henry Cardozo discussing "the rewards and

Introduction XXV

results of a well directed ambition" and Richard S. Holloway reflecting on the "advantages accruing from a cultivated mind."[59] The minutes represent these orations as a ritual celebration of the society's aspirations.

The orations are sometimes presented as evidence of speakers' own intellectual qualities. For example, William O. Weston was a quarterly orator in August 1849, when he was about seventeen years old. He spoke on education, and the minutes record that his speech was "the grandest proof of the advantages derived from the attainment of the same." The next year, when Augustus L. Horry spoke, the record stated that he "displayed a depth of intellect worthy of being cultivated."[60] Thus the topical selections reinforced the purposes of the society, and individual performances offered evidence of its success, available for audience assessment.

Although the lectures described in the Clionian Debating Society minutes are similar to those delivered at other mutual-improvement societies, celebrating the virtues of personal commitments to learning, on one occasion a link to contemporary racial politics was more clearly in evidence. In 1855, when William O. Weston was society secretary, he recorded of Benjamain Roberts's annual oration: "The ascendant star in the galaxy of Palestine's hopes was burnished with a sun-like aspect by this son of Clio & the not far distant day when Ethiopia too shall stretch forth her hands, appeared but as the 'morrow before the phrophetic touch of the speaker."[61] In his elaborate literary style, Weston pointed to Roberts's focus on learning as the basis for the global spread of Christianity, and the allusion to Psalm 68:31—"Ethiopia shall soon stretch out her hands unto God"—links his observations with one strand of nineteenth-century Black nationalism, signaling hope for the evangelization of Africa and revival of African power.[62] Although the nuances of Roberts's position remain elusive, the reference does illustrate an imagined connection with the peoples of the African diaspora broadly.

Library Acquisitions

The Clionians not only emphasized debating and lecturing but also the reading and study necessary for competent oral performance and intellectual growth. Beginning in December 1848 they began discussing the establishment of a collection of print publications, and the minutes record additions to this library from 1849 through 1855 (see appendix D). The library was accessible to members, and on anniversary occasions it was displayed for visitors.[63] Members were assessed fees for purchases, but the collection grew primarily through donations. Sometimes the minutes simply record the addition of "pamphlets of good speeches" or "several valuable works," but they do identify many of the holdings.[64] The Clionians and their network of patrons simultaneously sought standard works and locally significant texts.

A few books held by the Clionians were ubiquitous in mutual-improvement associations of the time, especially Noah Webster's famous dictionary and the autobiography of Benjamin Franklin.[65] Like other societies, the Clionians in their choice of published texts emphasized religious and historical themes, along with transatlantic intellectualism. The library was inaugurated when Job G. Bass gave the society a Bible in January 1849. Religious themes persisted, from the group's purchase in 1850 of Francis Hawks's *Monuments of Egypt,* which argues that archaeological discoveries in Africa reveal the truth of scripture, to the donation in 1855 of the works of the first-century Jewish historian Flavius Josephus.[66] Other works emphasized European history and echoed the debating questions. The library included two volumes of Thomas Babington Macaulay's *History of England,* Thomas Carlyle's *French Revolution,* William Grimshaw's *History of France,* and Richard Swainson Fisher's *Book of the World.*[67] Military and political history dominated the library's holdings, but in 1850 the group purchased Elizabeth Starling's *Noble Deeds of Woman* just four months after supporter Emma Farbeaux gave the society three unnamed books by "distinguished Authoresses."[68] The Clionians held primarily nonfiction, although in 1849 Bass donated a volume by American writer James Kirke Paulding, and in 1851 the local schoolteacher Frances Pinckney Bonneau presented works of the Irish poet Thomas Moore.[69]

Books like these were standards of the day, common in libraries across the nation.[70] Yet the Clionians also established a collection of local print materials published by white intellectuals. The group owned copies of pamphlet speeches such as an address on the value of education delivered by Francis W. Capers when he was a professor at the Citadel, a lecture on geology delivered to the South Carolina legislature by Professor Richard T. Brumby of South Carolina College, and a sermon by James W. Miles, an Episcopal minister and a professor of Greek and history at the College of Charleston.[71] In 1854 Henry Cardozo gave the society a copy of a book by John Bachman, a Lutheran minister and a College of Charleston professor of natural history, entitled *The Doctrine of the Unity of the Human Race Examined on the Principles of Science.* Published in 1850, Bachman's book intervened in ongoing public debates about whether different races of people derived from a single origin or multiple origins. The multiple-origins—or polygenist—position was a powerful resource for pro-slavery advocates, and Bachman, a monogenist although he defended chattel slavery and white supremacy, criticized the polygenist perspective. Cardozo's donation implies an interest in promoting engagement with Bachman's ideas

Introduction xxvii

among debating society members.[72] The Clionians' library seems to have lacked works supporting polygenism, despite their easy availability.[73]

Contemporary US politics was not a theme of the society's library holdings, and even Bachman's book was presented as scientific scholarship, not a political polemic. One exception occurred in April 1850, however, when the society planned the purchase of "Five political speeches recently delivered in the Senate."[74] If the term "the Senate" refers to the national legislature, then these speeches may have concerned topics like the Fugitive Slave Act, the abolition of slavery in the District of Columbia, or the imprisonment of free Black seamen in southern ports.[75] In their acquisition of print media, the Clionians may have tracked the ongoing sectional crisis and its local effects.

Creating an Archive

The Clionians not only amassed publications, but they also created a written history of their own activities, which they preserved with care. The two detailed volumes recording society proceedings are a case in point. These volumes also refer to documents that are no longer extant, such as a book of rules, treasurers' records, and copies of correspondence. Further, the Clionians asked orators to supply handwritten texts of their orations for the society's collections, and many speakers complied instantly, indicating that speaking from a prepared text was ordinary practice.[76] Much less customary was a request for a debater's notes, although in 1848 the society asked William E. Marshall for a copy of his arguments against restraining the liberty of the press and Simeon W. Beaird for his arguments concerning the justice of the Mexican–American War.[77]

Recordkeeping was a common activity of nineteenth-century debating societies, but the Clionian minutes are more explicit about the goals of preservation than most records. In 1849, for instance, Beaird minuted his motion following Weston's quarterly oration: "S. W. Beaird now rose to move the Society, request a copy of the beautiful speech just delivered, that they may always preserve its valuable and sound contents among the relics of the body."[78] The Clionians lived in a city already deeply invested in its history. In 1848 the white elite had celebrated the centennial of the Charleston Library Society with much fanfare about the significance of historic preservation and of establishing a record of excellence available for future emulation.[79] Furthermore, contemporaneous organizations within the free Black community in Charleston also kept detailed minutes; records still extant include those of the Brown Fellowship Society, the Friendly Moralist Society, and the Friendly Association.[80] The Clionians' efforts to capture and preserve records of what they did and said, like the archiving efforts of other local groups, were a performative assertion of their own worth xxviii *Introduction*

and the value of their activities. Even now, their minute books assert the group's presence, aspirations, and actions.

A Green Oasis

On July 20, 1853, Augustus L. Horry attended a Clionian Debating Society meeting. He had joined the society in 1849 and had participated actively, appearing regularly in debates, serving on committees of correspondence, and once, in 1850, delivering a quarterly oration. Horry had given gifts to the society: a maple table and four armchairs, some "valuable works" for the library, and a decorative picture. Then in December 1852, by letter from Philadelphia, Horry informed the group that he "had left the State 'probably for life'" and thus, with regret, must resign. He promised to send a "Gilt Frame Mythological Picture" as soon as possible. The society unanimously elected Horry an honorary member. But then he returned to Charleston, and he was invited to the July 20 meeting of the Clionian Debating Society as an "especial guest." Horry spoke at this meeting, and William O. Weston noted in the minutes that he concluded with gratitude, saying "that this memorable scene would be one that he would be able to point out as being a green oasis in the history of his life."[81] The metaphor of this meeting as a "green oasis" resonates with the sense of the society generally as a place of safety, growth, and sustenance. Yet the metaphor is not only spatial; Weston did not record Horry's having said "a green oasis in the desert of my life." The oasis is also temporal, an experience shared with others along an unfolding path, to be carried into the future. If the young men of the Clionian Debating Society created an oasis in space and time, how might we summarize its features? This oasis can, I believe, be understood as a place of renewal more than as a place of escape.

The living waters of this oasis were practices of literacy—reading, writing, speaking, debating—that were widely accepted as substantive education of the day. Across the nation, those who lacked access to formal institutions of higher education—as well as those few white men who had received collegiate training—created societies for themselves where intellectual culture could flourish, whether in coastal cities or interior settlements. These groups tended to be comparatively homogenous in gender, racial identification, and social standing. The Clionians operated consistently with other groups of ambitious young men in formalizing their procedures for action, in debating questions both abstract and concrete, in displaying their goals through oratory, in establishing library resources, and in generating scribal texts that asserted their own presence and intellectual capacities. They practiced their developing skills in the context of male camaraderie, and their minutes repeatedly referred to "our brotherlike

Introduction xxix

assemblage," "this brotherly Institution," and the "beloved Society."[82] The positive value of the young men's collaboration was regularly endorsed by men and women of their community.

Yet the members of the Clionian Debating Society performed these conventions of learning within a context of oppression, to which their 1858 phrase "present *political* disadvantages" elusively alludes. This phrase is a rare signal of the free Black community's precarious situation within a decade's worth of society minutes. It may be tempting to conclude that the Clionians chose conventional foci to distinguish themselves from enslaved people and to deflect white society's suspicions of potential subversion, but such an assessment assumes that white elites were a primary audience for the Clionians' activities.[83] Although the society's minute books could have withstood the surveillance of white elites suspicious of Black revolt, neither the minutes nor the activities they describe rhetorically invoke a surveilling audience. The language of these minutes was written to be read by the Clionians themselves: literally because meetings began with the reading of the previous meeting's minutes and also conceptually because the minutes carefully recorded items of significance to the participants and even contained oblique insider language, like Weston's references to "the President's hat" as the sign that the time for debate was at an end.[84] That is, an important way to read these minutes is as their language implies: as records created by young men reporting their activity *to and for themselves.* Likewise, the activities they minuted are represented as members' displays for one another and occasionally for supporters. These are displays of thoughtfulness and rectitude. In their study of Black American manhood, Darlene Clark Hine and Earnestine Jenkins note that in the pre–Civil War urban North, free Black men often valued a vision of manhood that emphasized "honor and integrity . . . and being responsible for oneself, one's family, and the community."[85] In the urban South, the Clionians similarly enacted self-respect and, as their minutes stated, "usefulness to ourselves and to others."[86]

Furthermore, we should be careful not to collapse the Clionians' emphasis on Western educational forms into a simple alliance with whiteness. It is true that classical subjects were the same as those taught by and to the white male elite, yet it does not necessarily follow that an interest in Western classical antiquity—or in debating, for that matter—was motivated by a desire for duplication. Instead, such an interest lays claim to the heritage of world culture generally, not defined by biological attributes but owing to curiosity and imagination. In 1903 W. E. B. Du Bois wrote in *Souls of Black Folk:* "I sit with Shakespeare and he winces not. . . . From out the caves of evening that swing between the strong-limbed earth and the tracery of the stars, I summon Aristotle and

xxx *Introduction*

Aurelius and what soul I will, and they come all graciously with no scorn nor condescension. . . . Is this the life you grudge us, O knightly America?" In rhetorical scholar Kirt H. Wilson's interpretation, Du Bois's book "redirects racial inquiry from biology to discourse—the process of perception, interpretation, meaning, and communication."[87] Read beside the poetic genius of Du Bois, the everyday minutes of the Clionian Debating Society from a half century before seem to resonate with an impulse similar to Du Bois's. In 1851 Clionian member Stephen J. Maxwell delivered a lecture on education, showing, as the minutes say, "the importance of Learning in preparing Man to act his part in the great drama of life and in opening his mental eyes to the works of nature particularly as exhibited in the Starry firmament above."[88] On this reading, the Clionians, as they turn skyward, join a project of self-determination and, implicitly, of resistance to racist ideologies. Debating and lecturing and writing letters and reading books and voting on the rules become what Hine and Jenkins call one of "the myriad ways in which slaves and free people in the Americas, against all odds, kept alive the will to survive, for themselves and their descendants, with their humanity intact."[89] This oasis, then, is a place to perform freedom, as individuals and as a collective. The form of freedom that was possible to perform, however, was severely limited, as elliptical references to "difficulties and discouragements" and "*political* disadvantages" demonstrate.[90]

There are further paradoxes. This group—like others of its day—was exclusionary along multiple axes, and the society simultaneously corresponded with Black abolitionists and made honorary members of Black men who held other people in bondage. Topics of racial justice were not explicit subjects of debate, although some queries suggest the possibility that they were discussed. Roberts's oration hints at a sense of identification with people of the African diaspora broadly, and the donation of Bachman's book and the apparent plan to acquire US Senate speeches suggest that discussions of race were not entirely deflected.

Three years after the Clionian Debating Society dissolved, the Confederate bombardment of Fort Sumter in Charleston Harbor began the bloody war that would end chattel slavery and, as Hine and Jenkins note, would "politiciz[e] black men."[91] It is one of the ironies of history that several men of the Clionian Debating Society, who in the 1850s had no prospect of political participation, would deploy their linguistic skills in and for US institutions.[92]

Three examples demonstrate this. First, Conrad D. Ludeke (1835–1895) left Charleston for New York in 1860. In 1861 he enlisted in the Union Army—perceived as a white man with a "dark complexion"—and he served until 1866, achieving the rank of captain and serving as an adjutant, keeping infantry

Introduction

xxxi

records. After a stint as the chief clerk of the Metropolitan Police of New Orleans, Ludeke returned to Charleston in 1871, where he worked as a butcher and, later, a US pension agent, before his death in 1895.[93] Second, Henry Cardozo (1830–1886) went to Cleveland in 1858, where he worked as a tailor. Ten years later he returned to South Carolina, and he served in the state legislature during the 1870s. He was a Methodist minister and a trustee of Claflin University.[94] Finally, Simeon W. Beaird (1826–1894), having taught clandestinely in Charleston in the 1850s, also taught Black children during and after the Civil War in Augusta, Georgia. A Republican politician, he was elected to Georgia's state constitutional convention in 1867, and in 1870 he chaired a delegation to the White House to alert President Ulysses S. Grant to the dire situation of Georgia's Black citizenry. By 1873 Beaird was a Methodist minister in Aiken, South Carolina, and treasurer of Aiken County.[95] Perhaps he was also the one who kept the Clionian minute books safe before they entered the rare book trade.

The common features of these careers are practices of literacy, both written and oral, from recordkeeping to exhortation. Perhaps, like Horry, these men found the Clionian Debating Society to be "a green oasis" in the history of their lives as well. If so, their stint at the oasis may have given them space and time to hone their rhetorical skills. Extant records supply suggestive evidence of the practical benefits of learning for these men and many of their fellows. The minutes of the Clionian Debating Society thus offer strong and important evidence of the educational interests and investments of Black male leaders in the postwar South.

Yet that is not the whole story. Whereas from 1847 to 1858 members of the Clionian Debating Society might readily have envisioned that their practice in self-governance, debating, speaking, reading, and writing was preparing them for leadership within the free Black community in Charleston, they could not have known the results of the cataclysmic war on the horizon nor have self-consciously equipped themselves for leadership in national Reconstruction. Indeed, not all of them survived to see the war come. One society member, Alexander C. Forrester, died of tetanus in 1853, only two months after leading the affirmative side in a debate on the question "Does the distance of a Country's dominions weaken the force of its Laws therein?"[96] He had little chance to deploy his skills in broader arenas. The vagaries of time and experience duly caution us to imagine what participation in the debating society could have meant at the time the members were meeting and not only to focus on practical results across time. From 1847 to 1858 the Clionians had fun together, learning and speaking and developing their skills. We would do well to imagine that

xxxii   *Introduction*

pursuing knowledge in society, not solitude, was not simply instrumental preparation for the future but also an experience of joy.

NOTES

1. Entry for September 18, 1850, in Clionian Debating Society (Charleston, SC), Proceedings, 1847–1851, Charleston Library Society, Charleston, SC (hereafter CDS-CLS); the "afflictions" query was selected on September 11. In this introduction, nonstandard spellings within quotations are not marked with *sic*.

2. John Garrison Marks, *Black Freedom in the Age of Slavery* (Columbia: University of South Carolina Press, 2020), 120.

3. Charleston Library Society, "Clionian Debating Society," 2023, https://charleston librarysociety.omeka.net/collections/show/15; ad, Augustus Wilfrid Dellquest, *Historic Augusta* (Augusta, GA: A. W. Dellquest Book, 1917), 21; ad, *The Biblio,* July 1921, 24; CDS-CLS, seller's card, inside front cover. In 1847 Greer's shop was at 135 King Street.

4. "Business Notes," *Publishers' Weekly,* July 8, 1922, 82; inside front cover and entries for September 22, 1851, January 14, 1858, in Clionian Debating Society (Charleston, SC), Proceedings, 1851–1858, David M. Rubenstein Rare Book and Manuscript Library, Duke University, Durham, NC (hereafter CDS-Duke); "Annual Reports, 1931–1936," box 17, George Washington Flowers Collection of Southern Americana Records, Rubenstein Library, Duke University; *The Centennial Exhibit of the Duke University Library, Consisting of Material from the George Washington Flowers Memorial Collection of Books and Documents Relating to the History and Literature of the South, April 5–June 5, 1939* (Durham, NC, 1939), 5.

5. Angela G. Ray, "Warriors and Statesmen: Debate Education among Free African American Men in Antebellum Charleston," in *Speech and Debate as Civic Education,* ed. J. Michael Hogan, Jessica A. Kurr, Michael J. Bergmaier, and Jeremy D. Johnson (University Park: Pennsylvania State University Press, 2017), 25–28.

6. See the flyleaf of W. H. Seat, *The Confederate States of America in Prophecy* (Nashville, TN: Southern Methodist Publishing House, 1861), http://catalog.hathitrust .org/Record/000778241, image 3.

7. This introduction uses the present-day term *free Black person* interchangeably with the common term in pre–Civil War Charleston, *free person of color,* while recognizing that some of the people associated with the Clionian Debating Society would have chosen other terms, such as *brown.* The minutes themselves use no racial descriptors, and public records associated with these individuals use a range of terms to designate race, color, or ethnicity: *black, brown, colored, dark, free person of color* or *FPC, mulatto, Negro, West Indian,* and *white.*

8. For the Act of 1834, see David J. McCord, ed., *The Statutes at Large of South Carolina* (Columbia, SC: A. S. Johnston, 1840), 7: 468–70.

9. Theodore D. Jervey to E. Horace Fitchett, May 13, 1939, reproduced in E. Horace Fitchett, "The Free Negro in Charleston, South Carolina" (PhD diss., University of Chicago, 1950), 18; Edmund L. Drago, *Initiative, Paternalism, and Race Relations: Charleston's Avery Normal Institute* (Athens: University of Georgia Press, 1990), 27; Bernard E. Powers Jr., *Black Charlestonians: A Social History, 1822–1885* (Fayetteville: University of Arkansas Press, 1994), 52; Michael O'Brien, *Conjectures of Order: Intellectual Life and the American South, 1810–1860,* vol. 1 (Chapel Hill:

Introduction   xxxiii

University of North Carolina Press, 2004), 424. A revised edition of Drago's 1990 book appeared as Edmund L. Drago, *Charleston's Avery Center: From Education and Civil Rights to Preserving the African American Experience,* rev. ed., rev. and ed. W. Marvin Dulaney (Charleston, SC: History Press, 2006), see esp. 35–38. On my research trajectory, see Angela G. Ray, "Rhetoric and the Archive," *Review of Communication* 16, no. 1 (2016): 43–59; and Angela G. Ray, "Archival Profusion, Archival Silence, and Analytic Invention: Reinventing Histories of Nineteenth-Century African American Debate," *Transactions of the American Philosophical Society* 112, no. 3 (2023): 95–114.

10. Harriet Jacobs, *Incidents in the Life of a Slave Girl,* ed. Lydia Maria Child (Boston, 1861), 286.

11. Thomas S. Harding, *College Literary Societies: Their Contribution to Higher Education in the United States, 1815–1876* (New York: Pageant, 1971), 19, 21, 89; J. Jefferson Looney, *Nurseries of Letters and Republicanism: A Brief History of the American Whig–Cliosophic Society and Its Predecessors, 1765–1941,* foreword by Tina Ravitz and Donald E. Stokes (Princeton, NJ: Trustees of the American Whig-Cliosophic Society, Princeton University, 1996), 4. See also David Potter, *Debating in the Colonial Chartered Colleges: An Historical Survey, 1642 to 1900* (New York: Teachers College, 1944), 64–93; David Potter, "The Literary Society," in *History of Speech Education in America: Background Studies,* ed. Karl R. Wallace (New York: Appleton-Century-Crofts, 1954), 238–58; David Potter, "The Debate Tradition," in *Argumentation and Debate: Principles and Practices,* ed. James H. McBath, rev. ed. (New York: Holt, Rinehart and Winston, 1963), 14–32; W. Martin Bloomer, "Controversia and Suasoria," in *Encyclopedia of Rhetoric,* ed. Thomas O. Sloane (New York: Oxford University Press, 2001), 166–69; David Zarefsky, "Debate," in *Encyclopedia of Rhetoric,* 191–97; W. Martin Bloomer, "Declamation," in *Encyclopedia of Rhetoric,* 197–99; B. Evelyn Westbrook, "Debating Both Sides: What Nineteenth-Century College Literary Societies Can Teach Us about Critical Pedagogies," *Rhetoric Review* 21, no. 4 (2002): 339–56; and Carly S. Woods, *Debating Women: Gender, Education, and Spaces for Argument, 1835–1945* (East Lansing: Michigan State University Press, 2018).

12. Angela G. Ray, *The Lyceum and Public Culture in the Nineteenth-Century United States* (East Lansing: Michigan State University Press, 2005), esp. 13–33; Carl Bode, *The American Lyceum: Town Meeting of the Mind* (Carbondale: Southern Illinois University Press, 1956).

13. As historian Joseph F. Kett observes, Holbrook "did not invent the popular literary society; rather, he baptized existing societies as lyceums"; Kett, *The Pursuit of Knowledge under Difficulties: From Self-Improvement to Adult Education in America, 1750–1990* (Stanford, CA: Stanford University Press, 1994), xvii.

14. Dorothy B. Porter, "The Organized Educational Activities of Negro Literary Societies, 1828–1846," *Journal of Negro Education* 5, no. 4 (October 1936): 555–76; Elizabeth McHenry, *Forgotten Readers: Recovering the Lost History of African American Literary Societies* (Durham, NC: Duke University Press, 2002). See also, e.g., Emma Jones Lapsansky, "'Discipline to the Mind': Philadelphia's Banneker Institute, 1854–1872," in *A Question of Manhood: A Reader in U.S. Black Men's History and Masculinity,* ed. Darlene Clark Hine and Earnestine Jenkins, vol. 1 (Bloomington: Indiana University Press, 1999), 399–414; and Shirley Wilson

Logan, *Liberating Language: Sites of Rhetorical Education in Nineteenth-Century Black America* (Carbondale: Southern Illinois University Press, 2008).

15. CDS-CLS, November 9, 1847.

16. CDS-CLS, December 17, 1848, January 2, February 15, September 6, December 26, 1849, January 1, December 2, 1850, January 1, 1851; CDS-Duke, September 25, December 22, 1851, January 1, December 30, 1852.

17. The minutes identify twenty-nine men who were members or who were considered for membership, twenty men who were honorary members or considered for that status, and six additional supporters. One person, Augustus L. Horry, was a member first and later, after he left Charleston for Philadelphia, an honorary member.

18. For example, "a brilliant assemblage of both sexes" attended the 1854 anniversary meeting; CDS-Duke, January 2, 1854.

19. Drago, *Charleston's Avery Center,* 34; Powers, *Black Charlestonians,* 48–53; James B. Browning, "The Beginnings of Insurance Enterprise among Negroes," *Journal of Negro History* 22, no. 4 (1937): 417–32; Robert L. Harris Jr., "Early Black Benevolent Societies, 1780–1830," *Massachusetts Review* 20, no. 3 (1979): 603–25; Robert L. Harris Jr., "Charleston's Free Afro-American Elite: The Brown Fellowship Society and the Humane Brotherhood," *South Carolina Historical Magazine* 82, no. 4 (1981): 289–310; Michael P. Johnson and James L. Roark, "'A Middle Ground': Free Mulattoes and the Friendly Moralist Society of Antebellum Charleston," *Southern Studies* 21, no. 3 (1982): 246–65; Marks, *Black Freedom in the Age of Slavery,* 117–53.

20. See, e.g., Michael P. Johnson and James L. Roark, eds., *No Chariot Let Down: Charleston's Free People of Color on the Eve of Civil War* (Chapel Hill: University of North Carolina Press, 1984), 3–20; Drago, *Charleston's Avery Center;* Powers, *Black Charlestonians;* Amrita Chakrabarti Myers, *Forging Freedom: Black Women and the Pursuit of Liberty in Antebellum Charleston* (Chapel Hill: University of North Carolina Press, 2011); Marks, *Black Freedom in the Age of Slavery;* Warren Eugene Milteer Jr., *Beyond Slavery's Shadow: Free People of Color in the South* (Chapel Hill: University of North Carolina Press, 2021); and Kerri K. Greenidge, *The Grimkés* (New York: Liveright, 2023).

21. Myers, *Forging Freedom,* 83; Drago, *Charleston's Avery Center,* 43–44.

22. Powers, *Black Charlestonians,* 46.

23. On Cardozo, see Eric Foner, *Freedom's Lawmakers: A Directory of Black Officeholders during Reconstruction,* rev. ed. (Baton Rouge: Louisiana State University Press, 1996), 40; and *Minutes of the Annual Conferences of the Methodist Episcopal Church: Spring Conferences of 1887* (New York: Phillips and Hunt, 1887), 84. On Weston, see Foner, *Freedom's Lawmakers,* 226; and William H. Lawrence, "A Sketch of the History of the Reorganization of the South Carolina Conference, and of Centenary Church," in *The Centenary Souvenir, Containing a History of Centenary Church, Charleston, and an Account of the Life and Labors of Rev. R. V. Lawrence, Father of the Pastor of Centenary Church* (Charleston, SC, 1885), xvi.

24. The two are called Henry Cardozo Jr. and Henry J. D. Cardozo. The former's handwriting in the Clionian minutes is similar to writing of the Reverend Henry Cardozo from the 1870s, but this identification is speculative. See Henry Cardozo to Charles Holloway, September 7, 1875, in Holloway Family Scrapbook, Holloway Family Collection, Avery Research Center for African American History and Culture, College of Charleston, Charleston, SC.

Introduction

XXXV

25. Larry Koger, *Black Slaveowners: Free Black Slave Masters in South Carolina, 1790–1860* (Jefferson, NC: McFarland, 1985), 143, 148–49, 226.

26. Koger, *Black Slaveowners;* Loren Schweninger, *Black Property Owners in the South, 1790–1915* (Urbana: University of Illinois Press, 1990), 104–8; Powers, *Black Charlestonians,* 39; Myers, *Forging Freedom,* 122–28.

27. Drago, *Charleston's Avery Center,* 46–47; C. W. Birnie, "Education of the Negro in Charleston, South Carolina, Prior to the Civil War," *Journal of Negro History* 12, no. 1 (1927): 19; Ronald E. Butchart, *Schooling the Freed People: Teaching, Learning, and the Struggle for Black Freedom, 1861–1876* (Chapel Hill: University of North Carolina Press, 2010), 21; Myers, *Forging Freedom,* 101–2; Daniel Alexander Payne, *Recollections of Seventy Years* (Nashville, TN: A.M.E. Sunday School Union, 1888), 15, 36; Francis A. Mood, *For God and Texas: Autobiography of Francis Asbury Mood, 1830–1884: Circuit Rider, Educator, and Founder of Southwestern University, Georgetown, Texas,* ed. Mary Katherine Metcalfe Earney (Dallas, TX: Listo, 2001), 40–50; Claude Carr Cody, *The Life and Labors of Francis Asbury Mood, D.D.* (Chicago: F. H. Revell, 1886), esp. 75–80, 92, 104–9. The obituary of Simeon W. Beaird stated that he was educated in the school of "the Rev. Mr. Mood, of the M. E. Church"; this may refer to John Mood (1792–1864), the father of John Amos, Francis, and William, or possibly to Henry Mood (1819–1892), their elder brother. See "The Rev. T. [*sic*] W. Beaird," *Southwestern Christian Advocate,* January 24, 1895, 5.

28. Payne remembered these curricular materials in his *Recollections of Seventy Years,* 15. He fled South Carolina in 1835 after white authorities closed his school (27–40). Payne was named an honorary member of the Clionian Debating Society in 1847, when he was living in Baltimore, and the members corresponded with him in 1849–1850; see CDS-CLS, December 22, 1847, May 21, 1849, May 29, July 31, August 14, 1850. In addition to serving as AME bishop, Payne was a founder and early president of Ohio's Wilberforce University.

29. Drago, *Charleston's Avery Center,* 38–44; Michael P. Johnson and James L. Roark, *Black Masters: A Free Family of Color in the Old South* (New York: Norton, 1984), 153–94.

30. Marks, *Black Freedom in the Age of Slavery,* 120.

31. Catherine R. Squires, "Rethinking the Black Public Sphere: An Alternative Vocabulary for Multiple Public Spheres," *Communication Theory* 12 (2002): 459, 460.

32. CDS-CLS, partial entry, preceding February 2, 1848; see also February 2, 4, 9, 10, March 1, 1848. The pages recording the troubled meeting were torn from the minute book, following the society's decision on March 1 to "blot [the record of the February 1 meeting] from off the proceedings of the Society." Hence it is not possible to discern the reasons for the conflict.

33. CDS-Duke, January 14, 1858. The minutes are not specific about the committee's tasks; presumably the men would dispose of the society's treasury and find homes for its library, record books, and other possessions.

34. CDS-Duke, February 23, July 1, October 25, December 16, 1852, February 14, March 23, July 20, December 21, 1853, July 12, 1854, January 22, 1855, April 7, 1856, January 14, 1858.

35. Marina Wikramanayake, *A World in Shadow: The Free Black in Antebellum South Carolina* (Columbia: University of South Carolina Press, 1973), 48–54.

xxxvi *Introduction*

36. Angela G. Ray, "The Permeable Public: Rituals of Citizenship in Antebellum Men's Debating Clubs," *Argumentation and Advocacy* 41, no. 1 (2004): 5n5.

37. CDS-CLS, December 2, 1850 (query), January 6, 1851 (debate).

38. CDS-CLS, November 23 (query), December 1, 1847 (debate).

39. Drago, *Charleston's Avery Center*, 36; Powers, *Black Charlestonians*, 52; Marks, *Black Freedom in the Age of Slavery*, 137; Mood, *For God and Texas*, 49–50. Drago lists nine questions debated by the Clionian Debating Society alongside similar questions debated by the Chrestomathic Literary Society at the college. Yet in only one case (question 6) did the collegians debate the question prior to the Clionians' debate. Compare CDS-CLS; and Books 1, 2, and 3 (#173/4, 5, 6), Chrestomathic Literary Society Minute Books, College of Charleston Archives, Special Collections, College of Charleston, Charleston, SC. The debating records of the other College of Charleston debating society of the time, the Cliosophic Society, are not extant. At this time the members of each society at the college debated among themselves, not yet against the other group. The Chrestomaths first began to discuss the possibility of a debate between the two societies on January 20, 1858; see Book 3 (#173/6).

40. Charles Morley, *A Guide to Forming and Conducting Lyceums, Debating Societies, &c, with Outlines of Discussions and Essays, and an Appendix, Containing an Epitome of Rhetoric, Logic, &c.* (New York: A. E. Wright, 1841), 26, 49.

41. Frederic Rowton, *The Debater: A New Theory of the Art of Speaking; Being a Series of Complete Debates, Outlines of Debates, and Questions for Discussion* (London: Longman, Brown, Green, and Longmans, 1846); James N. McElligott, *The American Debater: Being a Plain Exposition of the Principles and Practice of Public Debate* (New York: Ivison and Phinney, 1855).

42. CDS-CLS, September 18 (query), December 26, 1848 (debate); CDS-Duke, March 14 (query), March 28, 1854 (debate).

43. CDS-Duke, July 20, 1853. Secretary Henry Cardozo noted what he called, positively, "the usual share of interest that historical questions generally afford"; CDS-Duke, June 14, 1852.

44. On Charlemagne and Caesar, see CDS-Duke, December 13, 1852 (query), January 12 (debate), September 14 (query), September 28, October 12, 1853 (debates). On Napoleon, see CDS-CLS, February 23 (query), March 1 (debate), March 22 (query), April 5, June 7, 1848 (debates), March 14 (query), March 21, 1849 (debate), February 3 (query), March 31, 1851 (debate); CDS-Duke, June 28 (query), October 25, 1852 (debate).

45. CDS-CLS, December 1 (query), December 8, 22, 1847 (debates), September 27 (query), October 4, November 5, 1849 (debates); CDS-Duke, October 27 (query), December 8, 29, 1851 (debates).

46. CDS-Duke, June 2, 1856 (query), February 2, 1857.

47. Ray, "Permeable Public," 12; Richard L. Weaver II, "Forum for Ideas: The Lyceum Movement in Michigan, 1818–1860" (PhD diss., Indiana University, 1969), 164.

48. Entries for December 19, 1849, in Book 1 (#173/4), February 21, 1855, in Book 2 (#173/5), October 8, 1856, February 11, April 22, June 3, 1857, in Book 3 (#173/6), Chrestomathic Literary Society Minute Books.

49. On war with Mexico, see CDS-CLS, November 16 (query), November 23, 1847 (debate), June 7 (query), September 18, 1848 (debate); CDS-Duke, September 22 (query), October 13, 1851 (debate). See also Drago, *Charleston's Avery Center*, 40.

Introduction **xxxvii**

50. In 1836 Robert Y. Hayne, then mayor of Charleston, sent for the minutes of the Brown Fellowship Society to determine whether the group should be permitted to meet; Theodore D. Jervey, *Robert Y. Hayne and His Times* (New York: Macmillan, 1909), 433–34; see also Susan M. Bowler and Edmund L. Drago, "Black Intellectual Life in Antebellum Charleston," April 7, 1984, p. 11, box 8, folder 7, Eugene C. Hunt Papers, AMN 1047, Avery Research Center. Free persons of color in 1850s Charleston would thus be well aware of the threat of surveillance.

51. CDS-CLS, June 20 (query), June 27, July 5, 1849 (debates); CDS-Duke, May 11 (query), June 8, 22, 1853 (debates); Ray, "Permeable Public," 12; Angela G. Ray, "Learning Leadership: Lincoln at the Lyceum, 1838," *Rhetoric and Public Affairs* 13, no. 3 (Fall 2010): 383n48.

52. Drago, *Charleston's Avery Center,* 38.

53. CDS-Duke, June 14 (query), June 28, 1852 (debate).

54. CDS-Duke, April 12 (query), April 26, 1852 (debate); CDS-CLS, July 8, 1850. See Ray, "Permeable Public," 11; Bjørn F. Stillion Southard, *Peculiar Rhetoric: Slavery, Freedom, and the African Colonization Movement* (Jackson: University Press of Mississippi, 2019); and Marks, *Black Freedom in the Age of Slavery,* 137.

55. CDS-Duke, May 11, 1853.

56. CDS-CLS, May 17, 1848.

57. On the symbolic significance of inaugurals, see Karlyn Kohrs Campbell and Kathleen Hall Jamieson, *Presidents Creating the Presidency: Deeds Done in Words* (Chicago: University of Chicago Press, 2008), 29–56.

58. CDS-CLS, December 26, 1848, December 26, 1849, August 14, 1850; CDS-Duke, July 26, 1854.

59. CDS-Duke, January 2, 1854, January 7, 1856.

60. CDS-CLS, August 15, 1849, August 14, 1850.

61. CDS-Duke, January 1, 1855. On Roberts's later ministerial career, see Lawrence, "A Sketch of the History," xiv; and A. W. Pegues, *Our Baptist Ministers and Schools* (Springfield, MA: Willey, 1892), 412. Pegues's focus is E. Rainey Roberts, son of Benjamain L. Roberts and Catherine Dereef Roberts, and the text provides useful detail about the family.

62. William R. Scott, "Ethiopianism," in *Encyclopedia of Black Studies,* ed. Molefi Kete Asante and Ama Mazama (Thousand Oaks, CA: Sage, 2005), 234–35.

63. See, e.g., CDS-Duke, January 2, 1854.

64. CDS-CLS, April 10, 1850; CDS-Duke, September 25, 1851.

65. CDS-CLS, December 26, 1849, December 2, 1850.

66. CDS-CLS, January 1, 1849, December 2, 1850; CDS-Duke, June 18, 1855.

67. CDS-CLS, October 8, December 26, 1849; CDS-Duke, December 8, 1851.

68. CDS-CLS, December 2, August 14, 1850. On Farbeaux, see Ray, "Archival Profusion," 109–13.

69. CDS-CLS, December 26, 1849, March 10, 1851.

70. Comparing the Clionian Debating Society's list of library acquisitions with catalogs now held at the American Antiquarian Society that were published by mid-nineteenth-century lyceums, young men's associations, and debating societies reveals considerable overlap, especially for works mentioned in the previous paragraph. Furthermore, two decades after the Clionians created their library, a number of the same texts were listed in Charles H. Moore's *What to Read, and How*

xxxviii *Introduction*

to Read, Being Classified Lists of Choice Reading, Appropriate Hints and Remarks, Adapted to the General Reader, to Subscribers to Libraries, and to Persons Intending to Form Collections of Books, Brought Down to September, 1870 (New York: Appleton, 1871).

71. CDS-CLS, April 17, May 1, 1850, August 11, 1851.

72. CDS-Duke, December 6, 1854.

73. See William Stanton, *The Leopard's Spots: Scientific Attitudes toward Race in America, 1815–59* (Chicago: University of Chicago Press, 1960); and, for texts, Robert Bernasconi, ed., *American Theories of Polygenesis*, 7 vols. (Bristol, UK: Thoemmes, 2002).

74. CDS-CLS, April 10, 1850.

75. Recent Senate speeches were available in published form; see, e.g., *Proceedings of the U.S. Senate, on the Fugitive Slave Bill,—the Abolition of the Slave-Trade in the District of Columbia,—and the Imprisonment of Free Colored Seamen in the Southern Ports: with the Speeches of Messrs. Davis, Winthrop and Others* ([Washington, DC]: T. R. Marvin, [1850]).

76. See, e.g., CDS-CLS, February 16, 1848; CDS-Duke, January 7, 1856.

77. CDS-CLS, January 26, October 1, 1848. The position that Beaird supported in the debate is not apparent from the minutes.

78. CDS-CLS, August 15, 1849.

79. James L. Petigru, *Oration, Delivered before the Charleston Library Society, at Its First Centennial Anniversary, June 13th, 1848* (Charleston, SC: J. B. Nixon, Printer, 1848), 3.

80. Brown Fellowship Society Records, 1794–1990, and Friendly Moralist Society Records, 1841–1856, both at the Avery Research Center; Friendly Association Records, 1853–1869, South Carolina Historical Society, Charleston, SC. See also Harlan Greene and Jessica Lancia, "The Holloway Scrapbook: The Legacy of a Charleston Family," *South Carolina Historical Magazine* 111, nos. 1–2 (January–April 2010): 5–33.

81. CDS-Duke, September 25, 1851, December 16, 30, 1852, July 6, 20, 1853; see also CDS-CLS, February 28, 1849, and passim.

82. CDS-CLS, December 17, 1848, May 22, December 2, 1850.

83. O'Brien, *Conjectures of Order,* 424. Cf. Marks, *Black Freedom in the Age of Slavery,* 120.

84. CDS-Duke, April 14, May 11, August 3, October 12, 1853, February 1, April 25, 1854.

85. Darlene Clark Hine and Earnestine Jenkins, "Black Men's History: Toward a Gendered Perspective," in *Question of Manhood,* ed. Hine and Jenkins, 1:22.

86. CDS-CLS, May 17, 1848.

87. W. E. B. Du Bois, *The Souls of Black Folk,* rpt., with an introduction and chronology by Jonathan Scott Holloway (New Haven, CT: Yale University Press, 2015), 83; Kirt H. Wilson, "Towards a Discursive Theory of Racial Identity: *The Souls of Black Folk* as a Response to Nineteenth-Century Biological Determinism," *Western Journal of Communication* 63, no. 2 (1999): 204. See also Kirt H. Wilson, "The Racial Politics of Imitation in the Nineteenth Century," *Quarterly Journal of Speech* 89, no. 2 (2003): 89–108.

88. CDS-CLS, April 14, 1851.

89. Hine and Jenkins, "Black Men's History," 2.

Introduction

xxxix

90. CLS-Duke, January 14, 1858.

91. Hine and Jenkins, "Black Men's History," 51.

92. Marks notes that the Clionians' hope in the viability of freedom within the United States may have come about directly "because of their affiliation with the society"; Marks, *Black Freedom in the Age of Slavery,* 137.

93. Entry for June 19, 1860, in Friendly Association Records, 1853–1869; Conrad D. Ludeke, Compiled Military Service Records, Records of the Adjutant General's Office, 1780s–1917, Record Group 94, National Archives and Records Administration, Washington, DC; Conrad D. Ludeke, Military Pension Application File, Records of the Department of Veterans Affairs, 1773–1985, Record Group 15, National Archives. See also Ray, "Rhetoric and the Archive," 50–56; and Angela G. Ray, "The Agency of the Archive and the Challenges of Classification," in *Recovering Argument,* ed. Randall A. Lake (London: Routledge, 2018), 64–65.

94. *Journal of the Senate of the State of South Carolina, Being the Regular Session, Commencing November 22, 1870* (Columbia, SC: John W. Denny, Printer to the State, 1870); Lawrence, "A Sketch of the History," xix–xlvii; *Minutes of the Annual Conferences of the Methodist Episcopal Church . . . 1887,* 84; Foner, *Freedom's Lawmakers,* 40; *Claflin University and South Carolina Agricultural College and Mechanics' Institute, Orangeburg, S.C., 1876–77* [Orangeburg, SC, 1877]. See also Neil Kinghan, *A Brief Moment in the Sun: Francis Cardozo and Reconstruction in South Carolina* (Baton Rouge: Louisiana State University Press, 2023).

95. "The Freedmen's Celebration," *Christian Recorder,* July 29, 1865, 1; "School Directory," *Loyal Georgian,* February 17, 1866, 3; Heather Andrews Williams, *Self-Taught: African American Education in Slavery and Freedom* (Chapel Hill: University of North Carolina Press, 2005), 110, 113, 128–29; J. T. Trowbridge, *The South: A Tour of Its Battle-fields and Ruined Cities* (Hartford, CT: L. Stebbins, 1866), 490–91; *Journal of the Proceedings of the Constitutional Convention of the People of Georgia, Held in the City of Atlanta in the Months of December, 1867, and January, February and March, 1868, and Ordinances and Resolutions Adopted* (Augusta, GA: E. H. Pughe, 1868); "Washington," *New York Tribune,* March 17, 1870, 1; "Appointments of South Carolina Conference," *Christian Recorder,* March 6, 1873, 2; *Annual Report of the Comptroller General of the State of South Carolina, for the Fiscal Year Ending October 31, 1874, to the General Assembly,* in *Reports and Resolutions of the General Assembly of the State of South Carolina, at the Regular Session, 1874–'75* (Columbia, SC: Republican Printing, 1875), 200; "Rev. T. W. Beaird." A photograph of Beaird's tombstone in Pinelawn Cemetery, Aiken, SC, appears on www.findagrave.com. Secondary sources sometimes confuse Simeon W. Beaird with Thomas P. Beard (1837–1918), a Black newspaper editor and politician in postwar Augusta, GA. See also Ray, "Warriors and Statesmen," 25–28.

96. CDS-Duke, June 8, 1853; see also February 23 (query), March 9 (debate). Forrester died on May 18, 1853, at age twenty-two; "South Carolina, U.S., Death Records, 1821–1971," Ancestry.com (online database), 2008, https://www.ancestry.com/search/collections/8741/.

NOTE ON TRANSCRIPTION

The secretaries of the Clionian Debating Society crafted their organizational proceedings with great care. Despite the passage of time and the inevitable deterioration of paper and ink, the two volumes are easy to read, owing primarily to the society secretaries' highly legible handwriting. In creating this transcription, I have worked with the original manuscripts as well as with reproductions. Whereas examining layers of ink in the originals can best reveal the gestures of writing and thus increase confidence in the accuracy of a transcription, inspecting facsimiles that can be enlarged assists in deciphering cramped or crossed-out material.[1]

The process of preparing a scholarly edition in print and digital form based on handwritten text is a technological translation rather than a replication; for example, graphical features of the secretaries' handwriting are lost. Nonetheless, I have relied on a theory of transcription with two goals in mind, both of which can promote learning about the debating society as an educational endeavor.[2] First, I have sought to convey accurately the propositional content of the minutes, and second, insofar as possible, I have retained evidence of the society secretaries' compositional practices and decisions about revisions, whether made at the moment of inscription or as part of collaborative review in a society meeting. In keeping with those goals, I have maintained original punctuation and spelling, and material that the society secretaries crossed out in the original, where it is decipherable, is presented here, struck through; words that the secretaries overwrote or erased to the point of illegibility are not noted. Original interlineations are marked as such with carets (for example, "Annual Orator ^for 1852^"). Repeated words are reproduced, followed by [*sic*]. Occasional nonstandard spellings (for example, "thier" for "their") are followed by [*sic*] at the first appearance and retained unmarked thereafter. Grammatical errors, which usually involve subject-verb disagreement or unconnected clauses, are preserved without comment.

At the same time, I occasionally refined the text to facilitate reading. Using brackets, I have added letters or words when omissions are obvious: "defer[r]ed,"

xli

"regular monthly [meeting]." Some graphical choices are standardized: Although society secretaries wrote "Mr." and "M^r," "Jr." and "J^r," "Wm." and "W^m," "4th" and "4th," this transcription presents these abbreviations consistently without superscripts. Likewise, secretaries' sporadic use of the long *s* (*ſ*), common in eighteenth-century print and some nineteenth-century handwriting, appears here as its modern equivalent (for example, *business,* not *busineſs*).

Numbered endnotes offer my own explanations of usage or historical details. To encourage attentiveness to the minutes themselves, I have kept these interventions to a minimum. Footnotes created by society secretaries in the original minutes are marked with an asterisk (*) at the insertion point, as the secretaries did it; the substance of asterisked notes occurs here within the main text, at the end of the entries in which the asterisks appear.

Finally, readers will soon see that as rich as these meeting minutes are, they regularly call attention to documents that are no longer extant. For example, the minutes refer to the manuscripts of members' orations and to the society's constitution, bylaws, rules, lists of resolutions, lists of elected officers, and financial records; at the time of this writing, those materials have not resurfaced. Yet evidence of absence invites our attention as well.[3] The Clionians once created manuscript orations and formal society documents; whether or not those materials ever reappear, recognizing their creation and use constitutes substantive knowledge of ambition and a cooperative practice of learning.

Yet in this case we do not have to investigate absence alone. So much can be learned from presence. The survival of these two volumes of society proceedings is remarkable. They are an incomparable treasure, even as their distinctiveness illuminates the histories of limits on Black freedom and the politics of archiving.

I now invite you to read them with me, to remember, and to imagine.

NOTES

1. For the volume in Charleston, I used the original and also reproductions in the form of microfiche and, during a later proofreading stage, a digital facsimile posted online at Charleston Library Society, "Proceedings of the Clionian Debating Society," 2023, https://charlestonlibrarysociety.omeka.net/items/show/1263. For the volume at Duke, I relied on the original, on scanned images I created at the library, and, for later proofreading, on a digital facsimile posted online at Duke University Libraries, "Continued Proceedings of the Clionian Debating Society, 1851–1858," https://idn.duke.edu/ark:/87924/r47949881.

2. On transcription processes, see W. W. Greg, "The Rationale of Copy-Text," *Studies in Bibliography* 3 (1950/1951): 19–36; Robert N. Gaines, "The Processes and Challenges of Textual Authentication," in *The Handbook of Rhetoric and Public Address,* ed. Shawn J. Parry-Giles and J. Michael Hogan (New York: Wiley, 2010), 134–56; and Modern Language Association, "Guidelines for Editors of Scholarly Editions,"

last revised May 4, 2022, https://www.mla.org/Resources/Guidelines-and-Data /Reports-and-Professional-Guidelines/Guidelines-for-Editors-of-Scholarly-Editions.

3. See, e.g., Odai Johnson, "The Size of All That's Missing," in *The Routledge Companion to Theatre and Performance Historiography,* ed. Tracy C. Davis and Peter W. Marx (London: Routledge, 2021), 43–64.

*Proceedings of the
Clionian Debating Society,
November 5, 1847–January 14, 1858*

— 1847 —

[In this year the society was organized, the first officers were appointed, and the first debate was held. Secretaries minuted eight meetings, five with debates.—Ed.]

Clionian debating Society.
November. 5. 1847.

Proceedings of the Clionian Debating Society.
[November 9, 1847]

The meeting was called to order by the President.[1]—The Constitution was read, and approved of by the members, who affixed their signatures.[2] The President arose and intimated to the Body, that by their approval he would appoint Officers to fill the vacancies of the Society, (as it was the first meeting and the Officers would occupy the votes), which was carried without a dissenting voice. Accordingly the Officers were appointed—viz[3]—Messeurs S. J. Maxwell, F. H. Oliver and W. O. Weston—Committee of queries.—E. G. Beaird, Reporter;[4] and for the occupation of Reader's office, it was agreed upon to appoint a Reader protem[5] at a convenient season, and when necessary.

After the necessary business of the Society was finished—the President, Secretary and Vice President, expostulated in glowing terms their exemplary design, the honor confer[r]ed on them, and with much vehemence the perseverance, order and fortitude necessary for the promotion of their connection and the improvement of their intellect,—which was received by the members with repeated applause, and considered by the Body at large, as summum bonum[6] to their efforts. No further business appearing before the Society, the meeting was adjour[n]ed.

November 9th 1847. Signed—G. C. Greene—Secretary.

[November 16, 1847]

The meeting was called to order by the President—The roll first ^roll^ [sic] was called. The minutes read and approved. The debate opened by the regular

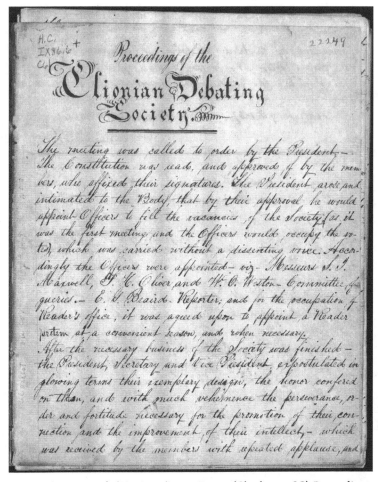

Figure 2. First page of Clionian Debating Society (Charleston, SC), Proceedings, 1847–1851, Charleston Library Society, Charleston, SC, reprinted by courtesy.

debatants, and kept up with much animation. The question was then decided in the affirmative.[7] The question for the next evening's debate was chosen, which reads as follows—'Whether the present War with Mexico, will be of any advantage to the United States of America. or not,'[8] The Secretary read the debatants for the next evening as follows—On the affirmative Master J. J. Greene Jr.,[9] on the negative Master Stephen J. Maxwell. No further business appearing before the Society—the Reporter made his report. The last Roll called, and the Society adjourned. Novr 16. 1847. Signed—G. C. Greene, Secretary

[November 23, 1847]

The meeting was called to order by the President. The first Roll called. The minutes read and approved. Mr. J. J. Greene Jr. proposed Mr. W. E. Marshall for admittance into the Society, which was unanimously received. Mr. S. W. Weston was appointed the regular quarterly orator. Mr. S. W. Weston motioned that the Society meet hereafter on Wednesdays, unanimously received. The debate opened by the regular debatants, and kept up with considerable annimation [sic]. The question was decided in the negative. The question for the next evening's debate was chosen,—which reads as follows—'Whether the (United States) was right in declaring her Independence.' The Secretary read the debatants for the next evening—as follows—Master F. H. Oliver on the affirmative, on the negative Master S. W. Weston. No further business appearing before the Society, the Reporter made his report. The last Roll called, and the Society adjourned.

Novr 23. 1847. Signed—G. C. Greene, Sec.

[December 1, 1847]

The meeting was called to order by the President. The first Roll called. The minutes read and approved. Mr. J. J. Green proposed Mr. J. M. F. Dereef ^lapsus pennae^[10] into the Society for admission,—unanimously received. The debate opened by the regular debatants, and was sustained principally on the negative. It was then decided in the negative. The question for the next evening's debate was chosen;—which reads as follows—"Which is the most desirable Literary or Military glory." The Secretary read the debatants for the next evening as follows—On the Literary Master W. O. Weston; On the Military Master E. G. Beaird. No further business appearing before the Society, The Reporter made his report. The last Roll called, and the Society adjourned.

Decr 1. 1847. Signed—G. C. Greene, Secry.

[December 8, 1847]

The meeting was called to order by the President. The first roll called. The minutes read and approved. Mr. S. W. Weston proposed Mr. G. Barrow for admission into the Society, unanimously received. The debate opened by the regular debatants but the subject was refer[r]ed for conclusion on the next meeting, which was also notified by the President, to be appropriated for the transaction of business. No further business appearing before the Society. The Reporter made his report. The last roll called, and the Society adjourned.

Decr 8. 1847. Signed—G. C. Greene, Sec.

[December 15, 1847]

The meeting was called to order by the President. The first roll called. The minutes read and approved. Mr. S. W. Weston motioned that the Society should return thanks to Mr. G. F. Barrow for his kindness in presenting the same with nearly a quire of paper;[11]—unanimously received. And also thanks to Mr. ^F.^ A. Mood for his kindness in tendering to us a code of Laws, and Lectures received from him, and Mr. Wm. Mood,—received without a dissenting voice. Mr. S. W. Weston motioned that an invitation be extended to Mr. John Mood Jr. on his arrival in the City, allowing him the privilege of attending meetings of the Society:—unanimously received.[12] He laid before the House the propriety of the Treasurer making a report at the expiration of his time, stating the ^sum^ received, and payed [sic] ~~away~~ from the Treasury: unanimously received. He also laid before the Society a bill to be annexed to the Constitution, which reads as follows. "That all monies received into the Society should be divided equally between the Literary box, and expenditures of the Society": unanimously received. He again motioned that the Rules be read quarterly, for the benefit of the Society: (to be annexed to the By Laws): Unanimously received. Again, that a Literary box be had at the expense of the Society,—unanimously received. That a Key be placed on the Library; which was carried. Mr. Wm. O. Weston laid for the consideration of the Society, a bill to be annexed to the Constitution; which reads as follows; "That all Officers of the Society except the President ~~be compelled to~~ be appointed regular debatants in their alphabetical order":—carried by a plurality of votes; but after a spirited debate it was repealed, as it was antagonistic to the 27th article of the Constitution. After a few remarks by the President the above motions connected with the Constitution were declared null and void, as the 27th art. of the Constitution required an evening's notice before any amendment or alteration can be made. The Society was therefore notified of the above motions, to be handed before the body at the next meeting. Mr. G. C. Green also notified the Body of a proposition to be made at the next meeting (to be annexed to the ~~Constitution~~ ^By Laws^); which re^a^ds as follows: 'That it shall require 1/3 majority to alter or amend any section of the By Laws, and the Society must have an evening's notice." The time being occupied by business the debate ^was^ defer[r]ed for the next evening. No further business appearing the Reporter made his report; the last Roll called, and the Society adjourned.

Decr 15. 1847. Signed, G. C. Greene, Secy.

Figure 3. Daniel Alexander Payne. Detail of *Bishops of the A.M.E. Church* (Boston: Printed by J. H. Daniels, [1876]), American Antiquarian Society, Worcester, MA, reprinted by courtesy.

[December 22, 1847]

The meeting was called to order by the President. The first Roll called. The minutes read and approved. The President declared to the body that as long as the present number of ~~of~~ members remain (11) 8 shall be considered 2/3 of the Society.[13] There being not 2/3 or 8 of the members present, there were no additions to the Constitution. The proposition~~s~~ offered, and of which the Society was

8   *Free Black Charlestonians in Debate*

notified by Mr. G. Greene, was unanimously carried. At the expiration of this time, a sufficient number of members being present, the propositions of which the Society ^was notified^ and offered by Mr. S. Weston were on motion unanimously carried. Mr. Weston also laid for the consideration of the House a list of Hon[or]ary Members—viz—Rev. Daniel Payne, Baltimore. Mr. B. Huger. W. W. Seymour. John Parker. John Mishaw, and (A. M. Bland of Philadelphia, Pen.)—unanimously carried. Mr. W. Gailliard[14] moved that a book committee be elected. Op^p^osed by Mr. S. Weston, as the business of a Book Committee is encumbent [*sic*] on ^the^ Reader. Mr. E. G. Beaird offered four Gentlemen to be annexed to the list of Honorary Members—viz—J. Weston. J. Green Sr. S. Weston, and F. H. Long. Opposed ^by^ Messrs. Gailliard and J. Green, but carried by a plurality of votes.[15] The subject, "Which is the most desirable Literary or Military glory," was then resumed, and after a spirited debate, it was decided that Literary glory is the most desirable. The question for the next Eevening's [*sic*] debate was chosen, which reads as follows,—"Whether a Republican or Monarchial government tends most to the happiness of a people." The Secretary read the debatants as follows—Master W. H. Gailliard on the Republican, and Mr. F. H. Oliver on Monarchial. No further business appearing the Reporter made his report. The last Roll called, and the Society adjourned. Decr 22. 1847. Signed—G. C. Greene, Sec.

Erratum[16]—Mr. J. J. Green Jr. notified the Society that he would motion that the number of Honorary members be restricted.

NOTES

1. The first president was Simeon W. Beaird. He was reelected on March 15, 1848.
2. The constitution is not extant. The minutes suggest that nine young men founded the society: Enoch G. Beaird, Simeon W. Beaird, William H. Gailliard, G. C. Greene, Jacob J. Greene Jr., Stephen J. Maxwell, F. H. Oliver, Samuel W. Weston, and William O. Weston.
3. *Videlicet,* abbreviated *viz.:* "namely."
4. For a list of members, honorary members, and supporters of the society, see appendix A.
5. *Pro tempore:* "for the time being." The society agreed to appoint a reader as the need for one arose. More commonly, the term *pro tem* in the minutes indicates a member's temporary appointment to a leadership role in the absence of an elected officer.
6. *Summum bonum:* "the highest good."
7. This is the only debating question unidentified in the minutes. For a list of debating questions and decisions, see appendix B.
8. US forces led by General Winfield Scott had captured Mexico City in September 1847, but the Treaty of Guadalupe Hidalgo, formally ending the war, would not be signed until February 1848.
9. The minutes use both Greene and Green to designate this member.

1847   9

10. *Lapsus pennae:* "slip of the pen." Greene may have been noting a slip in his inscription of Dereef's initials; the capital *F* is rendered ambiguously.

11. A *quire* is a measure of quantity, usually referring to twenty-four or twenty-five sheets of paper of the same size and quality.

12. Since the South Carolina legislature had outlawed school-keeping by free persons of color by an act of 1834, leaders of the free Black community in Charleston sought instruction for their children by hiring a series of young men of the Mood family, white Methodists, while they were students at the College of Charleston. Francis Asbury Mood, a college student between 1846 and 1850, was first an assistant to his elder brother John Amos Mood (the "John Mood Jr." mentioned in the minutes) and then later the principal teacher with his brother William as assistant. A member of the Cliosophic Literary Society at the college, he was known by his middle name, Asbury. See Francis A. Mood, *For God and Texas: Autobiography of Francis Asbury Mood, 1830–1884: Circuit Rider, Educator, and Founder of Southwestern University, Georgetown, Texas,* ed. Mary Katherine Metcalfe Earney (Dallas, TX: Listo, 2001), 40–50; and Claude Carr Cody, *The Life and Labors of Francis Asbury Mood, D.D.* (Chicago: F. H. Revell, 1886), esp. 75–80, 92, 104–9.

13. The minutes suggest the involvement of twelve individuals at this point: Gabriel F. Barrow, Enoch G. Beaird, Simeon W. Beaird, J. M. F. Dereef, William H. Gailliard, G. C. Greene, Jacob J. Greene Jr., William E. Marshall, Stephen J. Maxwell, F. H. Oliver, Samuel W. Weston, and William O. Weston. Possibly Simeon W. Beaird, the society president, was not counted here as a member.

14. The minutes use both Gailliard and Gaillard to designate this member.

15. Honorary members of nineteenth-century literary and debating societies tended to be older than regular members; regular members could appeal to them for advice or material assistance. Honorary members could attend society meetings, although they visited primarily on special occasions. The initial group of honorary Clionians, all men, included leaders of the free Black community in Charleston, such as brothers Jacob and Samuel Weston, Methodist tailors, as well as the Reverend Daniel A. Payne, then in Baltimore and soon to become the sixth bishop of the African Methodist Episcopal Church. Local honorary members included fathers of regular members; for instance, Samuel Weston was the father of William O. Weston, and Jacob Weston was the father of Samuel W. Weston. Several of the local honoraries belonged to the Brown Fellowship Society and the Friendly Union Society, and several held other people in bondage. On this generation, see Bernard E. Powers Jr., *Black Charlestonians: A Social History, 1882–1885* (Fayetteville: University of Arkansas Press, 1994), 36–72.

16. *Erratum:* "error." Greene is indicating that he neglected to include this item of business when entering the minutes of the meeting in the proceedings volume. He may have noted the error upon his initial entry or after the minutes were read for members' approval at the subsequent meeting.

— 1848 —

[In this year the society held its first election of officers, and the first oration was delivered. Secretaries minuted twenty-three meetings, including one later expunged from the records; thirteen meetings included debates, two included orations.—Ed.]

[January 5, 1848]

The meeting was called to order by the President. The first Roll called. The minutes read and approved. Mr. G. C. Green handed a copy of a Letter to be recorded, ^&^ to be addressed to Hon[or]ary members elect—unanimously received. He also notified the Committee of a meeting for the transaction of business assigned them. Mr. W. Gailliard offered Messrs. Job Bass, and J. Johnson as hon^or^ary members,—carried by a plurality of votes. The debate opened by the regular debatants, and kept up with little animation. The question was then decided in favour of a Republican government. The question for the next evening's debate was chosen, which reads as follows—'Which is the happier civilized or savage life.['] The Regular debatants—Messrs. S. & W. Weston. Mr. S. Weston for Civilized, and Mr. W. Weston for savage. No further business appearing the Reporter made his report. The Last Roll called, and the Society adjourned.

Jan 5. 1848. Signed—G. Greene, Sec.

[January 12, 1848]

The meeting was called to order by the President. The first Roll called. The minutes read and approved. Mr. J. Mood Jr. having accepted the invitation extended him, and being present, the President addressed him in laconic and appropriate terms, welcoming him to the Society. The debate opened by the regular debatants and kept up with much annimation. The question was then decided that a "civilized life was the happier." The question for the next evening's debate was chosen, which reads as follows—"Which excelled the more in literary pursuits, the Moderns or Ancients."[1] The Secretary read the debatants

10

as follows—Mr. E. G. Beaird for Moderns, and Mr. J. J. Green Jr. for Ancients. Mr. J. Mood then addressed the Society in beautiful and expressive terms, commending their advancement, and advising them to continue in their laudable engagement &c. No further business appearing before the Society, the Reporter made his report. The last Roll called, and the Society adjourned.
Jan 12. 1848. Signed—G. C. Greene, Sec.

[January 19, 1848]

The meeting was called to order by the President. The first Roll called. The minutes read and approved. The meeting was honored by the presence of Mr. A. F. [F. A.] Mood. The debate opened by the debatant for the Moderns (the other being absent) and kept up with much annimation. The question was decided,— "that the Moderns excell [*sic*] the Ancients." The question for the next evening's debate was chosen—which reads as follows—"Whether the liberty of the press should be ~~allowed~~ restrained or not." The Secretary read the debatants as follows—Mr. W. H. Gailliard on the affirmative, and Mr. W. E. Marshall on the negative. Mr. A. Mood made several appropriate and instructive remarks on the debated question, which were multum in parvo.[2] No further business appearing the Reporter made his report—the last Roll called—and the Society adjourned.
Jan. 19, 1848. Signed—G. C. Greene, Sec.

[January 26, 1848]

The meeting was called to order by the President, the first Roll called, the minutes read and approved. The debate opened by the regular debatants and kept up with much animation. The question was then decided in the negative. Mr. S. Weston motioned that Mr. W. Marshall furnish the Society a copy of his debate,—unanimously carried. The question for the next evening's debate was chosen which reads as follows—Which is the most useful[,] literary or romance reading.[3] The Secretary read the debatants as follows—Mr. G. Barrow on the affirmative and Mr. F. H. Oliver on the negative. No further business appear-
[At least two leaves were removed from the proceedings volume at this point. A meeting occurred on February 1, 1848, that was later declared "null and void." On March 1 the society voted to alter the minutes "so as to blot it from off the proceedings."—Ed.]
~~Correction~~ (what was not added.) Mr. ^Jacob^ Green during the meeting shoved Mr. Gailliard against the mantle peice [*sic*]. ~~which was very~~

[February 2, 1848]

The meeting was called to order by the President; the seats of the Secretary and Treasurer being vacant the President appointed Mr. W. O. Weston Secretary protem and Mr. E. G. Beaird Treasurer protem—the first roll was then called—the minutes of the "extra" meeting was not read, it being doubtful to the members whether they should be read or not as the meeting was extra and deferred, that the proceedings might also be deferred by a vote of the society—they all being of one opinion—by motion of Mr. S. W. Weston it was put to the house to determine by thier [*sic*] sanction what should be done, whereupon it was carried unanimously that the proceedings should be passed at the next "extra" meeting. The Reporter being appointed Treasurer protem, Mr. G. Barrow was appointed Reporter protem; the Reporter informed the society of two gentlemen about the premises wishing to become members of the same—being represented by Mr. Barrow as gentlemen which in all respects would meet the demands of the "Constitution," they were accordingly ballotted [*sic*] for and unanimously elected, in names they stand Messers. [*sic*] R. Legare and I. Hyames[4]—being introduced by the com[m]ittee appointed, and having heard the Constitution read they subscribed themselves as members. The President then opened the floor for any member; as he stated at the last meeting that the debates would be concluded at this meeting; after being treated on to some extent by a part of the members, it was decided that "Literary reading is the most useful." The question chosen for the next meeting's debate, reads thus, "Whether ^the^ application of steam to machinery has been of any ^dis^advantage to mankind or not." The secretary then read the debatants as follows Mr. S. W. Weston on the affirmative and Mr. William O. Weston on the negative. The Presdt gave notice that as the debatants had already been appointed, and next meeting being the meeting for the quarterly oration, we would then be obliged to listen to the "Orator" on the meeting following the next. The President again stated that the thanks of the house be offered to Mr. G. Barrow for the gift of two sperm candles,[5] which through his not being aware of the gift is the reason of it not being offered before, as it was presented several meetings ago; which upon motion the thanks of the house was returned to the gentleman. All the business being conducted with the greatest "<u>harmony</u>," and no farther appearing the Reporter protem made his report; the last roll called and the society by motion was adjourned. February 2nd 1848. Signed, W. O. Weston, secretary pro-tem

[February 4, 1848]

Extra Meeting

The meeting was called to order by the President, the first Roll called; the minutes read and approved; and some gentlemen haveing [sic] voted con, the President asked for their reasons; which were immediately given. The Protest read, on which a spiritly [sic] debate ensued, occupying the time allowed by the Constitution, without coming to a conclusion, or descision [sic]. No further business appearing, the extra meeting was adjourned sine die.[6]

Erratum—The proceedings of the last extra meeting read, (being defer[r]ed) and corrections made.

Feb 4th 1848. Signed, G. C. Greene, Secr.

[February 9, 1848]

The meeting was called to order by the President, the seats of the Secretary and Treasurer being vacant, Mr. W. O. Weston was appointed to fill that of the Secretary, and Mr. W. H. Gailliard that of the Treasurer. The first roll was then called—the minutes of the last "extra" meeting read, and after alteration of date, was approved—being favoured with the presence [of] Messers. Job G. Bass. and F. H. Long, honorary members; the Secretary by order read the "Constitution" for thier hearing; after which the regular debatants were read—and after treating the subject for some time, it was decided that "application of steam to machinery has been of advantage to man." The President gave notice that as on the next meeting the "Quarterly Orator" would address the Society; that no questions for discussion would be proposed until the next meeting. No farther business appearing—the Reporter made his report—the last roll was then called—and the Society by motion was adjourned.

February 9th 1848. Signed, William O. Weston, (sec) pro tem

[February 10, 1848]

At an extra meeting of the Clionian Debating Society, the house was called to order by the President, the minutes read, and approved. After which, ~~the protest~~ the Protest which had been defer[r]ed, was laid before the Society for discussion. Mr. F. H. Oliver requested the Secretary to read the proceedings of Feb. 2; in which he ~~sho detected~~ discovered a clause relative to the protest having been carried. A debate ensued; and finally it was decided that the meeting of Feb. 1. be considered "null and void," in strict conformity with the "Protest." No further business appearing, on motion the house adjourned.

Feb 10. 1848. Signed—G. C. Greene, Sec.

[February 16, 1848]

The meeting was called to order by the President—the first Roll called—the minutes read and approved. Several of the honorary [members] being present, the Secretary ~~was authorized to~~ read the Constitution ~~and for~~ ^according to "By Laws"^ their benefit ^also^. Mr. S. W. Weston the 'Quarterly orator' greeted the Society with ^a^ commendable address;[7] and after the conclusion the Society requested a copy, and in compliance to request the original was immediately transfer[r]ed to the same. About this time the seat of the Secretary being vacant, by leaf [*sic*] of absence—Mr. I. Hyames was appointed Secretary protem. The polls for the Election of Quarterly Orator were opened—and after the Manager's report—Mr. E. G. Beaird was declared to have been elected, by a plurality of votes, the next Quarterly Orator. The question for ^the^ next evening's debate was chosen, which reads as follows,—"Which was the greatest and most virtuous general, Washington or Alexander?["][8] Mr. S. Weston notified the Society that he would offer a bill for the alteration of two sections of the Constitution—Art. 12 & 14.—The President ^notified^ the Society that the number of members having increased to fourteen, ten shall be considered as 2/3.[9] No further business appearing the Reporter made his report, the last Roll called, and the Society adjourned.

Feb 16. 1848. G. C. Greene, Sec.

Erratum—E. G. Beaird on affirmative of the question, and G. Barrow on the negative.

[February 23, 1848]

The meeting being called to order by the President, the first roll was then called, the minutes of the last meeting read, and after little alteration approved. (Mr. R. F. Legare was appointed to fill the vacant seat of the vice President; Mr. W. O. Weston to fill that of the Secretary, and Mr. I. Hyames that of the Treasurer.) A letter of resignation was received from Messrs. S. W. Weston. G. C. Greene. ~~and~~ J. J. Greene and F. H. Oliver, which being put was unanimously carried. The Secretary then read the debatants; which after the conclusion of thier arguments; it was decided that "Washington was the greatest and most virtuous general." The debatants for the next meeting were read; viz. Mr. I. Hyames for Hannibal and Mr. R. Legare for Napoleon. The question (before which reading) was carried, reads thus "Which was the most skilful general Hannibal or Napoleon."[10] Mr. W. Weston notified the society of an alteration* to 12th & 14th Rules of the Constitution; from the specified day to "first meeting." No farther buisness [*sic*] appearing the Reporter made his report—the last roll called, and the Society by motion adjourned.

Feb 23rd 1848. Signed—W. O. Weston, acting secretary

*He would propose to be made at the next meeting.

[March 1, 1848]

The meeting was called to order by the President—the first roll was then called—the proceedings of the last meeting read and approved—the debate opened, and kept up by many members—after which it was decided that "Napoleon was the most skilful general." The question chosen for the next meeting's discussion, reads thus, "Which is of the most service to man, those machines that ply upon the water or land." The regular debatants were read, viz. Mr. W. H. Gailliard on the first portion of the question, and Mr. W. O. Weston on the latter portion. Mr. W. O. Weston then offered the alterations to the Constitution, of which the Society was notified at the last meeting, which being put was carried; he also ~~offe~~ gave notice that at the next meeting he would offer the following additions to the Constitution. First; "All such wishing to become members shall apply by letter with two recommenders, which letter cannot be read; except 2/3 of the members be present; and no applicant can be eligible except at the age of 16 or more years." Second; "The President shall not be allowed any vote; unless there is an equal number on each side. Then he is allowed the casting vote." Third; "The Constitution and Bye Laws, shall be strictly enforced at every meeting whether "Regular or Extra" as far as they are applicable." Fourth; Every officer at the expiration of his term shall be required, to have finished all buisness incumbent on his office, and report its completion to the President; and the President shall notify the Society of the same. Fifth; "The first meeting in February, the first in May, and first in August and the first in November, shall be the times for the hearing of the "Quarterly Orator," and the election of another. Any orator elect that shall refuse ^or fail^ to serve, shall forfeit 12 1/2 cts."[11] He also notified an alteration to the 7th Article; that instead of Six; five members shall form a quorum. After which notifications, he moved that as the meeting of Feb 1st was protested and carried, that a black line be drawn over every line, so as to blot ~~if~~ it from off the proceedings of the Society; Messers. Legare and Hyames then offered thier resignation to the Society; stating and giving many reasons for so doing; not that they found any fault with it or its members; but for its benefit principally; which by thier request was received; but not until many members, viz. Messers. E. G. Beaird W. H. Gailliard and W. O. Weston; spoke earnestly in thier regret for thier leaving and

16   *Free Black Charlestonians in Debate*

bidding them a friendly farewell. No farther business appeared—the Reporter was called upon for his report, which being made—the last Roll was called—and the Society by motion was adjourned.

March 1st 1848. Signed, W. O. Weston, secretary pro-tem.

[March 15, 1848]

The meeting being called to order by the President, the first roll was called—the minutes of the last meeting read and approved—the President gave notice that the debate would be deferred to the next meeting as they had to go immediately by Constitution into an election for officers—after which the "ballotting box" was opened—and by report of Poll managers the following gentlemen were declared unanimously elected—as follows. S. W. Beaird re-elected President—W. E. Marshall Vice President elect—W. O. Weston secretary elect—S. J. Maxwell, Treasurer elect—E. G. Beaird. W. H. Gailliard and G. Barrow Committee of Queries elect—and J. M. F. Dereef Reporter elect.[12] Mr. W. O. Weston then offered his additions to the Constitution and one alteration, of which the Society had been notified; which were immediately carried. He also moved an alteration to the Honorary member's letter, from plurality of votes to elected which was also carried; he then offered Mr. C. H. Holloway as an Honorary member ~~which~~ who was unanimously elected;[13] he again offered a letter to be written to members elect, which was carried. After which no more business appeared—and the house by motion adjourned.

March 15th 1848. Signed, William O. Weston, Secretary

Erratum. The Reporter was called on for his report which was made.

[March 22, 1848]

The meeting was called to order by the President; the first roll called—The President, Secretary and Committee of Queries being present, they were respectively inaugurated; after which the regular debatants were called upon, which after they concluded and treated on by all present; it was decided; that as far the word "ply" meant in the question; "that those machines that ply on the water ~~was~~ were the most serviceable." The Committee then handed in thier questions; the one chosen reads as follows. "Was it ambition that led Napoleon to battle or not." Mr. E. G. Beaird for the affirmative, and Mr. ~~W. Gailliard~~ G. F. Barrow for the negative. No farther ^business^ appearing the Reporter by call made his report, the last roll called—and the house adjourned by motion.

March 22nd 1848. Signed, William O. Weston, sec.

Erratum. The minutes of last meeting read and approved.

[April 5, 1848]

The meeting being called to order by the President; the first roll was then called; the Treasurer-elect being present was respectively installed; the debate then began by the regular debatants, but not being concluded at the regular hour, it, by the discretion of the President ^was^ deferred to next meeting; the Presdt then explained the 6th Art. of the Constitution; notifying the Society that after the expiration of this official term; that the office of Secretary and Treasurer shall by ~~Constional~~ Constitutional authority be held by one member; no farther buisness appeared, the Reporter made report; the last roll was called and the Society by motion adjourned. (The minutes of last meeting was read and approved.)

April 5th 1848. Signed, W. O. Weston, secretary

[May 17, 1848]

The meeting was called to order by the President; the first roll was then called: There being no meeting since April 5th in consequence of many members being unavoidably detained from forming a quorum through many circumstances; the President for this cause deferred the subject, as no one was prepared to continue it at that moment; for it was already a deferred subject and no one could be compelled to debate. After which the following Preamble and Resolution was offered in the names of Messers. G. Barrow and E. Beaird. They read thus, "Whereas we the members of the "Clionian Debating Society["]; knowing "education" to be one of the most important of duties devolved upon man, and the improvement thereof to be most essential. Rather than give up the good fight of usefulness to ourselves and to others.[14] We would offer a "resolution" to our fellow members; As circumstances will not permit us to assemble together as often as we would desire and often as we should meet. Hoping that for the present, it may be of benefit to us all, members in one common bond of "Love." "Therefore be it Resolved; That on and after the passage of this "Resolution," this Society in compliance with the above Preamble, do meet on the first Wednesday in every month for discussion of ^(regular)^ subjects among its members, and that the Article which requires it to meet every week, be held in suspension; until a quorum of the members can make it convenient to comply with the 22nd Art., and on thier reporting such wishes to the Society; this resolution can be dropped; and the 22nd Art. complied with: But be it further Resolved that the President can call intervening meetings for the passage of any resolution, the election of any applicant or the performance of any business, [a few words obliterated] at his discretion; And that the Secretary shall summon the members regularly, after receiving orders from the President." The above "resolution" was passed unanimously. The following addition ~~was~~ to the Constitution was then read, as a notification for its being put at the next meeting; it thus reads, "The President shall not be allowed to take any part in the regular debates. But if there is discussion among the members; concerning matters of interest to the Society, such as the alteration or augmentation of the "Rules" of the Constitution, the passage of any resolution or the carrying of any motion; &c &c; when he rises to put ~~it~~ any such matters to the Society, after the members have ended thier opinions on the subject; he can also state his opinion likewise.["] After this notification the President rose, and addressed the Society for some length of time on "the benefits derived from a connexion with such a body, as ~~as~~ a Debating ^Society^, showing the vast improvement it makes in the human mind by compelling studious research into subjects of vast import, that would never once before have claimed our attention, he concluded by asking earnestly that every member would study his debate thoroughly before every meeting, for that by such, he would expect to see our star of improvement in the ascendant. He then motioned that every member that would second his request would rise from thier ^seats^, upon which every one present rose with one consent. There being no more business to engage the body; the last roll was called; the report made and the Society adjourned by motion, to meet according to passed "Resolution." May 17th 1848. Signed, W. O. Weston, secretary

(The minutes of last meeting read and approved.)

[June 7, 1848]

The meeting was called to order by the President—the first roll was then called—the minutes of last meeting read and approved.—The regular debates then commenced which after conclusion, it was decided that it was ambition that led Napoleon to battle. The question chosen for next meeting reads thus. Which nation fought on the most just side the United [States] or Mexico, Mr. ~~Barrow~~ Gailliard on the first portion and Mr. Maxwell on the latter. The Presdt then informed the body that they were notified of the election of "Annual Orator" at the last meeting, but through mistake omitted in the regular proceedings, the polls were opened for ann. orator, which after report of managers ^Honorary Member^ Mr. J. Parker was declared unanimously elected. By vote of the body, power was given the Presdt to instruct the Secty, to alter the specified time if he thought proper; notice was then given to the Society, that the election for officers would take place at next meeting. No farther business appearing, the last roll was called; the Reporter made his report and the Society by motion adjourned.

June 7th 1848. Signed, William O. Weston, sec.

[July 19, 1848]

At this date, the ~~second~~ third regular [word obliterated] ^election^ meeting of the Clionian Debating Society was held. Which being called to order by the President; the first roll was called; the minutes of last meeting read and approved; there being but little time to remain in body after the above business; the President by permission deferred the debates to the next general meeting; & so as to give time for the election ^of^ officers for the third term, as the second term expired by constitution. The President rose, and addressed the meeting, asking them to receive kindly, his resignation of the Presidential authority; as there were others fully capable of holding it, and whom he would be glad to see performing such duties.[15] After which the polls were opened; and upon report of managers appointed, the following named gentlemen were declared unanimously elected to fill the following offices for the next term. viz. Mr. E. G. Beaird Presdt. Mr. W. E. Marshall Vice. Mr. S. W. Beaird Secretary & Treasurer. Messrs. G. F. Barrow, W. H. Gailliard, & W. O. Weston Committee of Queries; Mr. S. J. Maxwell, Reporter. The Secretary, Committee of Queries &c being present were duly installed, each returning thier thanks in appropriate remarks. The President elect not being in the city; Mr. W. H. Gailliard was appointed Presdt. protem; to act with the same powers untill the arrival of the President or his Vice. No farther business appearing; the Report was made of the order of the body during meeting; the last roll was then called and the house adjourned by motion.

July 19th 1848. Signed, S. W. Beaird, Secretary

[September 18, 1848]

The meeting being called to order by the Presdt pro-tem; the first roll was called; the proceedings of last monthly meeting read and approved. The regular debating then commenced; and after being kept up with much animation for some time, it was finally decided that in the last war the United States fought on the most just side. At this time Mr. S. W. Beaird offered a resolution to the Society, which was preceded with a few remarks, which being put was unanimously carried. (See rule book 3rd resolution with this date)[16] The Presdt under authority of the resolution appointed S. W. Beaird as chairman of the committee, it being moved by Mr. W. O. Weston and seconded by Mr. G. F. Barrow. For which appointment S. W. Beaird returned his grateful thanks to his fellow members. Mr. Barrow now moved that the Presdt do authorize the secretary to write a letter to all non-attending members, notifying them that if they do not attend the meetings, that thier names shall be struck off the list of membership. Which was opposed by S. W. Beaird, he endeavouring to show that it was not in thier power to expel any member without he committed some flagrant act, and also endeavouring to exhibit the bad results that would follow such expulsion; after which Mr. Barrow withdrew his motion. Mr. Weston moved that the members be notified of the change of the hour according to Constitution from Eight to Seven O'clock untill [*sic*] March, after the seconding of which; the members were notified and requested always to be punctual. The committee of Queries now handed in thier "Questions." Mr. Barrow's question was put and carried; but a mistake made by the Presdt caused confusion in the votes; and the questions were again ~~ballotted~~ put to the house; where-upon Mr. Weston's question was carried by plurality of votes; which reads thus "Will the acquisition of California be of any great use to the U.S."[17] S. W. Beaird stood as next regular debatant on the affirmative, and G. F. Barrow on the negative of the question. No farther business demanding the attention of the assembled body; the Society was by motion adjourned.

(September 18th 1848) S. W. Beaird, Secretary

[October 1, 1848]

~~At~~ an extra meeting of the Society was called at this inst;[18] to ^take^ into consideration, the contents of a letter received from Honorary member J. S. Parker, Annual orator elect. Which after its reading, it was found only to ask for the deferring of the appointed time, to at least three weeks later; after which Sect. Beaird moved that the time of the celebration, be on the 26th of December; following his motion with a few words to show that no other time would suit the circumstances of either the members, or the community at large at this season of the year; which motion being seconded by W. Weston Esq., upon its being put to the house was unanimously carried; and the Secretary ordered to answer and notify Mr. Parker immediately. Mr. Barrow ~~requested~~ moved that the Society ~~do~~ request the debate of S. W. Beaird, at last meeting on the justice of the Mexican war; being seconded by W. O. Weston and being put was unanimously carried; whereby the debatant met the request by presenting his debate. No farther ^business^ presenting itself; the Society was by motion adjourned.

October 1st 1848. S. W. Beaird, Secretary

[December 17, 1848]

Another "extra" ^intervening^ meeting of this Society was held on this date. Which after being called to order by the President, the business for which it was called was begun. The Semi-Annual arrear list was called over and paid.[19] The Society then went into an election for officers, which upon report of Managers. The whole ticket for the last Four months was re-elected (See officers book). The

Secretary then read the last passed resolution, and received authority to destroy the "Original." Nearly all of the officers being present, they were duly qualified. Upon motion of S. W. Beaird seconded by W. O. Weston, it was unanimously carried that an invitation be extended to the Enterpean Debating Society to attend the hearing of our Annual address; and the Secty was ordered to perform the duty as soon as practicable. No farther business demanding the attention of our brotherlike assemblage; it was by motion adjourned.

Dec 17th 1848. S. W. Beaird, Secretary

[December 19, 1848]

Another "Extra" intervening meeting of this Society, was held for the purpose of considering the answer of Honorary Member J. S. Parker which, after the Chairman ^of the Committee^ on General interests had informed the Society that he had received a communication, from him, stating that extreme sickness had prevented him from attending to the duty devolved upon him, and humbly asking to be excused from the performance of his duty to at least three weeks hence; which was to address the Society on its Anniversary ^the^ day. ^of^ Dec 26th 1848. When upon motion it was unanimously Resolved. That this Society do excuse Mr. J. S. Parker. But the deference of the time could be no longer than the 1st day of January. And further as he cannot perform the duty on that day; that we if possible must endeavour to secure the services of another honorary member. Whereupon Mr. Job G. Bass was offered and unanimously elected, and the Committee on General interests ^was^ instructed to go immediately and wait upon ^him^, and thereby receive his verbal answer. When upon thier return; they reported that he had willingly accepted. The chairman of the Committee was then ordered to notify Mr. Parker of the Society's decision. Mr. Weston then offered Mr. Wm. McKinlay as an addition to the list of Honorary Members, and upon he being ballotted for, was unanimously elected. S. W. Beaird then offered the following resolutions, which were also unanimously carried. 1st Resolved. That the Committee on general interests; be instructed to report to the Assemblage, on the Anniversary day, the exact state of the Treasury department: and the manner in which such funds are raised. And further that they report our need of a "Library" and earnestly ask the assistance of the audience in the procurement of one. 2nd Resolved. That the management of all election polls be encumbered on the Committee on general interests, as a duty. 3rd Resolved That the clause, contained in Amendment No. 2 reading, "And no applicant can be eligible except at the age of 16 or more years." Be forever stricken out. After the passage of the above resolutions. The Secretary was ordered by vote of the Society, to extend ^an invitation^ to the community

22   *Free Black Charlestonians in Debate*

and also to every honorary member to attend the hearing of our Anniversary address on the 1st of January 1849. No further business appearing; the Society was by motion adjourned.

December 19th 1848. Simeon W. Beaird, Secretary

[December 26, 1848]

A regular monthly meeting of this Society, was held at this date. Which being called to order by its President; the first roll was called and the minutes of all meetings from the last monthly; were read, all of which were approved by the body. The regular debating then commenced, and being ^kept up^ for a good length of time, with much animation by nearly every member present; after the conclusion of which, ~~The~~ It was decided on the affirmative side; that the "acquisition of California will be of great advantage to the U.S.["] The Com^m^ittee of Queries now handed in thier questions; of which the one chosen reads thus, "Which country presents ^the^ brightest prospects for future happiness and permanency the U.S. or Great Britain." The Secretary by request then introduced his President as the regular "Quarterly Orator."[20] After which the President rose, and addressed the Society to some length on the importance of, and the advantages derived from good and careful reading: He having concluded Mr. S. W. Beaird moved the Society request a copy of his address, being seconded by Mr. W. O. Weston & put it was unanimously carried. Where-upon he immediately presented the "Original."[21] The Secretary then read the Constitution; by authority from the same. After which the Society went into a regular election for another "Quarterly Orator." And upon report of "poll" managers, Mr. Wm. H. Gaillard was declared elected and he was notified of the same. The ~~Sect~~ Secretary then read many beautiful letters received from "Honorary Members": which in thier contents were not only advising, but also very encouraging. The last roll was now called; as no farther business appeared; the Reporter made his report and the Society was by motion adjourned.

December 26th 1848. Simeon W. Beaird, Secretary

Erratum: Mr. R. E. Dereef; was offered by Mr. W. H. Gaillard; as an 'Honorary Member' to the Society; and he being ballotted for, was unanimously elected.

NOTES

1. "Ancients" in this question indicated writers of Western classical antiquity.
2. *Multum in parvo:* "much in little," that is, of much significance in a few words or in a short time.
3. In the nineteenth century, the term *literature* encompassed writings on science, history, religion, geography, and politics, not only poetry and fiction; *romance* signaled fictional compositions, especially stories of adventure, heroism, and love.

1848   23

4. The Clionian minutes use both Hyames and Hyams to designate this member. On March 20, 1854, he was serving as secretary of the Friendly Association and signed his own name as Isadore A. Hyames; Friendly Association Records, 1853–1869, South Carolina Historical Society, Charleston, SC.

5. Sperm candles were made from oil harvested from a whale's spermaceti organ.

6. *Sine die:* "without an appointed time for resumption," "indefinitely."

7. For a list of elected orators and orations, see appendix C.

8. The question compared US general and president George Washington (1732–1799) and Macedonian king Alexander the Great (356–323 BCE).

9. New members added since December 22, 1847, were Isadore A. Hyames and R. F. Legare. Evidently the society president was counted as a member in this enumeration.

10. Another comparative question, this one matched the Carthaginian general Hannibal (247–ca. 183–181 BCE) and French emperor Napoleon I (1769–1821).

11. The United States minted half-cent coins between 1793 and 1857.

12. All current members were elected officers.

13. The debating society ordinarily met on the Holloway family property on Beaufain Street. Charles H. Holloway (1814–1885), son of Richard Holloway and Elizabeth Mitchell Holloway, was a carpenter and harness maker and a Methodist class leader; he was among the free Black Charlestonians who held other people in bondage. See Harlan Greene and Jessica Lancia, "The Holloway Scrapbook: The Legacy of a Charleston Family," *South Carolina Historical Magazine* III, nos. 1–2 (January–April 2010): 5–33; Larry Koger, *Black Slaveowners: Free Black Slave Masters in South Carolina, 1790–1860* (Jefferson, NC: McFarland, 1985), 143; and Holloway Family Scrapbook, Holloway Family Collection, Avery Research Center for African American History and Culture, College of Charleston, Charleston, SC.

14. The term "the good fight" resonated with Christian scripture: for example, the Apostle Paul admonished Timothy, "Fight the good fight of faith, lay hold on eternal life, whereunto thou art also called, and hast professed a good profession before many witnesses" (1 Timothy 6:12, KJV); then, nearing the end of his life, Paul wrote, "I have fought a good fight, I have finished my course, I have kept the faith: Henceforth there is laid up for me a crown of righteousness" (2 Timothy 4:7–8, KJV).

15. Simeon W. Beaird resigned the presidential office at this point, having held the role since the society's inception. The new president, Enoch G. Beaird, was Simeon's younger brother.

16. Although the rule book is not extant, it is likely that this resolution created the Committee on General Interests, an appointed committee that managed the business affairs of the society and conducted elections.

17. Part of the Mexican Cession, California was ceded to the United States in 1848 as a result of the Mexican–American War. By the time of this debate, the California Gold Rush had begun.

18. *Instant,* abbreviated *inst.:* "occurring in the present month."

19. An arrear list identified members of the society who had not yet paid required fees.

20. The president at this time was Enoch G. Beaird.

21. Speaking from a written text, a common method of formal speechmaking, was a skill practiced regularly by members of nineteenth-century literary and debating societies.

— 1849 —

[In this year the society held its first anniversary event and began acquiring publications for a library. Secretaries minuted thirty-five meetings; twenty-two included debates, four included orations.—Ed.]

Anniversary Day, January 1st 1849

The ~~regular~~ "Anniversary day" being ^deferred^ until this date by circumstances; It was accordingly celebrated at this time at the "Hall" over the Society's meeting room:[1] where a beautiful and enlightened audience attended. After prayer by Honorary Member S. Weston; the first annual report was read by the Chairman of "Committee on general interests["]; which being concluded The President introduced Honorary Member J. G. Bass, to the assemblage, as the "Orator." He then arose and addressed not only the Society in the most beautiful, and yet the plainest of language; but the audience itself felt the force of his remarks ~~and~~, in the truths represented and contained therein. In concluding his beautiful, forcible, plain, advising and encouraging address; he stepped from off the stage, with the "Book" of all books in his hand, as a present to the Society, and the first that should enter thier contemplated "Library."[2] Before presenting it, he addressed the President in the most glowing terms of the importance and value of such a prize; after which he placed it into the President's hands. The President then responded in ^a^ most satisfactory manner, in which he expressed the gratefulness of the Society to him for such a valuable present and assured him, "that upon it the Society's principles should be based." After the conclusion of all the above; the Committee received a liberal collection from the audience ^for a Library^, and many promises; which showed that all was well pleased with our actions on our first celebration, and gives us great encouragement to continue on. Peaceableness having crowned the whole proceeding; the benediction was pronounced. And the delighted ^audience^ moved homeward with ~~spl~~ pleasing smiles upon thier cheeks.
Simeon W. Beaird, Secretary

[January 2, 1849]

An "Extra" meeting was now called. The Presdt having demanded order. The business of the meeting was begun. Mr. W. Weston moved that the Society do request a copy of Honorary member J. G. Bass' ~~sp~~ address before the Clionian Debating Society on the 1st of January 1849; and in addition a copy also of his address before the Christian Benevolent Society in May 1848, which being seconded by Mr. G. F. Barrow, was put and unanimously carried.[3] The Secretary was then ordered to make the request by letter. S. W. Beaird then moved that the Society ask a copy of the President's response to Mr. Bass on his presenting the Bible to the Society—which also being put was unanimously carried; and the request was immediately made to the President, which was accordingly met. Mr. Weston having seconded the motion ~~No farther~~ The Secretary acknowledged the reception of a letter from the Enterpean Debating Society, accepting the invitation extended to them to attend the Anniversary celebration. No farther business calling the attention of the body, it was by motion adjourned. January 2nd 1849. Simeon W Beaird, Secretary

[February 7, 1849]

A regular monthly meeting of the Clionian Society was held at this date. The Presdt having called it to order; the first roll was called and the proceedings of the last monthly and extra ^meetings^ were in conjunction, read, and approved. After which the regular debatants commenced to kindle the flame of discussion, which being nursed until the very hour of adjournment ^by every member^ was by request deferred until the next meeting for continuation. The following resolution was then offered by S. W. Beaird, which being seconded, was unanimously carried. Resolved: That after the passage of this resolution; Every member shall contribute monthly, the sum of 6/4 cts. for the ever continuing purchasing of books for the benefit of the body. The chairman of the "Committee on general interests" submitted his Annual report; having given ^reasons^ for not doing it at the regular time. No farther business appearing the Reporter made his report; the last roll was called and the house adjourned by motion.

February 7th 1849. Simeon W. Beaird, Secretary

[February 15, 1849]

An "Extra meeting" was now called. Which after having been called to order, was notified by the President that he had received a letter directed to the President, Officers and Members of the Clionian Debating Society. Which after opening; he turned over to his Secretary to read. Having first discovered that it

26 *Free Black Charlestonians in Debate*

contained the excellent sum of 2 Dollars sent as a gift from the Utopian Debating Society to aid in purchasing a Library. After the reading of the contents by the Secretary (which were found to be truly beautiful) S. W. Beaird immediately rose and moved, that a "Committee of response" be appointed to answer the letter instantly in due expressions of gratefulness and thankfulness; which after being seconded was unanimously carried. Where-by the following gentlemen were appointed to perform the honourable duty. Viz. Simeon W. Beaird Chairman. Messers. Gabriel F. Barrow, Wm. H. Gaillard, & Wm. O Weston Committee. The following resolution was now submitted by S. W. Beaird, which after being seconded was unanimously carried. Resolved That in order to preserve all the writings of this Society. A true copy of every ~~thing~~ written article sent either to or from this Society be kept in the Library. ~~No farther bus~~ The Chairman of the "Committee on general interests["] notified the body that the collections were going on finely and that as soon as they have finished receiving payment of promises. He would submit a true and exact report of the Same. No farther business demanding attention The meeting was by motion adjourned. Feb 15th 1849. Simeon W. Beaird, Sect.

[February 28, 1849]

Another intervening meeting of the "CDS" was held at this date. The President calling it to order, stated the objects for which the body assembled. After which he received two letters addressed to the President & Members, ~~from~~ ^through^ Mr. W. Weston, which after being read, were found to contain the applications of two gentlemen for membership; Viz. Messrs. Henry Cardozo Jr. & Augustus L. Horry. These gentlemen being fairly represented by thier recommenders; were ballotted for, & unanimously elected. Mr. S. Beaird then gave notice, that at the next meeting he would submit a set of "Rules" for the "Library Department." After which the Secretary gave the formal Weekly notice of the general election of officers and orators at the next meeting. Several motions were made, which after some misunderstandings and explanations, the business of the meeting closed, and upon motion the Society adjourned.
Feb 28th 1849. Signed, Simeon W. Beaird, Sec.

[March 5, 1849]

Still another "intervening" meeting of this Society was held at this time. The President called it to order and stated the objects of it. After which he opened a letter directed to the Society and handed it over to his Secretary for reading, which was discovered to contain in its contents the re-application of Mr. I. A. Hyames, for membership into the Society; he being declared fit to meet every

Figure 4. The Reverend Henry Cardozo, photograph by Walter C. North, Cleveland, OH, in Francis Lewis Cardozo Family Papers, 1864–1968, Manuscript Division, Library of Congress, Washington, DC, reprinted by courtesy. Henry Cardozo and his family lived in Cleveland from 1858 to 1868.

demand of the Constitution by his recommenders, was ballotted for and unanimously re-elected. Messrs. Beaird & Weston, now in succession rose and endeavoured to show and explain the terms upon which Mr. Hyames resigned, concluding by showing that he would not be required again to pay the entrance fee but only the regular arrears that would have been due by him had he continued. All of which was received by the members. Mr. Weston now moved that the President be requested to defer the debates of the next meeting to the next anticipated weekly meeting, which request was duly granted by the President, with the consent of every member; as at the next meeting there would ^be^ so much business on hand as not to allow sufficient time to attend to the debates in a proper manner. Mr. Beaird now gave notice of his intention to introduce at the next meeting an augmentation to the Constitution, for the regular appointment of a "Committee" to examine the books and money department of the Sect & Treas at every election and report thereof to the Society. No farther business appearing, the meeting adjourned by motion.

March 5th 1849. Simeon W. Beaird, Sec.

[March 7, 1849]

A regular meeting was now held; the Presdt called it to order; the first roll being called; the minutes of the last regular and all intervening meetings were read and approved. The members elect being present and introduced, now gave audience to the Constitution, after which they in succession subscribed themselves; paid all monies required, and received congratulations both from President and members; the monthly "Library" list was called over and almost altogether paid up. Mr. S. Beaird now submitted the "Rules" for the "Library Department" of which he had notified the Society, which were all unanimously carried ("See Library Department"). He also moved that the blank in Art. 9th of those Rules, be not yet filled, but that we for a little time yet still comply with the 6th Resolution which was carried. Mr. W. O. Weston offered a resolution which was unanimously carried (See Resolutions No. 8). Mr. W. H. Gaillard offered another which was carried in the like manner. (See Resolutions No. 9). Mr. Beaird now submitted the Amendment No. 8 of which he had notified the Society was intended to be added to the Constitution, which also was unanimously carried (See Amendments). The term of the present seated officers having now expired and the ^Sect^ having already before given the formal notice; the President after having occupied his seat for 2 terms, now willingly resigned it, which was received by the body, with reluctance, yet hoping that she[4] still had members who would endeavour to fill it, with as much impartiality and sound judgment as her now retiring President had done. The body after having gone into an election

for officers; the chairman of the Poll managers declared the following ticket unanimously elected (See officers' book). Mr. W. Weston was also declared unanimously elected as the next Quarterly Orator, and Honorary member Benjamin Huger as next "Annual Orator." Nearly every officer ᵇ elect being present, they were respectively installed; and such was the excitement of feelings at the time, that not an officer elect fell short of receiving a complimentary speech from his President, ^&^ which he did not fail to answer in return. Mr. Weston offered a "petition" in conformity with Resolution 1st for the changing of the meetings from "monthly" to "weekly" which was unanimously adopted and the members notified of the above change. No farther business demanding the attention of this brotherly conducted meeting; the Reporter made his report; the last roll was called and the Society adjourned by motion.
March 7th 1849. Simeon W. Beaird, Secretary

[March 14, 1849]

According to the adopted petition from many members, at last meeting; the first regular of the "Weekly" meetings took place. The President called it to order; the first roll was called; the minutes of last meeting were read and approved. The debates on the deferred question were begun and continued until the very hour of adjournment, when upon the President's decision, the United States and her supporters came off as winners. The Committee having now handed in thier questions; the following one was carried. Viz. "Was England right in banishing Napoleon Bonaparte to the Island of St. Helena?"[5] On the affirmative; S. W. Beaird was read as supporter, and E. G. Beaird on the negative. The Secretary now read the copy of the letter sent by him to Honorary Member B. Huger, which was received as the property of the Society. No more business appearing; the Reporter made a favourable report; the last roll was called and the Society, by motion adjourned.
March 14th 1849. Simeon W. Beaird, Sect.

[March 21, 1849]

A regular "Weekly" meeting was held at this date. The President having called it to order; the Secretary called the first roll; and read the minutes of the last meeting which were approved. The regular debating now commenced in its usual animating style, which being kept up for a length of time, was upon the President's rising, decided favourable to the affirmative supporters. The questions being handed in, and acted upon; the following one was chosen, "Are there any benefits derived from riches?" Mr. H. Cardozo was read out, on the affirmative, and Mr. W. Gaillard on the negative. No other business appearing to demand

30   *Free Black Charlestonians in Debate*

attention; the last roll was called and absentees called on for excuses, which being done; the Reporter presented his report; and this harmonious meeting adjourned by motion.

March 21st 1849. S. W. Beaird, Sec.

[March 28, 1849]

At this date and at the usual hour, the regular Weekly meeting of this Society was called to order by its President. The first roll being called; the minutes of the last were read and approved. The "Debatants" were now read out, who accordingly rose in succession; after which the floor being opened, the heat of discussion began to be more sensibly felt, which lasted until the <u>very</u> hour of adjournment. When the President rose, and, by deciding with great impartiality on the "Affirmative" lessened it in a very great degree. The Committee being called on, handed in thier questions. The one chosen reading thus "Is the Republic of France likely to remain permanent?"[6] Mr. G. Barrow was read on the affirmative and Mr. I. Hyames on the negative. No more business presenting itself; the Reporter being called on made his report; the last roll was called and this encouraging meeting was by motion adjourned in harmony.

March 28th 1849. Simeon W. Beaird, Secretary

[April 4, 1849]

A regular Weekly meeting of the CDS being held at this time, it was called to order by the President. The first roll was called; the minutes of the last meeting read and approved. The affirmative debatant being read out, rose and supported himself for a good length of time; after which the negative gentleman being called upon, was announced to be absent; whereupon the floor was opened, and successive gentlemen rose "pro" and "contra" until the subject was almost exhausted when the adjourning hour came and stopped thier movements. The President rising, decided on the negative part of the question. The question chosen of those handed in, reads thus.—"Has the Pope's banishment been or is likely to be of any advantage to Rome?"[7] Mr. A. L. Horry was read on the affirmative & Mr. S. W. Beaird on the negative. No more business demanding the attention of the body. The Reporter made his report. The last roll was called and this harmonious meeting adjourned by motion.

April 4th 1849. Simeon W. Beaird, Sec.

[April 11, 1849]

A regular meeting of this Society was held and called to order by the President. The first roll was called; and the minutes of the last, read, and approved. The debatants now in succession rose with considerable warmth on both sides, and being supported in a most able manner by every one present until past the adjourning hour, ~~they~~ ^they^ thus placed the President in a doubtful position, until at last he acknowledged and gave way to the superiority of the "Negatives." The questions being handed in by the Committee, the following was chosen "Was Brutus right or wrong in condemning his sons to execution, when tried before him for conspiring against the government?"[8] Mr. E. G. Beaird was read on the first portion and Mr. G. F. Barrow on the latter. No farther business appearing; the Reporter made his report; the last roll was called and the Society was adjourned by motion.

April 11th 1849. Simeon W. Beaird, Sec.

May 21st 1849

A ~~regular~~ meeting of the Clionian D. Society was held on the above date; which owing to sickness; affliction; inclemency of weather and other preventing circumstances was, though attempting to meet at ~~many~~ ^various^ times, kept, from so doing. All hindrances being now removed, the President called a meeting at this time to bring the members together before the next regular meeting, which was attended exceedingly well. Being called to order by the President; the first roll was called; the minutes of the last meeting were read and approved. The debating on the last chosen question having commenced was continued for some time with much animation, after the conclusion of which it was decided on the first portion of the question. As there was much business to be attended to on the next meeting, the President by request of members, appointed it as "Business meeting." The Secretary gave notice of the elections of two orators to take place at the next meeting, he also gave notice of the contributions that would be ~~required at~~ ^called for^ at the meeting which have become due. Mr. S. Beaird, seconded by Mr. E. Beaird, moved that a "Committee of Four" be appointed to address a communication to Honorary member Daniel A. Payne, at Baltimore, which after the Committee was augmented from "Four" to "Eight" was unanimously carried, and the following gentlemen appointed. Viz. S. W. Beaird Chairman, Messrs. H. Cardozo, A. L. Horry, E. G. Beaird, G. F. Barrow, J. M. Dereef, W. H. Gaillard and I. A. Hyames Committee. Several other motions were made, but which after being objected to by others and shown to be out of place were withdrawn. No more of business appearing, the Reporter made his report. The last roll was called, and the Society by motion was adjourned.

Simeon W. Beaird, Sec.

May 23rd 1849

A regular ^meeting^ being held was called to order by its President; the first ^roll^ being called and the minutes of the last meeting read and approved, the Society, according to motions carried at last meeting, went immediately to the transaction of business. The Monthly "Book" contribution list was called over and partly paid; the Semi-annual contribution list was also called over and partly paid. The Secretary, by orders from the President, now read the contents of a letter received from Mr. Benjamin Huger, Honorary Member; "Annual Orator elect" which after reading was found to contain information of his declining to serve, giving very sufficient reasons for so doing; the letter was then put to the house, which was unanimously carried.[9] The Presdt now ordered the 'Polls' to be opened by the managers; for the election of both an Annual and a Quarterly orater [sic]. After a space of time the 'Managers' through thier chairman, declared the following gentlemen elected by votes. Viz. Mr. Enoch G. Beaird "Annual orator" for January 1st 1850; and Mr. S. W. Beaird, "Quarterly Orater" for August 1849. The gentlemen being present were notified of the above results. The coming meeting being the one for the hearing of the Quarterly Orator; the Society was notified by its President that there would be no debating. No more of business being brought forward; the Reporter made his report; the last roll was called and the Society having observed the greatest order through the whole of its business was by motion adjourned.

Simeon W. Beaird, Sec.

'CDS,' May 30th 1849

In conformity with notice given at last meeting, this Society convened in all its strength, ~~to~~ being [word obliterated] ^favoured^ with the presence of many of its Honorary Members, to listen to the strains of oratory, which were to be poured forth by one of the 'Members.' Being called to order by the President; the first roll was called; the minutes of the last meeting were read ^&^ approved. As there was no question chosen at last meeting in consequence of the special business of this meeting, the 'Committee' was called upon for questions; the first question moved for, was lost; the second one was also lost; when upon putting the 'third,' it was carried by votes. Which reads thus "Which will a man hear first the prayer of his wife or mother?" The President now introduced Mr. W. H. Gaillard, as the 'Orator,' who addressed the 'Body' for some length of time upon the subject "Neglected Genius" in the most beautiful and figurative language that ever was heard from a member before, just at the conclusion of which every member sighed; thus regretting that it ended so soon. Mr. S. Beaird seconded by Mr. G. Barrow, after a few remarks moved that the Society request a copy of the address, which being put was unanimously carried. Whereupon the Speaker immediately presented the original. Upon the chosen question Mr. H. Cardozo stood as regular debatant on the first portion of the question, and Mr. W. H. Gaillard on the last. No more of business appearing, the Reporter made his report, the last roll was called and this more than agreeable meeting adjourned by motion.

Simeon W. Beaird, Sec.

'CDS,' June 6th 1849

A regular meeting of this Society was called to order by its President. The first Roll being called; the minutes of the last were read and approved. The debatants now rose in succession, who together with thier supporters kept up a lively house for some time; after which upon the rising of the President, the decision was altogether in favour of the 'Wife.' The Committee now handed in thier questions, when upon putting them to the house; the First, the Second and the third one were lost; whereupon a substitute for them was introduced which was unanimously carried. It thus reads "Were the Athenians, right in condemning Socrates to death"[10]—on the affirmative S. W. Beaird was read out and E. G. Beaird on the negative. No more business appearing; the Reporter upon call, made his report; the last roll was called, and this Society by motion was adjourned.

Simeon W. Beaird, Sec.

'CDS,' June 20th 1849

This meeting was called to order by the Vice President; the Presdt being absent through sickness. The first roll was called and the minutes of the last were read and approved. Mr. E. G. Beaird was called upon to fill the vacancy of the Vice's seat. The debating now commenced, which being kept up to the adjourning hour, received the decision in favour of the negative portion of the question. The following question was chosen for the next evening's debate "Which tends most to the diminution of ~~crime~~ ^murders^ 'capital' punishment or 'life-time' imprisonment.["]11 Mr. H. Cardozo stood next as affirmative and Mr. W. H. Gaillard as negative. No more business appearing the Reporter made his report & the Society by motion adjourned.

S. W. Beaird, Sec.

'CDS,' June 27th 1849

This regular meeting was called to order by the President; the first roll being called and the minutes being read were approved. The regular debatants having

34   *Free Black Charlestonians in Debate*

arisen and continued to demand attention for some time; after which the adjourning hour having arrived, it was moved that the President defer the question for further discussion at next meeting, which being put was unanimously carried. The next evening for meeting being the 4th of July, it was moved by S. Beaird that the members choose by votes, either an evening after or before that time; whereupon Mr. H. Cardozo, seconded by Mr. E. Beaird, moved that the Society meet on Monday evening 2nd of July at the usual hour, which was carried. No more of business appearing, the Reporter made his report, ~~and~~ the last Roll was called and the Society adjourned by motion.
Simeon W. Beaird, Sec.

'CDS,' July 5th 1849

In consequence of there being no meeting on Monday 2nd inst. as was expected; The Presdt ordered a meeting on this evening, which being well attended was called to order by him. The first roll was called and the minutes of last meeting were read and approved. The deferred question was now given to the floor for any member. Upon which nearly every one present arose, and assisted in rekindling the flame, whose heat was felt until ~~at~~ the adjourning hour brought upon it the cooling influence of the President's decision in favour of "Capital punishment." The following question was chosen from among those handed in, thus reading "Which tends most to the ruin of the human race, Dishonesty or Intemperance." Mr. Hyames stood on the first portion as regular and Mr. Horry on the latter. The Secretary gave the formal notice to the Society of the election of officers at the next meeting. No more business appearing, the Reporter made his report; the last roll was called and the Society by motion was adjourned.
Simeon W. Beaird, Sec.

'CDS,' July 10th 1849

This meeting was called to order by the President. The first roll was called, and the minutes of the last were read and approved. The regular debates ~~were~~ commenced and continued to the very hour of decision; when before such action; (several members that had not spoken and ^others^ that were not exactly exhausted of discussive matter,) rose successively with different motions for the decision, others for continuing and many for deferring. All of which being put were successively lost; at last Mr. Cardozo moved 'That the Society cast its votes for officers this evening, and meet to morrow evening to conclude the debates; count the votes and declare the result of the election.' Which being seconded and put, was carried by the majority. After the managers had opened the polls ^&^ received the votes, they immediately closed; and no more business appearing; the Reporter made his report, the last roll was called and this well conducted meeting adjourned over to ~~tom~~ Thursday evening 12th inst. for the finishing of business.

Simeon W. Beaird, Sec.

'CDS,' July 12th 1849

This protracted meeting was called to order by its President. The first roll being called the minutes of the last meeting were read and approved. The floor was now given to any debatant, which after many had risen and contended for some time with great warmth; it was decided on the first portion of the 'Question.' The managers now opened the vote box and proceeded to the counting of the votes polled at the antecedent meeting. Which resulted in the following gentlemen being elected (see Officers' book, July 1849). Notice was given that the officers elect, would be installed at the next regular meeting; at which time there would be no debates. No farther appearance of business being to demand attention, the Reporter made his report; the last roll was called; and the Society adjourned by motion.

Simeon W. Beaird, Sec.

'CDS,' July 25th 1849

This meeting was called to order by the President. The first roll was called and the minutes of the last meeting read and approved. The house now gave mute silence, to give due attention to the ceremonies of the presentation of a beautiful maple painted turned feet Table and Four very suitable and comfortable arm chairs. Which was presented to the Clionian Debating Society, by Augustus L. Horry, in behalf of the greater portion of interested members. His manner of speech being altogether adapted to the occasion ~~and~~ ^being^ well arranged and suitable for the hearing of such a body. The installation of officers now began to take place. The President in a few brief remarks resigned his cares and responsibilities into the hands of the President elect, to which he in return made a few pertinent remarks. The President elect now began his duties by installing the remaining officers elect, all of which being present, received thier various ^offices^ in very flattering terms from thier superior in office, each of which prefaced the taking of thier office oaths with very becoming remarks. The question now arose, whether the next meeting should be for the hearing of the Quarterly oration or for general debates? as circumstances did not seem very favourable to the 'Oration'; it was moved by Mr. H. Cardozo which after a little amendment was seconded by S. Beaird that it be a debating meeting; which being put was unanimously carried. The question chosen from those handed in by the committee, reads thus "Which the more useful Telegraphic or Steam power?["] Mr. S. J. Maxwell was read out on the first portion of the question and Mr. W. Marshall on the last. After the conclusion of all business the President elect addressed his large assemblage of members in ^a^ most beautiful and eloquent style, adorning language with her most suitable ornaments; which were all received with great applause by every one present. No more of business appearing to demand the attention of this orderly fraternity, after the Reporter made his report and the last roll was called, this well conducted meeting adjourned under ^the^ weighty influence of good feeling and order.

Simeon W. Beaird, Sec.

'CDS,' August 1st 1849

This meeting having been called to order by the President. The first roll was called, and the minutes of the last meeting read and approved. The anticipated lengthly [*sic*] and heated debate now commenced, and continued even over the adjourning hour, until noticed by the President, and stopped. He having now arisen seemed for a while doubtful, and appeared if somewhat embar[r]assed for want of decision; at length as if confused he pronounced in favour of the first portion. This being concluded the following question was chosen from among those handed in, "Was the treatment of the English to the Irish tyrannical?" Mr. W. Weston was read out on the affirmative and S. Beaird on the negative. S. Beaird now read two proposed augmentations to the Library Department of Rules, both of which were prefaced, and notice given of their intended offering at the next meeting. No more business appearing; the Reporter made his report; the last roll was called and the meeting adjourned by motion.

Simeon W. Beaird, Sec.

'CDS,' August 8th 1849

This meeting being called to order by the President; the first roll was called; and the minutes of the last meeting read and approved. The regular debates were now began by its appointed supporters which lasted for some length of time. the floor being opened for all, the debates commenced to show itself in a s[t]ill more and more animated form which was continued even over the hour of adjournment; it being the time, the President arose to pronounce his decision, which was on the 'Affirmative.' The body having decided that the next meeting should be devoted to the 'Quarterly Oration'; the 'Committee' therefore handed in no questions. The 'Committee on general interests,' ~~forming~~ forming a 'Committee on contracts and building' now submitted thier report through thier 'Chairman,' of all monies received, all contracts made and of all the work completed; which was unanimously adopted. The Secretary was now ordered to extend invitations for the next meeting's oration. There not being a sufficient number present to act upon the augmentations notified of at last meeting, they were thereby postponed. No more of business appearing to demand attention. The Reporter upon call, made his report. The last roll was called and this orderly meeting adjourned by motion, in harmony.

Simeon W. Beaird, Sec.

C.D.S., August 15th 1849

This overflowing and enthusiastic meeting, was called to order at the usual hour. The first roll being called was answered by every member that was in the city. The minutes of the last meeting were read and approved. There being a great number of the Honoraries present; the Secretary according to Constitution was ordered to read the same to the hearing of all present. Which being concluded, the President introduced Mr. Wm. O. Weston as the 'Orator'; whereupon he proceeded to the performance of his task. In which he paid many compliments, attributed many honors, and confirmed many wise opinions on that sublime subject, 'Education,' his oration being the grandest proof of the advantages derived from the attainment of the same. Having received all attention for almost 20 minutes he sat down amid great applause. S. W. Beaird now rose to move the Society, request a copy of the beautiful speech just delivered, that they may always preserve its valuable and sound contents among the relics of the body, which being seconded by E. G. Beaird, and put, was unanimously carried, whereupon the Presdt in a ^few^ neat and appropriate remarks made the request, which after being responded to by the 'Orator,' he complied and immediately presented the original. The whole body being now present, the 2 notified augmentations to the Library Department were submitted by S. W. Beaird, which being put was unanimously carried. The whole of which meeting can be said to be among one of those most encouraging and exacting ones ever celebrated by the CDS. The presence of so many old and experienced heads pointed to the past; while the members young and gay told of the present and the future. Not all the ornaments of wreaths and flowers and mottoes could ever have made so lasting ~~and~~ an impression. Every thing being ~~now~~ ^so far^ completed, the Honoraries took their respective leave of absence. The Society now proceeded to the choice of Questions. Which resulted in the following, "Which the better a Mechanical or Professional pursuit." Mr. E. G. Beaird being read on the first portion and Mr. G. F. Barrow on the last. All of business being now brought forward and finished. The ~~last~~ Reporter made his report ~~and~~ the last ~~Society~~ roll was called over and this Society adjourned in the most joyful and agreeable manner.

Simeon W. Beaird, Sec.

CDS, August 22nd 1849

A regular meeting being held at this date, was called to order by its President. The first roll was called and the minutes of the last meeting were read and approved. The anticipated heated debate now commenced; being supported by all the strength of powerful arguments and carried on with most animating spirits. The hour at length arrived for a decision, which only, put a stop to this beautiful discussion. The President having weighed well the arguments decided most satisfactorily on the latter portion of the 'Question.' The following question was now chosen from those handed in. "Were the French right in interfering with the late affairs at Rome."[12] Mr. H. Cardozo stood as next regular on the affirmative and Mr. I. Hyames on the negative. No more business appearing to demand attention; the Reporter made his report and the last roll was called, and the meeting adjourned.

Simeon W. Beaird, Sec.

(Omission) At this meeting there were many Honorary Members present.

C.D.S., August 29th 1849

This date bringing with ^it^ another part of the assemblage of Honorary Members, witnessed another of the Clionian's joyful meetings. Being called to order by the President. The first roll was called, and the minutes of the last meeting were read and approved. The regular debates were now opened by successive supporters, and continued to the very exhaustion of the subject; when the President arose to give his conscientious decision. Which was, on the negative portion of the question. The Committee of Queries, having now handed in thier questions the following was chosen from among them "Which the greater protection against a foreign foe; a nation's Military or Naval force?["] Whereupon Mr. A. L. Horry was read out as regular supporter of the first portion and Mr. S. J. Maxwell of the latter. "The Committee on general interests" reported favourably to the covering of the Library, and chairs, on certain conditions, which was unanimously carried to sanction the proceedure [*sic*] to the work. No more business appearing, The Reporter made his report and the society adjourned by motion.

Simeon W. Beaird, Sec.

C.D.S., September 6th 1849

A regular meeting being held at this time, was called to order by the President. The first roll was called and the minutes of the last meeting were read and approved. The regular debates were now commenced, which continued to the adjourning hour; when it was requested of the President to defer; which was in conformity done. The President opened a letter directed to the President & Members, when upon giving it to his Secretary to read and it being read was found to contain an invitation from the Utopian Society, to attend thier first ~~celeb~~ Anniversary celebration which was unanimously received, and upon motion a Committee of Four was appointed to return an answer to the same, and ~~again~~ upon ~~a~~ ^another^ motion it was ordered them to invite that Society to form in our Hall. The Committee consisted of Mr. Henry Cardozo Chairman Messrs. E. G. Beaird, A. L. Horry, and S. W. Beaird Committee. Messrs. S. W. Beaird and E. G. Beaird were appointed Corresponding Marshals to receive all orders for the Clionian Society from the Utopian Marshals. No more of business appearing. The reporter made his report and the meeting by motion was adjourned.

Simeon W. Beaird, Sec.

'C.D.S.,' September 13th 1849

The meeting being called to order by its President, The first roll was called and the minutes of the last meeting were read and approved. The continuation of the defer[r]ed debates was begun and being concluded; was decided in favour of "Naval protection." The following question was chosen from those handed in by the Committee. "Which the greater incentive to exertion punishment or rewards?["] Upon which Mr. W. E. Marshall was read out for the first portion and Mr. W. O. Weston for the latter. Mr. William B. Clark was offered by S. W. Beaird as an Honorary Member of the Society, who upon being ballotted for was elected by a unanimous voice. A letter of 'Thanks' to Mrs. Emma K. Farbeaux,[13] for her many gifts to the Society and also for the especial notice taken of the Society by her, was moved by Mr. S. W. Beaird and being ^seconded^ by Mr. E. G. Beaird was put and with great applause unanimously carried for a committee of Four to be appointed to perform the duty. Whereupon Mr. S. W. Beaird was appointed Chairman and Messrs. H. Cardozo, E. G. Beaird and W. O. Weston Committee. The Society having Unanimously voted to abandon the present Latin Motto,[14] it was moved and unanimously carried that a Committee be appointed to report to the Body another of fewer words and greater meaning. Whereupon Messrs. S. W. Beaird, H. Cardozo, W. Weston

40   *Free Black Charlestonians in Debate*

and E. G. Beaird were appointed. No farther business appearing; the Reporter made his report; the last roll was called and the house adjourned by motion. Simeon W. Beaird, Sec.

'C.D.S.,' September 27th 1849

A regular meeting being held at the usual time; it was called to order by the Presdt. The first Roll was called and the minutes of the last meeting read and approved. The regular debatants rose in succession in support of the respective sides, which ~~was~~ being concluded (after much warmth) at the adjourning hour; it was decided in favour of 'Rewards.' The following question was chosen "Which the more interesting Ancient or Modern history." Upon which S. W. Beaird was read out on the first portion and E. G. Beaird on the last. The 'Committee of Thanks to Mrs. E. K. Farbeaux,['] reported the completion of the task devolved on them and submitted a true copy of the communication sent, which was unanimously received. A letter was also opened, which contained the response of that lady, which upon reading was found to be truly regardful and affectionate. Another letter was received from Mr. Robert L. Deas; containing an application for membership; upon which the constitutional number 2/3 being present; ^&^ he having received ^a^ report favourable from the Committee on general interests; he was balloted for and unanimously elected. No more of business appearing to demand attention; the Reporter made his report; the last Roll was called and the meeting adjourned by motion. Simeon W. Beaird, Sec.

C.D.S., October 4th 1849

This regular meeting being held; it was called to order by the ^Vice^ President at the usual hour. The President being absent, and the Vice occupying his chair, caused a vacancy of the Vice's seat which was filled by Mr. Hyames. The first roll being called and the minutes being read and approved. The regular debating hour arrived; which debates after some continuation, were, by request of members present, deferred. Mr. I. Hyames submitted a letter of application for membership from Mr. Benjamin E. K. Hampton, which being properly addressed, and he being fairly represented by the recommenders; was balloted for and unanimously elected. W. O. Weston gave notice of intention to submit an alteration to clause 4th of Bye-Laws at next meeting. S. W. Beaird moved that the Society on immediate vote, do change its meetings from Weekly to Monthly in compliance with Resolution 1st and that Monday evenings be substituted for Wednesdays as long as the Resolution be in force; which being seconded by E. G. Beaird was unanimously carried. W. O. Weston also notified the

Society of his intention to submit an alteration to clause 14th of Constitution as far as relates to the election of Annual Orator. No more business appearing to demand attention; the Reporter made his report; the Last Roll was called and the meeting was adjourned by motion.
Simeon W. Beaird, Sec.

C.D.S., October 8th 1849

Extra Meeting

Having been called to order by the President. The first Roll was called and the minutes of the last meeting were read and approved. Messrs. R. L. Deas and B. E. K. Hampton, members elect, being present, were introduced and the Secretary by orders, read the Constitution to thier hearing, after the conclusion of which, they successively signed. The alteration to clause 4th of Bye-Laws was submitted which in substance was the election of Members by ballott instead of 'Viva Voce,'[15] which being put was unanimously carried by an over Constitutional requirement of number. The alteration of Clause 14th of Constitution was also submitted ^and carried in the same manner^; in substance the election of the Annual Orator 12 months previous to his hearing, and immediately after the conclusion of the Antecedent Orat[i]on and the change of the name of the Month from April to January. The Committee appointed to select a new motto for the Society, made thier report of the one selected which was unanimously and with great applause received by the Body. (See Constitution.) A letter was read, received from Mr. F. A. Mood which contained information of a present of two volumes of Macaulay's history of England[16] and also a portion dedicated with very suitable and well received advices; which was again unanimously received by the Society, and upon motion of S. W. Beaird and seconded by E. G. Beaird a response of 'Thanks' was immediately noted to be sent by an appointed 'Committee.' Mr. Hampton moved a committee of Three and S. W. Beaird one of Four including a Chairman, which last being seconded by W. O. Weston was unanimously carried. Whereupon S. W. Beaird was appointed Chairman and Messrs. Benjamin Hampton, Robert L. Deas and Henry Cardozo, Committee. No more of business appearing to demand the attention of this punctual body, The Reporter upon call made his report. The 'Last Roll' was called and by motion the Society adjourned.
Simeon W. Beaird, Sec.

"C.D.S.," November 5th 1849

This regular ^monthly^ meeting of the above Society was at the usual hour, called to order by the Vice President. The first Roll was called and the proceedings

of the last ~~monthly~~ Extra meeting were read and approved. The debates were begun by the appointed debatants and supported at large for a length of time; when concluded, it was decided in favour of the first portion of the question. The following question was chosen from among those handed in by the Committee "Is war the proper means for the gratification of national revenge?" Upon which Mr. G. F. Barrow was appointed upon the ~~first aff~~ affirmative and Mr. Henry Cardozo on the negative. The polls were now ordered to be opened and the Society went immediately into an election for officers. Which upon report of the Managers the following gentlemen were declared elected (See Officer's book). Mr. Henry Cardozo was also elected Quarterly Orator for February 1850. Notice was given that at the next meeting there ~~we~~ would be no debating; as the installation of the officers elect would take place. The Semi-Annual contribution ~~list~~ and the Monthly Book contribution lists were called over and mostly altogether paid up. The "Committee of Thanks" through thier Chairman read the copy of the letter sent to Mr. F. A. Mood which was unanimously received by the Society. No more business appearing to demand attention, the last Roll was called; the Reporter made his report; and the Society adjourned in peace.
Simeon W. Beaird, Sec.

'C.D.S.,' December 3rd 1849

This regular monthly meeting was held at the usual time and hour. Which being called to order by the President went immediately to business. The first Roll was called and the minutes of the last meeting were read and approved. The regular installation began by a complimentary address by the President to the President-elect, who upon returning thanks for the honors thus conferred was duly installed by oath of allegiance to 'Constitution.' After the conclusion of which nearly every officer elect being present was also installed, to which every one more or less showed forth his abilities to some extent. The Society was notified that Mr. Cardozo being elected President, stood then as a regular debatant for next meeting, whereupon Mr. J. M. F. Dereef being next in turn was read upon the Negative of the question.[17] The Secretary read the report of 'Committee' appointed to examine his books and the state of the Treasury, which report being favourable and correct, was adopted unanimously. No more business appearing; the Reporter made his report; the last Roll was called and the Society by motion adjourned.
Simeon W. Beaird, Sec.

"C.D.S.," December 26th 1849

This meeting being called for the purpose of hearing one of the regular Quarterly orations delivered was attended in full number by the members, and also by

1849 43

many of the Honorary Members. The Presdt having called it to order; the first Roll was called and the minutes of the last meeting were read and approved. The President now announced to the Assemblage the name of Simeon W. Beaird as the Orator; upon which he rose and in the course of his remarks endeavoured to support the bright principles of Industry, Perseverance and Patience. After the conclusion of which Mr. Wm. H. Gaillard rose and moved that the Society request a copy of the address, which being seconded by Mr. G. F. Barrow was unanimously carried. Whereupon the President in a few brief remarks requested the copy and which was immediately given. S. W. Beaird presented to the Society as a present from Mr. Jacob Farbeaux; Webster's unabridged Dictionary;[18] and at the same time moved that a Committee of Four be appointed to return the thanks of the Society; which being seconded by Mr. B. E. Hampton was unanimously carried. And the following gentlemen appointed Viz. Messrs. S. W. Beaird Chairman, Messrs. A. L. Horry, E. G. Beaird and I. A. Hyames Committee. S. W. Beaird again presented to the Society Six volumes as a present to the Society from Mr. Job G. Bass, Honorary Member. Viz. Scenes in Spain: Paulding Works: Sketches of the Seminole War: 2 Vols Carlyle French Revolution: & Grimshaw's France.[19] Which was unanimously received and upon his motion of a Committee of Four be appointed to return thanks and being seconded by Mr. B. E. Hampton was carried and the following gentlemen appointed Viz. Wm. H. Gaillard Chairman and Messrs. B. E. Hampton, R. L. Deas and W. O. Weston Committee. The Society's interests and dignity as far as her relationships to Mr. Wm. E. Marshall was concerned was now brought up for discussion and being argued for some time with much ability by many members;[20] that a "committee of seven["] be appointed to ask his candid intentions of acting, as he had been for some time a non-attending and non-arrear-paying member, upon motion being seconded was unanimously agreed upon and the following gentlemen appointed as a Committee of request Viz. Simeon W. Beaird Chairman Messrs. W. O. Weston; I. A. Hyames; E. G. Beaird; G. F. Barrow; B. E. Hampton and Robt. L. Deas were app Committee. Mr. S. W. Beaird now moved that the Utopian; Brown Fellowship; Cotarae; Friendly Union; and Select Convivial Societies be and the Cadet Riflemen Band[21] be invited to attend the Second Anniversary celebration of this Society, which being seconded and put was unanimously carried. The question arose whether we shall ask for contributions on the celebration day, which being put, was decided by a majority of votes in the negative. No more business appearing to demand the attention of this punctual body. The Reporter made his report; the Last Roll was called and the Society by motion adjourned.

Simeon W. Beaird, Secretary

NOTES

1. The society met on the Holloway family property on Beaufain Street.
2. Bass presented a Bible. For the Clionians' library acquisitions, see appendix D.
3. Job G. Bass (1816–1901) was a community and religious leader respected for his speaking skills. On September 13, 1841, the records of the Friendly Moralist Society had praised Bass for "that modest yet dignifyed strain of Orratory for which that Gentleman is Remarkable"; Friendly Moralist Society Records, 1841–1856, Avery Research Center for African American History and Culture, College of Charleston, Charleston, SC.
4. Members of many nineteenth-century men's groups used feminine pronouns to refer to their societies. William O. Weston, when he was Clionian secretary, sometimes identified the debating society explicitly with Clio, the Greek Muse of history.
5. After his defeat at the Battle of Waterloo in 1815, Napoleon was detained on the South Atlantic island of St. Helena, where he remained in exile until his death in 1821.
6. The French Second Republic (1848–1852), established after the Revolution of 1848, would dissolve after Napoleon's nephew Louis-Napoléon Bonaparte overthrew the republic in an 1851 coup d'état, creating the Second Empire in 1852.
7. Owing to an Italian nationalist rebellion, Pope Pius IX (1792–1878) fled Rome for the kingdom of Naples in November 1848.
8. Lucius Junius Brutus (fl. sixth century BCE), a semilegendary Roman consul, is reported by the Roman historian Livy to have had his sons executed for their participation in a conspiracy to restore the Tarquin kings.
9. After Huger declined to deliver the annual oration for 1850, the society elected a regular member for that duty. Thus, with the exception of honorary member Job G. Bass, who delivered the first annual oration in 1849, regular members delivered all of the society's formal orations.
10. The trial and execution of the Greek philosopher Socrates by the Athenian democracy in 399 BCE has remained controversial and widely debated since that time.
11. Capital punishment was often debated in nineteenth-century debating societies. See Angela G. Ray, "Learning Leadership: Lincoln at the Lyceum, 1838," *Rhetoric and Public Affairs* 13, no. 3 (Fall 2010): 383n48.
12. This query refers to the recent Siege of Rome (April–July 1849). French forces sent by Louis-Napoléon Bonaparte ultimately defeated the short-lived Roman Republic, and Pope Pius IX returned from exile. In the defense of the republic, Giuseppe Garibaldi became an Italian nationalist hero.
13. Emma K. Farbeaux (ca. 1806–1881), wife of Jacob Farbeaux (ca. 1801–1874), was enslaved at the time of her birth. In 1849 she paid state capitation tax as a "free Negro" and was providing domestic service in the Broad Street home of the wealthy white Charlestonian Eliza Neufville Kohne, where Jacob Farbeaux was a coachman; in 1850 Emma and Jacob would relocate with Kohne's household to Philadelphia. See Angela G. Ray, "Archival Profusion, Archival Silence, and Analytic Invention: Reinventing Histories of Nineteenth-Century African American Debate," *Transactions of the American Philosophical Society* 112, no. 3 (2023): 95–114.
14. The society's Latin mottoes are unknown.
15. *Viva voce:* "orally."

16. Volumes 1 and 2 of Thomas Babington Macaulay's five-volume *History of England from the Accession of James the Second* were published in 1849.

17. Since the society president judged debates, the person occupying that office could not serve simultaneously as a debater.

18. By 1849 several of Noah Webster's dictionaries of American English were in circulation.

19. *Scenes in Spain* was published in New York in 1837; multiple volumes of the works of the American writer James Kirke Paulding appeared in the 1830s; *Sketch of the Seminole War* was published in Charleston in 1836; Thomas Carlyle's *The French Revolution* appeared in three volumes in 1837; and several printings of William Grimshaw's *History of France,* first published in 1828, were available by 1849.

20. The concern may have been that Marshall was participating in another debating society at the same time, a practice to which some Clionians objected. See the entry for October 6, 1851.

21. The Utopian Debating Society is mentioned elsewhere in the Clionian minutes. On the Brown Fellowship and Friendly Union Societies, see *Rules and Regulations of the Brown Fellowship Society, Established at Charleston, S.C., 1st November, 1790* (Charleston, SC: J. B. Nixon, Printer, 1844); Robert L. Harris Jr., "Charleston's Free Afro-American Elite: The Brown Fellowship Society and the Humane Brotherhood," *South Carolina Historical Magazine* 82, no. 4 (1981): 289–310; Bernard E. Powers Jr., *Black Charlestonians: A Social History, 1882–1885* (Fayetteville: University of Arkansas Press, 1994), 51–52; John Garrison Marks, *Black Freedom in the Age of Slavery* (Columbia: University of South Carolina Press, 2020), 119–40; and *Constitution and By-Laws of the Friendly Union Society of Charleston, S.C., Organized May 4th 1813* (Charleston, SC: Karrs and Welch, 1889). On the Select Convivial Society, see "Select Convivial Society," *[Charleston] South Carolina Leader,* November 17, 1866, 3; this announcement indicates a likely founding date around 1839. On the Cadet Riflemen Band, see Edmund L. Drago, *Charleston's Avery Center: From Education and Civil Rights to Preserving the African American Experience,* rev. ed., rev. and ed. W. Marvin Dulaney (Charleston, SC: History Press, 2006), 33.

— 1850 —

[In this year the society acquired most of the books and pamphlets for its library. Secretaries minuted twenty-eight meetings; twenty included debates, three included orations.—Ed.]

2nd "Anniversary Celebration"
C.D.S., January 1st 1850.

This auspicious day, bringing with it much delight and pleasure, was hailed with great joy by the Clionian Society. In the afternoon about 3 O'clock the Society assembled in all its strength in thier meeting 'Hall.' And about 4 O'clock being joined by the Utopian Society, marched in procession to the School Hall above; where a large and enlightened audience were waiting in profound silence, to greet them. Being seated; the ceremonies were begun by prayer, from Mr. Job G. Bass, an Honorary member; after the conclusion of which; the President in arising announced to the anxious assemblage Enoch G. Beaird ^a member^ as the Society's 'Orator.' The distinguished member in doing honor to his beloved Society; while attempting to meet thier every expectation; did truly do great honor to himself. Having kept the vast assemblage in strict attention for some time; while portraying in the most beautiful language and ^in^ the most eloquent st manner, the many happy effects resulting from the pursuit of an Energetic and Persevering mind. Interspersing his ~~oration~~ ^remarks^ with the most striking examples of bright and virtuous characters. Nor did he fail in the concluding parts to recommend every virtuous action to the favour of his fellow members. Assuring them that though no reward was offered them, to insure the duration of thier existence; yet through thier labours and toils they have been crowned with abundant success in time past; Which together with a due reverence and respect to the bright principles of Christianity they may ever yet entertain brilliant hopes of the continuance of the duration of thier Society's existence. Having concluded amid numerous and great applauses both from every member and the whole audience; after the benediction was pronounced the assemblage was invited in the Society's Hall where they were entertained by the members, for more than an hour, while exhibiting to them, the various articles; books, Library &c. in the possession of the Society. After which this multitude of enlightened ^people^ took up thier line of march for home, having enjoyed a pleasant New Year's afternoon in the Hall of a Debating Society. After wishing the Society all success in thier Third year's embarkation. They silently and peaceably departed; leaving thier lovely smiles in the recollection of every member and the well wishing of thier favourable voices, still sounding in the ear. Thus was joyfully and peaceably begun, conducted and ended the celebration of the Second Anniversary of the ~~Cl~~ ever prosperous Clionian Debating Society.

Simeon W. Beaird, Sec.

C.D.S., January 7th 1850

A regular monthly meeting of this Society was held on the above date. Being called to order by the President; the first Roll was called and the minutes of the last meeting and also of the Anniversary celebration were read and approved. The debating commenced by the regular appointed and continued to receive very great support to the very moment of adjournment. The President arising decided in favour of the "Affirmative." The following question was chosen by votes from those handed in by the Committee. "Which tends most to a nation's benefit, its agricultural or commercial advantages?" Upon which Mr. W. Gaillard was read out for the first portion and Mr. I. Hyames for the latter. Mr. W. O. Weston presented to the Society for Mrs. Emma K. Farbeaux, 2 Volumes of Rollin[']s Ancient history, being in cost 3 Dollars out of Five given by her for the purpose of binding some volumes which only costed Two Dollars.[1] He also after a few remarks moved that the thanks of the Society be extended by letter, which upon being seconded by Mr. S. W. Beaird that a Committee of Six be appointed to perform the honourable duty, was put and unanimously carried. Whereupon the following members were appointed Viz. W. O. Weston Chairman Messers. S. W. Beaird; R. L. Deas; B. E. Hampton; E. G. Beaird; and G. F. Barrow Committee. The Chairman of the Committee appointed to write a letter of request to Mr. Wm. E. Marshall a member now read the answer to said letter, and he Mr. Marshall having appeared and met all demands, upon motion of S. W. Beaird and being seconded, the letter was put and unanimously received. A motion was made by Mr. W. H. Gaillard, that the Society go into an immediate election for the next Annual Orator, but it being rather late, he withdrew his motion. The monthly Book list was called and almost altogether cleared. No more of business appearing; the Reporter made his report; the last Roll was called and the Society by motion adjourned.

Simeon W. Beaird, Secretary

'C.D.S.,' February 4th 1850

This regular monthly meeting of the above Society being held on the above date at the usual hour, was called to order by the President. The first Roll was called and the minutes of the last meeting were read and approved. The regular debating commenced and was continued to the hour of adjournment though not altogether exhausted, was decided in favour of the first portion of the question. The following question was chosen from those handed in Viz. "Who was the most patriotic Demosthenes or Socrates?["][2] Upon which Mr. Augustus L. Horry was read out for the first portion and Mr. B. E. K. Hampton, for the latter. The polls were now opened for the election of an Annual Orator; when upon report of managers, Mr. Wm. H. Gaillard was declared elected, for January 1st 1851. The Chairman of the committee on the letter of thanks to Mr. Jacob Farbeaux; as also the chairman of another to Mrs. Emma K. Farbeaux, read each respectively the contents of thier letters which were all unanimously received by the body. Due notice was given that at the next regular meeting the present term of Officers shall have expired and that a general election will then take place. No more of business appearing to demand attention. The Last Roll was called ~~an~~. The Reporter made his report and the Society by motion adjourned.
Simeon W. Beaird, Sec.

'C.D.S.,' March 4th 1850

This regular monthly meeting being called to order by its President. The first Roll was called and the minutes of the last meeting were read and approved. The regular debating having commenced was continued to the adjourning hour, when upon the President's decision the supporters of the latter portion of the Question came off Victors. The following question was chosen from among those that were handed in by the Committee reading thus "Whether a man condemned to die, though unjustly, can, without a crime escape from justice & the laws?" Upon which Mr. Stephen J. Maxwell was read out upon the affirmative and Mr. W. E. Marshall on the negative. Mr. Wm. H Gaillard, Chairman of the Committee of Thanks to Honorary member Job G. Bass, for his gift of many valuable volumes; now read the contents of the letter bearing the signatures of the Committee, which being put was unanimously received as the property of the Society.

Protracted Meeting, March 11th 1850

As soon as this meeting was called to order by the President, and the first Roll was called; upon the vacancy of the Vice's ^seat^ Mr. Weston was requested to act. The Secretary gave notice to the body that he was not compelled to read the proceedings of the last meeting at a Protracted meeting and also as he understood that a portion it was to be protested at this meeting he did not deem it requisite to write them and therefore for such reasons omitted so doing. After which Mr. Wm. O. Weston arose and presented the anticipated "Protest" signed by many others, all of whom took part in supporting its claims for a length ^of time^ and which was opposed by others.[3] The Protest having created a very different feeling from what was expected and tending towards evil consequences; was upon motion by S. W. Beaird laid aside. And the following resolution carried in its stead. "'Resolved' That as the Protest has become by the expressed opinions of many members the creator of very different feelings from what it was intended to produce, and before it should be attended with evil consequences Be it carried that it be not considered at all. And that as that portion of the proceedings of the last meeting as far as the election, was constitutional, that portion still remain legal. And as the after portion is acknowledged by all to be unconstitutional, that portion be reconsidered and re-acted upon at this meeting." Which being put after being seconded was carried; and the Society immediately went into an election for Officers which resulted as follows. (See officers book dated March 1850) Notice was given that at the next meeting called by the President the installation of officers would take place. No more business appearing. The Reporter made his report. The last Roll was called and the Society adjourned.

Simeon W. Beaird, Secretary

'C.D.S.,' March 20th 1850

This intervening meeting was called by the President, for the purpose of the installation of officers elect. Being called to order; the first Roll was called and the minutes of the last meetings, were read and approved. Upon the reading of the list of officers elect; the President Vice & Assistant Librarian declined, which upon a motion for its acceptation being seconded and put, was carried. The polls were then ordered to be opened and upon report of managers, it resulted in the choice of Messrs. Enoch Beaird; W. H. Gaillard & R. L. Deas, to fill said respective vacancies. The result of the above election required the resignation of Mr. E. Beaird as Reporter and as a member of the "committee of queries" he being elected President. When upon motion of S. W. Beaird, being seconded said resignation was accepted. The polls were again opened by order, to fill the vacancies, and upon report of managers Mr. Hampton was declared as elected Reporter and Mr. H. Cardozo Jr. as a member of the Committee of Queries. After the conclusion of the above portion of the business. The regular installation began by the relinquishing of the chair by the then incumbent

50   *Free Black Charlestonians in Debate*

attended with a few brief, yet well applied remarks to his fellow members as well as to his successor in office. The President elect returned the compliment paid him by his predecessor, in a becoming style, after which he accepted the chief seat in the body upon honour of word. The installation of the remaining portion of officers now successively took place according to station, all of whom allowed not the high compliment paid them by the President to pass unnoticed, but returned them in a manner that would speak well of every "Clionian." Mr. W. H. Gaillard now took an opportunity to return his thanks to the body for having elected him as thier next representative as an Orator. A petition was brought forward by S. W. Beaird in accordance with Resolution 1st that, that Resolution which required Monthly meetings be, according to its own wording, dropped. And that the Art. 22nd of Constitution which called for Weekly meetings on every Wednesday evening be complied with. Which being seconded by Mr. W. O. Weston was put and carried. Notice was given to the members that on next Wednesday evening 27th inst. the regular Quarterly Oration would be delivered. S. W. Beaird Secretary & Treasurer, requested of the Presdt, that he would appoint, in accordance with the requisitions of the Constitution the Committee of Three to examine and report the state of his books and the Treasury Department. Whereupon Messrs. Hampton, Deas, & Cardozo were appointed. It being in the power of the President to appoint a chairman of the "Committee on general interests," he accordingly appointed Mr. Henry Cardozo Jr. as that Chairman. No more of business appearing to demand attention. The Reporter made his report the Last Roll was called and the Society by motion adjourned to meet hereafter on every Wednesday evening. Simeon W. Beaird, Secretary

'C.D.S.,' March 27th 1850

This first of the regular Weekly meetings, being held for the purpose of hearing the regular Quarterly Oration delivered; and being well attended both by members common & Honorary; was called to order by the President. The first Roll was called and the minutes of the last intervening meeting were read and approved. The President in arising, announced to the Body the name of Mr. Henry Cardozo jr. as the 'Orator.' Anxiously and earnestly did every member listen to the first display made by their fellow Clionian. And well did he meet thier every expectation; in handling his subject as manfully as one more accustomed to the performance of such tasks. The "true happiness of man" received additional weight of importance from the many stresses and illustrations placed upon it by the venturesome Orator. Having concluded his remarks, Mr. W. O. Weston rose and in a few words moved that the Society request a copy of said address, which being seconded by S. W. Beaird, was put and unanimously carried; whereupon the President made the request in behalf of the Society, which was immediately met by the presentation of the Original by the Orator. The polls were now ordered to be opened; and upon report of managers, Mr. Augustus L. Horry was declared elected as next Quarterly Orator. Mr. Cardozo gave due notice to the Society that at next meeting he would offer a Resolution providing for the hereafter election of Orators every Four instead of every Three months as it now is. The seat of the Vice President being vacant, Mr. Wm. E. Marshall was requested to occupy it. No more of business appearing to demand attention. The Reporter made his report. The last Roll was called and the Society adjourned by motion.

Simeon W. Beaird, Sec.

'C.D.S.,' April 3rd 1850

At the regular hour; this meeting was called to order by the President. The first Roll was called and the minutes of the last Weekly meeting were read and approved. The regular debating commenced, and continued to receive very great support, till even past the hour for its ceasing; though still ~~unh~~ unexhausted. The President in arising expressed an embarrassment in deciding, and for some time remained doubtful. At length he gave his decision in favour of the "negative." The Committee having handed in thier questions; the following was chosen, reading thus, "By whom has the most good been effected Martin Luther or George Washington?["]⁴ Upon which Mr. W. O. Weston was read out for the ~~affirmative~~ ^1st portion^ & Mr. G. F. Barrow for the latter portion of the Question. The Secretary & Treasurer, now read the result of the examination of his Departments by the Committee appointed; which reported thier correctness. Mr. Cardozo read out the names of those gentlemen that he as chairman of the "Committee on general interests" had appointed; to wit Messrs. S. Beaird; W. Weston; R. L. Deas & I. A. Hyames Committee. No more of business appearing to demand attention. The Reporter made his report. The last Roll was called and the Society adjourned by motion.

Simeon W. Beaird, Sec.

'C.D.S.,' April 10th 1850

The regular weekly meeting of the above Society, was called to order by the President. The first Roll was called and the minutes of the last Weekly meeting were read and approved. The discussion having commenced with much warmth was continued to its hour for ceasing, when the President decided favourable to the first portion of the question. The following question was then chosen from those handed in by the Committee, "Which [is] the more conducive to moral purity, a Country or City life?" Upon which Mr. Henry Cardozo jr. was read out in support of the former & Mr. J. M. F. Dereef for the latter portion. Mr. Wm. Weston presented to the Society Three pamphlets of good speeches & valuable letters; which upon motion of S. W. Beaird & seconded, the thanks of the Society were returned to Mr. Weston for his acceptable gifts. Mr. W. H. Gaillard moved that the Society, purchase the Five political speeches recently delivered in the Senate and now published,[5] which was put, after being seconded, & ^was^ carried. No more business appearing to demand the attention of the Body. The Reporter made his report ^the Last Roll was called^ and the Society adjourned by motion.

Simeon W. Beaird, Sec.

'C.D.S.,' April 17th 1850

At the usual hour on the above date, the regular Weekly meeting of the above Society was called to order by the President. The first Roll was called and the minutes of the last Weekly meeting were read and approved. The debates commenced in order, and was continued to its ceasing hour. When upon the upon the [sic] President's decision, the arguments in support of the first portion of the question were declared the most weighty. The following question was then chosen, reading thus "Who deserves the greater meed of praise, the Inventor or Improver of a project?" Upon which Mr. R. L. Deas was read out for the first portion of the question & Mr. W. H. Gaillard, for the latter. Mr. Deas presented to the Society a copy of an address of Professor F. W. Capers before the Citadel Cadets;[6] for which, upon motion of S. Beaird & being seconded by W. Weston the thanks of the Body was unanimously returned to the gentleman. Mr. S. Beaird now notified the Society that on next meeting there was a certainty of there not being a quorum of the members in the city;[7] and thereby moved that in consequence the Society postpone its meeting to the 'Week' after; which being seconded by Mr. Cardozo was put & unanimously carried. No more of business appearing. The Reporter made his report, The last Roll was called & the Society by motion adjourned.

Simeon W. Beaird, Sec.

'C.D.S.,' May 1st 1850

A regular meeting being held, it was called to order by the President at the usual hour. The first Roll was called, and the minutes of the last Weekly meeting were read & approved. The discussion commenced in order by the regular appointants and was continued with much warmth for a length of time by a portion of the members present; after which Mr. Cardozo arose and expressed his acknowledgement of the weight and importance of the subject and his utmost desire to participate, but through fatigue & indisposition was utterly prevented and thereupon moved the continuance of the discussion at next meeting. Mr. Weston in arising expressed himself as being placed in the same condition of the former gentleman and therefore seconded the motion; which being put was unanimously carried. Mr. Gaillard presented the Society with a copy of Professor B[r]umby's address on geology;[8] which upon motion of Mr. Weston and the same being seconded, it was carried that the thanks of the Body be returned to the gentleman. No more of business appearing to demand attention. The Reporter made his report. The last Roll was called & the Society by motion adjourned.

Simeon W. Beaird, Sec.

'CDS,' May 22nd 1850

Sickness having laid its afflicting hand on many of the members of this brotherly Institution. It was, for the last "Two" weeks kept from assembling as usual. But at this date there being an extra fine attendance; the President called it to order. The first Roll was called and the minutes of the last Weekly meeting were read and approved. The unfinished arguments in support of the continued weighty question from last meeting were now begun and continued with great & even more than expected warmth to the ceasing hour; when upon the President's decision, the supporters of the "Inventor's" claims came off triumphant. The following question was chosen from those handed in by the Committee "Was Caesar right, in usurping the government of the Roman Empire?["][9] Mr. I. A. Hyames was read out on the affirmative and Mr. A. L. Horry on the negative. Mr. R. L. Deas presented to the Society a copy of Mr. N. Mitchell's address before the 4th of July Association.[10] When upon motion of Mr. Weston and seconded by S. W. Beaird the & being carried; the thanks of the Body was returned to the presenter. The President gave notice that he had received a communication from Honorary member Job G. Bass accompanied with the requested address, which he delivered before the Society on its first Anniversary celebration in January 1849.[11] When upon motion of Simeon W. Beaird and being seconded and carried; the consideration of the same was laid over for the next meeting. No more of business appearing to demand the attention of the Assembly. The Reporter pro-tem made his report; the last Roll was called and the Society was by motion adjourned.

Simeon W. Beaird, Secretary

'CDS,' May 29th 1850

The President having called this regular meeting to order. The first Roll was called and the minutes of the last Weekly meeting were read and approved. The discussion on the last adopted and weighty question was now begun and continued for a length of time with much animation, until the hour for ceasing had nearly arrived, when Mr. Weston who had already spoken on the subject to some length, expressed his desire for its continuation, as he would not like such a subject so important to be passed over until it was exhausted. The President after having heard the views of other gentlemen, put the said request to the voice of the body, which was unanimously carried. He therefore accordingly gave notice that he had granted its continuation. S. W. Beaird, Chairman of the committee on the letter to the Revd. Dr. Daniel A. Payne of Baltimore, an Honorary Member: gave notice that he had received an answer through the kindness of Mrs. E. K. Farbeaux, directed to him for the Body. Mr. W. H. Gaillard moved that both the letters of Messrs. Bass & Payne be immediately read. Mr. Weston opposed the motion and moved that the reading of the letters be postponed until there was a larger assembly of the members present; as the recent fire of the morning had probably fatigued many and prevented them from attending.[12] After other explanations and the support of other gentlemen of Mr. Weston's views, Mr. Gaillard with all good humor withdrew his motion, and Mr. S. W. Beaird having seconded Mr. Weston's motion, it was put & unanimously carried. No more of business appearing to demand the attention of this punctual body The Reporter made his report. The last Roll was called and the minutes Society by motion was adjourned.

Simeon W. Beaird, Sec.

'C.D.S.,' June 12th 1850

There being a very good attendance of members, at this meeting. At the usual hour it was called to order by the President. The first Roll was called, and the minutes of the last Weekly meeting were read and approved. The floor was not given to any, for the continuance of the discussion on on the last important subject, which was begun, continued and ended with great warmth and interest. At the conclusion the decision was given in favour of the 'Affirmative.' The following question was chosen from among those handed in by the Committee "Whose learned men have contributed most to the advancement of civilization those of the Greeks or Romans?["] Upon which Mr. B. E. K. Hampton was read out for the Greek and Mr. S. J. Maxwell for the Roman portion of the question. All business demanding attention being now concluded. The last Roll was called ~~and~~. The Reporter made his report, and the Society was by motion adjourned.

Simeon W. Beaird, Sec.

'C.D.S.,' June 19th 1850

This persevering body again met at the usual hour on the above date for the transaction of business. Having been called to order by the President. The first Roll was called and the minutes of the last meeting were read and approved. The discussion on the last adopted question was now begun with considerable warmth and continued to receive support to near the hour of adjournment; when Mr. Cardozo requested the continuation of the subject to the next meeting, being supported by Mr. Weston as a second. The President put the said request to the voice of the house and it being unanimously agreed on, he granted the same. Mr. S. W. Beaird moved that the time for hearing our next quarterly oration be fixed on the meeting after the election and installation of officers in July next, which being seconded, was put and unanimously carried; and the Secretary was ordered to notify the orator of the same. The reason of this delay being, the fourth month resolution of Mr. Cardozo not yet being carried, though under consideration. No more of business appearing to demand attention. The last Roll was called and the Reporter made his report. And the Society was adjourned by motion.

Simeon W. Beaird, Sec.

'C.D.S.,' July 1st 1850

In obedience to orders received from the President, this body met on this Monday evening in the place of Wednesday evening. Being called to order by the President, the first Roll was called and the minutes of the last meeting were read and approved. The continuation of the last subject was begun and continued to the ceasing hour. When Greece with all becomingness received a decision in favour of her supporters. At this hour the Secretary gave due notice, that the general election and installation of officers would take place at the next meeting; therefore no questions were handed in by the Committee of Queries; as there would be no debating on that evening. The Secretary rose and requested the members at large not to consider him as a candidate for that responsible position any longer, as he had now occupied it for Six terms, including 2 years.[13] He was willing to behold it occupied by other gentlemen, in order that he might recreate, but not that he found, any task in the least burdensome, that his fellow Clionians might impose on him. The President in accordance with the Constitution appointed the following gentlemen a Committee to examine the

56   *Free Black Charlestonians in Debate*

Treasury Departments, as also the books, of the Secretary and Treasurer. Viz. Messrs. H. Cardozo; W. O. Weston; & W. H. Gaillard. No more of business appearing to demand attention. The Reporter made his report. The last Roll was called and the Society adjourned by motion.

Simeon W. Beaird, Sec.

'CDS,' July 8th 1850

According to previous notice this meeting was called for the special purpose, of the general election of officers for the Ninth Term. Having been called to order by the President. The first Roll was called and the minutes of the last meeting were read and approved. The Committee appointed to examine the books and Treasury of the Secretary and Treasurer made a favourable report. The polls were now ordered to be opened. And upon report of managers the following gentlemen were declared elected for the next term (See officers book). The adjourning hour having nearly arrived a motion was made by Mr. Wm. Weston and seconded by Mr. S. W. Beaird, that the Installation in order to be conducted properly, do take place on the meeting of next Wednesday 17th inst., instead of the present hour. Which being put was carried. Mr. Barrow gave notice that at the next meeting he would bring before the notice of the body, the utility of having Diplomas to present to members that may in time leave the State, which was received. At no election meeting before had there been so many candidates for the various offices, and yet proud we are to say that none had ever been conducted with more harmony and union than this. Which speaks well of the actions of this flourishing and laudable Institution. The hour for adjourning having arrived, and no more of business presenting itself to demand attention. The Reporter made his report. The last Roll was called and the Society adjourned over to the Installation meeting of the 17th inst.

Simeon W. Beaird, Sec.

'CDS,' July 17th 1850

The regular weekly meeting of this society was held on the above date, and being called to order by the President, the first roll was called, and the minutes of the last meeting was read and approved. The regular installation (which was deferred from the last meeting) now commenced by the President arising and after announcing the name of Mr. Simeon W. Beaird as President elect, he congratulated himself and his fellow members on the Harmony and good order which the society had enjoyed during his official term, and beleiving [*sic*] that his worthy successor would be capable of promoting the same harmony he willingly resigned to him the elevated position. The President Elect now returned his thanks for the honours conferred on him, and on accepting the office avowed his determination to adhere strictly to the constitution, and thus he became duly installed. The subordinate ^officers^ was then duly installed, most of whom being present, pledged themselves to perform the duties of their respective offices to the best of their abilities. This being concluded, the committee of Queries handed in their questions from among which the following was chosen "Was Themistocles right in committing suicide rather than assist an enemy of his country."[14] Mr. W. E. Marshall was read out on the affirmative and Mr. W. O. Weston on the negative. All business demanding attending being now concluded, The Reporter made his report, the last roll was called, and the society on motion adjourned.

Error. Mr. R. L. Deas moved that a letter of thanks be addressed to Mr. S. W. Beaird, for his valuable services as Secretary & Treasurer, which was unanimously adopted.

H. Cardozo Jr., Sec.

'CDS,' July 24th 1850

As usual this society held its regular meeting on the above date, and being called to order by the President, the first roll was called, and the minutes of the last meeting read and approved. The regular debates now commenced and was carried on with considerable ardour even beyond the ceasing hour, at the close of which The President arose and gave his decision in favor of the negative. The questions for the next meeting were then handed in among which the following was chosen "Who accomplished the greatest good for his country Demosthenes or Cicero."[15] Mr. E. G. Beaird was appointed on the affirmative and Mr. G. F. Barrow on the negative, all business of importance being now concluded, the Reporter made his report the last roll was called and the society on motion adjourned.

Error—Mr. Deas being absent at the regular installation meeting, was duly installed by the President at this meeting.

H. Cardozo Jr., Secretary

C.D.S., July 31st 1850

This society held its regular weekly meeting on the above date after being called to order by the President, the first roll was called, and the minutes of the last meeting were read and approved. The regular ^debates^ now commenced, and such was the spiritedness with which they were carried on that nought but necessity compelled them to close, after which the President arose and gave his decision in favor of the first portion of the question. The next meeting being

58   *Free Black Charlestonians in Debate*

agreed on by motion for the hearing of the quarterly Oration no questions were handed in. Mr. Deas gave due notice that at the next meeting he would offer a resolution to change the meetings from weekly to fortnightly. It was moved by Mr. Cardozo that the letters of Messrs. Bass & Payne be read at the next meeting which was agreed on. The President recommended to the society the purchase of certain valuable books for the Library which was agreed to by the members who instructed him (the President) to purchase said books. All business of importance being now concluded, the reporter made his report, the last roll was called, and the society on motion adjourned.

H. Cardozo Jr., Secretary

C.D.S., August 14th 1850

This exceedingly well attended meeting was held on the above date, and being called to order by the President the first roll was called, and the minutes of the last meeting were read and approved. The Vice President being absent from the city, Mr. Maxwell was called on to fill the chair. Mr. S. W. Beaird ^presented^ to the society for Mrs Emma K. Fa[r]beaux, three very valuable books written by distinguished Authoresses. Mr. R. L. Deas moved that a letter of thanks be returned ^for the same^ which after being seconded was put and unanimously carried. Whereupon the following members were appointed, viz. W. O. Weston chairman, Messrs. W. H. Gailliard, G. F. Barrow, A. L. Horry, and R. L. Deas, Committee. Mr. S. W. Beaird also presented to the society the valuable works which he was instructed by them to purchase, upon which he made a few very appropriate remarks, recommending the perusal of them, which was all well received. The desired period now arrived for the hearing of the quarterly Oration the President announced the name of Mr. Augustus L. Horry as the orator who with much self command delightfully entertained the audience for some time on the subject of "Perseverance["] in the course of which he displayed a depth of intellect worthy of being cultivated. After concluding Mr. W. O. Weston moved that a copy of the address be requested of him, which being seconded was put and unanimously carried. Whereupon the President in a few pertinent remarks made the request, the Orator after having returned his thanks for the manner in which his address was received presented the original. According to previous notice the letters of Messrs. Payne and Bass were read and the Annual Oration of the latter received and deposited in the Library. Mr. Cardozo gave notice that at the next meeting he would bring forward his resolution for len[g]thening the time for the Quarterly Oration. The questions were handed in, from among which the following was chosen Which was calculated to shed the brightest lustre and influence on Grecian manners and character, "The laws of Solon or

1850

Lycurgus."[16] Mr. H. Cardozo was appointed on the first and Mr. J. M. Dereef on the latter portion of the question. No more of business appearing to demand attention, the Reporter made his report the last roll was called, and this meeting which was graced with the presence of many Honoraries adjourned by motion. H. Cardozo Jr., Secty.

'CDS,' September 4th 1850

The prevailing epidemic having seized a majority of our members for its victims, they were consequently prevented from meeting for the last two weeks.[17] But on the above date there being a good attendance the President called the ^meeting^ to order, the first roll was called, and the minutes of the last meeting were read and approved. The vice President being absent from the city Mr. Maxwell was called on to fill the chair. The regular debates now commenced and was carried on with increasing ardor to the last moment possible. after its close the President gave his conscientious decision in favor of the first portion of the question. The committee then handed in their questions from among which the following was chosen. "Was Cromwell right in usurping the reins of Government in England."[18] Mr. Deas handed in his resolution "for changing our meeting from weekly to semi-monthly" which was postponed for the next meeting's consideration, the President gave notice that at the next meeting the election of Quarterly Orator would take place, no more of business appearing to demand attention, the reporter made his report, the last roll was called, and the society on motion adjourned.
H. Cardozo Jr., Sec.
'Error' Mr. Deas was appointed on the affirmative, and Mr. Gailliard on the negative portion of the question.

'CDS,' September 11th 1850

This punctual body assembled at the usual hour on the above date, the President called it to order, the first roll was called, and the minutes of the last meeting were read and approved. The regular debates then commenced and continued to receive a warm support till the limited time had passed, after its close the President arose and gave his decision in favor of the negative. Mr. H. Cardozo Jr. after due notice brought forward his resolution to lengthen the time for the delivery of the private Orations before the Society, it was seconded, put to the house, and unanimously carried. the polls were now opened for the election of regular Orator, the managers counted the votes and declared Mr. S. J. Maxwell orator elect. the committee of queries han[d]ed in their questions from among which the following was chosen "Are afflictions in any manner beneficial to

60   *Free Black Charlestonians in Debate*

humanity." Mr. Hyams was appointed on the affirmative and Mr. Horry on the negative portion of the question. Mr. Maxwell filled the seat of the Vice-President he being absent from the city. all business of importance being now concluded, the reporter made his report, the last roll was called, and the society on motion adjourned.

H. Cardozo Jr., Sec.

'C.D.S.,' September 18th 1850

The regular weekly meeting of this Society was held on the above date, it was called to order by the President, the first roll called, and the minutes of the [last meeting] was read and approved. Mr. Hampton who was absent from the city at the last Installation meeting, now appeared and was duly installed by the President. Mr. W. O. Weston Chairman of the committee appointed to return the thanks of the Society to Mr. S. W. Beaird for his valuable services as Secretary and Treasurer, now fulfil[l]ed his appointment (which was delayed for sometime on account of sickness) by the introduction of the following "Preamble and Resolutions."

"Preamble"

The prevailing sentiment of the present age unfortunately has been to blind or in a manner to place upon the same platform the services of those who are truly meritorious, with those who are merely of an ordinary character. Among those who stand prominent in performing duties of an unexceptionable character, and of a rightly deserving description, and whose qualifications are of the rarest character, there stands prominent the name of S. W. Beaird, endeared as he is to us all by the relations that has existed between us as members, but more particularly as the Secretary and Treasurer of the Clionian D Society. his actions need no commentary, they are indellibly [*sic*] written upon the minds of each and every one, they are as familiar as the records of the Society, he being associated with it in such a great degree, yea from its origin throughout its different phases, to its now flourishing condition, and we have always beheld for ourselves this good deportment his business activity and his timely counsel in the most requisite hour. Deeming then his services while in that capacity as truly beneficial in its tendency to enhance the prosperity of the institution, and that his ever untiring industry in every post of duty whether laborious or tedious has tended in a great degree to place upon a firm foundation the financial and the literary condition and the respectability of the Society's reputation, and above all nerving the cheerfulness with which he performed these onorous [*sic*] duties for the space of eight long terms,[19] it is meet[20] that we should show forth some token of our appreciation of his valuable services. Therefore be it resolved unanimously.

1st That we fully regard the long-extended services of our late Secretary and Treasurer, and tender to him our sincere thanks for the ability and the zeal which he always evinced in the discharge of his onorous duties.

2nd That we tender to him our best wishes for the fulfilment properly of the new sphere of duties which the Society has tendered him.

3rd That the following Preamble and Resolutions be entered upon the Journals of the Society.

Signed, W. O. Weston / R. L. Deas / W. H. Gailliard

The above Preamble and Resolutions were unanimously adopted by the Society. Whereupon Mr. S. W. Beaird arose and expressed his thanks to his fellow members for the high esteem which they has placed on his services. Mr. W. O. Weston Chairman also of the committee appointed to communicate the thanks of the Society to Mrs. Farbeaux for her late valuable gifts, fulfilled his duty, by reading a copy of the letter, which was unanimously ^received^ by the Society. The regular debates now commenced and was warmly supported on both sides until the ceasing hour checked its continuance, after which the President arose and gave his decision favorable to the Affirmative. The committee of Queries handed their question[s] from among which the following was chosen, "Who has the greatest chance to show forth his patriotism in time of war the statesman in the hall of power, or the soldier on the field of battle." Mr. Hampton was appointed on the first and Mr. Maxwell on the last portion of the question. Mr. Deas presented his resolution for changing our meetings from weekly to semi-monthly, which was put to the house and lost. All business of importance being now concluded, the reporter made his report, the last roll was called, and the Society on motion adjourned.

H. Cardozo Jr., Sec.

C.D.S., October 2nd 1850

The punctuality of our members was again manifested by attending the regular weekly ^meeting^ of the Society on the above date. Which was called to order by the President, the first roll called, and the proceedings of the last meeting were read and approved. The Vice President being absent on account of sickness, Mr. Barrow filled the chair. The regular debates commenced and was carried on with increasing animation till the adjourning hour checked its further continuance though unexhausted, after which the President gave his decision in favor of the latter portion of the question. The Committee of Queries handed in their questions from among which the following was chosen—"Was Caesar right in crossing the Rubicon or not."[21] Mr. W. E. Marshall was read out on the affirmative and Mr. W. O. Weston on the negative of the question. Mr. Cardozo gave

due notice that at the next meeting he would move to carry into effect the first resolution. All business of importance being now concluded, the Reporter made his report, the last roll was called, and the Society on motion adjourned.
H. Cardozo Jr., Sec.

'CDS,' October 14th 1850

An "extra meeting" of the Society was held on the above date, it was called to order by the President, the first roll called, and the minutes of the last meeting read and approved. The Vice President being absent Mr. Hyams filled the chair. The regular ^debates^ now commenced and was so spiritedly discussed that the adjourning hour was almost forgotten, it however closed from necessity after which the President impartially decided in favor of the negative portion of the question. The Committee of Queries han[d]ed in their questions from among which the following was chosen—'Was the conduct of the Roman General Regulus commendable or condemnable."[22] Mr. E. G. Beaird was appointed on the first and Mr. G. F. Barrow on the latter portion of the question. Mr. Cardozo moved that according to Resolution 1st our meetings do change from weekly to monthly, and that we meet on Monday Evenings instead of Wednesday Evening, as long as said Resolution continues in force which was seconded, put to the house, and unanimously carried. The President gave due notice that at the next meeting the present term would expire, and the election of new officers would take place, he also notified the officers that according to Constitution he would require of them a report of the completion of their duties. No more business appearing to demand attention, the Reporter made his report, the last roll was called, and the Society on motion adjourned.
H. Cardozo Junior, Sec.

CDS, November 4th 1850

The regular monthly [meeting] of this society being held at the usual hour, on the above date, ^it^ was called to order, by the Vice President, the first roll was called, and the proceedings of the last (Extra) meeting were read and approved. The regular debates then commenced, and was carried on warmly till the ceasing hour checked its continuance. After which, the President decided in favor of the first portion of the question. The polls were now ordered to be opened, and the Society went immediately into an election for officers. Which upon report of Managers the following gentlemen were declared elected. (See officers list) No questions were handed in as the next meeting would be occupied for the installation of officers. The Monthly and Semi-annual contributions list were called out and partly paid. According to previous notice the President called on all the officers for a report of the completion of their duties to which they respectively answered in the affirmative. All business of importance being now concluded, the Reporter made his report, the last roll was called and the Society on motion adjourned.

The President appointed the following committee to examine the books of the Sec. & Treas., W. O. Weston, B. E. Hampton, R. L. Deas.

H. Cardozo Jr., Sec.

C.D.S., December 2nd 1850

This Society held its regular Monthly Meeting on the above date. After being called to order, the first roll was called, and the proceedings of the last meeting were read and approved. Mr. S. W. Beaird presented to the Society the three following Books which he was instructed by them to purchase, viz. Hawks Egypt. Noble deeds of Women. and Franklin's Life.[23]

The President now proceeded to install the new President which he prefaced with a few very appropriate remarks, and which was suitably answered by the President elect in a few remarks in which he signify^ed^ his acceptance of the office. The installation of all the subordinate officers were then successively conducted by the President, all of whom were apparently willing to perform any duty for the advancement of their beloved Society. The President then appointed Mr. S. W. Beaird as Chairman of the Committee on General interests and after a short time the Chairman announced to the President the following gentlemen who would compose his committee (See officers list.) Mr. S. W. Beaird moved that we invite the Utopian Society to attend our approaching third Anniversary which was seconded, and unanimously carried. The contribution list were called and considerably cleared. The committee of Queries then handed in their questions, from among which, the following was chosen, "Is education beneficial to society." Mr. H. Cardozo was appointed on the affirmative and Mr. J. M. Dereef on the negative. All business of importance being now concluded the Reporter made his report, the last roll was called and this well attended meeting adjourned by motion.

H. Cardozo, Sec.

NOTES

1. Several multivolume English translations of the French historian Charles Rollin's eighteenth-century text, *The Ancient History of the Egyptians, Carthaginians, Assyrians, Babylonians, Medes and Persians, Macedonians, and Grecians,* were available in 1850.

2. This query compares the Greek statesman and orator Demosthenes (384–322 BCE) with the earlier Greek philosopher Socrates (ca. 470–399 BCE).

3. The reasons for this protest are unknown.

4. This query compares the German theologian Martin Luther (1483–1546), who sparked the Protestant Reformation, with President George Washington. Many US Protestants considered the founding of the United States to be a culmination of the Reformation; see Marjule Anne Drury, "Anti-Catholicism in Germany, Britain, and the United States," *Church History* 70, no. 1 (March 2001): 105–6.

5. Many US Senate speeches from early 1850 were published as pamphlets; topics included compromise resolutions, California's admission to statehood, the Fugitive Slave Act, the question of enslavement generally, and the potential for national dissolution.

6. Francis Withers Capers (1819–1892), professor at the Citadel until late 1847, addressed the cadets' Calliopean Society in 1846. The address was then published as a pamphlet entitled *State Military Academies*.

7. John C. Calhoun (1782–1850), the proslavery statesman serving as US senator from South Carolina, died in Washington on March 31. His remains were transported to Charleston, arriving on April 25. Plans for elaborate public demonstrations, processions, and funeral ceremonies in the city were well under way by mid-April, making it feasible for Beaird to predict that many Clionians would choose to be away. See "Telegraphic Intelligence: Reported for the Charleston Courier," *Charleston Courier,* April 17, 1850, 2; "Arrangements for the Funeral of Mr. Calhoun," *Charleston Courier,* April 22, 1850, 2; and "South-Carolina Mourns for Her Dead," *Charleston Courier,* April 27, 1850, 2.

8. Professor Richard Trapier Brumby (1804–1875) of South Carolina College delivered an address to the state legislature in 1849; it appeared as a pamphlet, *An Address on the Sphere, Interest and Importance of Geology.*

9. The query refers to Gaius Julius Caesar (ca. 100–44 BCE), Roman general, statesman, and dictator.

10. Local attorney Nelson Mitchell delivered a Fourth of July oration in 1848 that was published as a pamphlet in 1849, entitled *Oration Delivered before the Fourth of July Association, on the Fourth of July, 1848.*

11. Bass was likely writing from Toronto, Canada West (present-day Ontario). In 1889 he reported that he left Charleston in 1849. His first wife, Ellen Bass, died in Toronto in 1851. Serving as a chaplain in the 90th New York Infantry during the Civil War, Bass later worked as a Methodist minister and penitentiary chaplain in Brooklyn, New York, until his death in 1901. Job G. Bass, Pension Application File, and Job G. Bass, deposition, January 12, 1889, in Conrad D. Ludeke, Pension Application File, both in Records of the Veterans Administration, 1773–1985, Record Group 15, National Archives and Records Administration, Washington, DC.

12. A downtown fire began in the early hours of May 29 and destroyed several businesses and telegraph posts. Local newspapers blamed the fire on an arsonist and credited the decisive action of firefighters for saving the Charleston Hotel. See "Another Destructive Fire," *Charleston Mercury,* May 29, 1850, 2; "Destructive Conflagration," *Charleston Courier,* May 30, 1850, 2; "The Fire of Yesterday," *Charleston Mercury,* May 30, 1850, 2; and "The Telegraph," *Charleston Mercury,* May 30, 1850, 2.

13. By this time Simeon W. Beaird had served as the society's inaugural president for two terms and then as secretary and treasurer for six terms.

1850   65

14. In this query, the Clionians follow the tradition presuming that the death of Themistocles (ca. 524—ca. 460 BCE), Athenian naval strategist and politician, was an honorable self-sacrifice. See John Marr, "The Death of Themistocles," *Greece and Rome* 42, no. 2 (October 1995): 159–67.

15. This query compares two famous orators and politicians: Demosthenes in fourth-century BCE Greece and Marcus Tullius Cicero (106–43 BCE) in Rome.

16. The query compares Solon (ca. 630–ca. 560 BCE), an Athenian statesman and lawmaker, with Lycurgus, traditionally a Spartan lawgiver of the seventh century BCE.

17. An epidemic of a malady known as break-bone fever afflicted many people in Charleston in the hot summer of 1850, albeit with few fatalities. Symptoms included headaches, pain in muscles and joints, exhaustion, chills, fever, and nausea, followed by skin rashes and insomnia. See William T. Wragg, "History of the Break-bone Fever: An Epidemic which Prevailed in Charleston, in the Summer of 1850," *Charleston Medical Journal and Review* 6, no. 2 (March 1851): 153–82; and Christopher Happoldt, "Observations on the Epidemic Break-bone Fever of 1850, in Charleston," *Charleston Medical Journal and Review* 6, no. 5 (September 1851): 605–27.

18. Oliver Cromwell (1599–1658) led parliamentary forces in the English Civil Wars against King Charles I, helping to overthrow the Stuart monarchy. During the republican Commonwealth, Cromwell was lord protector of England, Scotland, and Ireland.

19. On July 1, 1850, Beaird recorded in the minutes that he had served as secretary-treasurer "for Six terms, including 2 years." Here Weston, Deas, and Gailliard have added the two terms Beaird served as president prior to assuming the secretarial role.

20. The adjective *meet* in this now-archaic usage means "proper" or "appropriate for the situation or context." The Clionians would have been familiar with the usage from the King James Bible, where it frequently appears. For example, the second Pauline epistle to the Thessalonians salutes its readers: "We are bound to thank God always for you, brethren, as it is meet, because that your faith groweth exceedingly, and the charity of every one of you all toward each other aboundeth" (2 Thessalonians 1:3, KJV).

21. In 49 BCE, Julius Caesar's forces crossed a small stream, the Rubicon, invading Cisalpine Gaul. The movement constituted a violation of law that precipitated a civil war in Rome, and "crossing the Rubicon" became a phrase indicating a purposive action from which there is no turning back.

22. Marcus Atilius Regulus (fl. third century BCE) was a Roman general and consul who fought against the Carthaginians. Legends of his capture, his being sent to Rome to discuss peace, his arguments against peace, and his return to Carthage to die a martyr's death have been celebrated and questioned.

23. Francis L. Hawks's *The Monuments of Egypt; or, Egypt a Witness for the Bible* appeared in 1850. Elizabeth Starling's *Noble Deeds of Woman,* first published in London in 1835, was often reprinted during the nineteenth century. When the Clionians bought their copy of the famous autobiography of Benjamin Franklin (1706–1790), the standard English edition was an 1818 version produced by Franklin's grandson William Temple Franklin.

— 1851 —

[In this year society secretaries minuted twenty-six meetings; fourteen included debates, two included orations.—Ed.]

3rd "Anniversary Celebration"
C.D.S., January 1st 1851

This joyous day, bringing with it pleasing recollections of the past; and bright anticipations of the future, was welcomed by the 'Clionian Society.' In the afternoon the Society assembled in their Hall below, and about 4 o'clock, accompanied by the Utopian Society, they proceeded to the Hall above, where a very respectable audience awaited them. After being seated the exercises were commenced with prayer by Mr. Charles H. Holloway an Honorary Member, after its conclusion, the President 'Pro-tem' announced W. H. Gailliard as annual orator. The speaker now arose, and appropriately introduced his subject with a few preliminary remarks and then proceeded to elucidate the manner in which Knowledge may be obtained, and eloquently portrayed the happy effects resulting therefrom, his subject was frequently brightened by the many striking historical illustrations brought forward, which rendered ^it^ doubly impressive, after enchaining the attention of the audience for a considerable time on this most interesting subject, he failed not to congratulate his fellow members on the return of another Anniversary, and to recommend to them [the] principle of ~~sef~~ self-application as the true path to Knowledge and consequently~~ly~~ usefulness. Having concluded he sat down amid repeated applauses ^which^ assured him of the manner in which his interesting address was received by the delighted audience. The exercises were then closed with the Benediction, and this bright ^assembly^ left for their homes saturated[1] with a rich intellectual repast. The Society then retreated to their hall below, when after a short time they too separated, but not without a mind doubly encouraged to pursue the path of 'learning and mental improvement' which has, and ever will be the sole object of the Clionian Debating Society.

H. Cardozo Jr., Sec.

C.D.S., January 6th 1851

The society held its regular monthly meeting on the above date, it was called to order by the President 'Pro-tem.' The first roll was called, and the proceedings of the last regular meeting and of the Anniversary Celebration was read and approved. The President 'Pro-tem' having been chosen to fill the seat, on account of the Vice President's absence, Mr. W. H. Gailliard was then appointed to ^act^ as Vice President. The secretary read the report of the Committee appointed to examine his books, which report being favorable, was unanimously adopted. Mr. Cardozo moved that a copy of Mr. Gailliard's annual oration be requested of him, which being seconded, was put to the house, and unanimously carried. The regular debates now commenced, and was warmly kept up for a considerable time, and would have been continued to exhaustion, were it not that the limited time allotted, checked its further continuance. After its conclusion the President decided in favor of the affirmative. The Committee of Queries handed [in] their questions from among which the following was chosen, "Which had the greatest influence on Grecian character their Poetry or Philosophy." Mr. R. L. Deas was read out on the ~~affirmative~~ ^first^ and Mr. W. H. Gailliard on the latter portion of the question. The Polls were now opened for the election of Annual Orator for 1852 upon the managers counting the votes Messrs. Weston and Cardozo were found to have an equal number of votes, the President therefore casted his vote in favor of the former, he was then declared duly elected. the contribution list were called and considerably cleared. No more of business appearing to demand attention. The reporter made his report, the last roll was called and the Society on motion adjourned.
H. Cardozo Jr., Sec.

C.D.S., February 3rd 1851

But one short month had elapsed when the Clionian Society (true to her purpose) had again assembled in their hall on the above date. The meeting was called to order by the President. The first roll called, and the minutes of the last meeting read and approved. Mr. Horry was called upon to fill the seat of the Vice-President. The regular debates then commenced and was carried on with increasing interest and life, till when at its height, and the minds of all became warmed in the subject, while all was life and animation the adjourning hour arrived, and both speakers and hearers had to give up their pleasures for the time being. After a short interval the President arose and gave his decision in favor of the latter portion of the question. The Committee handed in their questions, from among which the following was chosen, "Were the allied nations of Europe ~~right~~ justifiable in banishing Napoleon."[2] Mr. Hyams was

68   *Free Black Charlestonians in Debate*

appointed on the affirmative, and Mr. Horry on the negative of the question. Mr. W. O. Weston annual orator ^elect^ for '52; offered his resignation to that office—which by the unanimous voice of the body was not accepted, but upon being again urged by him, it was concluded that the office was vacant, and that they would go into an election for annual orator at the next meeting. The Secretary gave notice that at the next meeting the general election of officers for the eleventh term would take place. All business of importance being now concluded, the reporter made his report, the last roll was called, and the Society on motion adjourned.

H. Cardozo Jr., Sec.

'CDS,' March 10th 1851

A regular meeting of this Society was held on the above date. It was called to [order] by the President pro-tem, the first roll was called and the proceedings of the last meeting read and approved. Not having obtained a quorum until a comparatively late hour, it was moved that the regular debates which were to have taken place be deffered [*sic*] 'till ^the meeting^ after the election and installation of officers, ^which^ was seconded and unanimously carried. The Society then went immediately into an election of officers for the eleventh term. And upon report of Managers the following were declared elected (See officers list). The votes were also taken for Annual Orator ^for 1852^ which resulted in the election of Mr. S. W. Beaird. Upon motion of Mr. S. W. Beaird next Monday evening was appointed as the time for the installation of officers elect. He also moved that as the President and Vice President are absent from the city, that some one of the members be chosen to act as President on that occasion, which ^was^ seconded and unanimously carried. Whereupon Mr. W. H. Gailliard was proposed, and ^also^ elected. Mr. E. G. Beaird then presented Moore's Poetical Works, a most valuable gift from Miss Frances P. Bonneau to the Clionian Society.[3] Whereupon Mr. S. W. Beaird moved that a Committee of Six be appointed to return the thanks of the society by letter to the kind donor, which was seconded and unanimously carried, the President then appointed the following gentlemen, viz. S. W. Beaird, Chairman, E. G. Beaird, H. Cardozo Jr., W. H. Gailliard, S. J. Maxwell and R. L. Deas. The President also appointed the following gentlemen to examine the Books of the Secretary and Treasurer, and to report concerning them at the next meeting, viz. S. W. Beaird, W. H. Gailliard, and E. G. Beaird. No more of business appearing to demand attention the reporter made his report, the last roll was called, and the Society on motion adjourned.

H. Cardozo Jr., Sec.

C.D.S., March 17th 1851

An extra meeting of this Society was held on the above date for the purpose of installing the officers elect. The meeting was called to order by the President, the first roll called and the proceedings of the last regular meeting read and approved. The committee appointed to examine the Books of the Secretary & Treasurer made a favorable report thereon. The regular installation now commenced by the inauguration of the new President, who after having accepted the high and honorable charge entrusted to him, proceeded to install all the subordinate officers successively, all of whom expressed a cheerful willingness to perform any duty which the Society's welfare would demand of them, and thus ended the installation. The President then appointed Mr. W. O. Weston Chairman on the committee of general interests. Mr. S. W. Beaird notified the Society of his acceptance of the high and important trust committed to him as its Annual Orator for '52.' Mr. W. H. Gailliard moved that the constitution be read for the instruction of the members on the first meeting in April which upon being amended by Mr. S. W. Beaird that it be read after the hearing of the "Private Oration" was seconded and carried. The Secretary notified the Society that on Monday evening 31st March, the regular debates which were necessarily deferred will then take place. All business of importance being now finished, the Reporter made his report, the last roll was called, and the Society on motion adjourned.

H. Cardozo Jr., Secretary

'C.D.S.,' March 31st 1851

This Society held another 'extra' meeting on the above date for the purpose of hearing the deferred debates. it was called to order by the President. The first roll called, and the minutes of the last extra meeting read and approved. The regular debates then commenced, was warmly carried on, and ceased only on account of the expiration of the time allotted to it, after which, the President arose and gave his decision in favor of the negative portion of the question. The Committee of Queries then handed in their questions from among which the following was chosen, "Have the late Revolutions of Europe tended much to benefit the condition of the people of that Continent."[4] Mr. Hampton was read out as debatant on the affirmative, and Mr. Maxwell on the negative of the question. Mr. Deas presented to the Society two ^very^ valuable pamphlets, which upon motion was received and the thanks of the Society ^unanimously^ returned to the kind donor. Notice was given that on next Monday evening the 7th "proximo,"[5] the "regular" Oration before the Society would then be delivered. The Chairman on the "Committee of General interests" handed in his list

of those who should assist him in the performance of the duties incumbent on that office. All business of importance being now concluded, the Reporter made his report, the last roll was called, and the Society on motion adjourned.
H. Cardozo Jr., Secretary

'C.D.S.,' April 14th 1851

With their usual promptness the Clionian Society held a regular Monthly meeting on the above date. It was called to order by the Vice President—the first roll called—and the proceedings of the last 'extra' meeting read and approved of. The Vice President then appointed Mr. A. L. Horry as President 'Protem' who after having taken the chair, arose and announced to the audience the name of Mr. S. J. Maxwell as the Orator for the evening. The speaker then arose and introduced that most interesting subject "Education" with a few preparatory remarks, and then proceeded to show with great success the importance of Learning in preparing Man to act his part in the great drama of life and in opening his mental eyes to the works of nature particularly as exhibited in the Starry firmament above, which the happy speaker proved to be the source of the greatest exercise of the mind, and the highest flights of the Imagination. After having illustrated his subject with many beautiful figures, and striking facts, he closed his excellent address, which from beginning to end was characterised by great depth of thought, and a flow of elegant language, that would do honour to one of greater advantages, and thus he sat down amid the applause of the audience, after which Mr. W. H. Gailliard arose and paid a deservedly high compliment to the speaker and then moved that a copy of his address be requested, which was ^seconded^ by Mr. S. W. Beaird, put to the house, and unanimously carried. The President accordingly made the request, which the speaker promised to comply with in a few days. Mr. S. W. Beaird, Chairman on the committee of thanks to Miss F. P. Bonneau presented to the Society a copy of his letter written to that Lady which was unanimously received by the body. All business of importance being now concluded, the Reporter made his report, the last roll was called, and this meeting of members both Honorary and private adjourned by motion.
H. Cardozo Jr., Secretary

C.D.S., May 7th 1851

A regular meeting of this Society was held on the above date, after being called to order by the President, the first roll was called, and the proceedings of the last meeting read and confirmed. The Vice President and Secretary being absent on account of sickness their seats were respectively filled by Messrs. S. W. Beaird and W. O. Weston. Mr. S. W. Beaird then moved that the regular debates for this evening be deferred to the next regular meeting, which being seconded was carried. According to previous notice the polls were now opened for the election of Semi-Annual Orator. the votes were polled, counted, and upon report of Managers Mr. R. L. Deas was declared elected unanimously. Mr. S. W. Bea[i]rd now moved that for the present our meetings be changed from once a month to twice a month and that it be the 1st and 3rd Mondays of the Month, Mr. E. G. Beaird seconded the motion but moved the latter portion by substituting the 2nd and 4th Mondays of the Mondayth which being acceded to was put to the house and carried. Mr. S. W. Beaird notified the Society of his intention to bring before it at its next meeting the alteration of an amendment of Bye Laws determining the time of reading the Constitution quarterly, that it be changed to every installation meeting as being the most convenient and proper time. The Semi-annual and Monthly contribution list were called, and partly paid. All business of importance being now concluded, the Reporter made his report, the last roll was called, and the Society on motion adjourned.

H. Cardozo Jr., Sec.

C.D.S., June 9th 1851

This Society held its regular Semi-Monthly [meeting] on the evening of the above date. it was called to order by the President, the first roll called, and the proceedings of the last meeting read and confirmed. The Vice President being absent from the city Mr. A. L. Horry was called on to fill his seat. Mr. R. L. Deas then arose and expressed to the Society his extreme reluctance to inform them that he would be unable to serve them in the capacity of Semi-Annual Orator, and therefore begged that they would accept his declination. The time now arrived for the commencement of the regular debates, the appointed ^debatants^ was called out and reported to be absent. Whereupon the President arose and opened the house for the members at large, the chanced[6] was embraced, the debates commenced and was carried on with considerable warmth until the last moment allowable was used, after its close, the President arose and gave his decision in favor of the affirmative portion of the question. The committee of Queries now produced their questions from among which the following was chosen "Will the World's Fair bring about the contemplated union of intercourse among the nations of the earth."[7] Mr. W. E. Marshall was read out on the affirmative, and Mr. W. O. Weston on the negative of the question. Mr. S. W. Beaird explained to the Society the alteration to the amendment of Bye Laws he intended to offer but for the want of time he would defer 'till the next meeting. No more of business appearing to demand attention, the Reporter made his report, the last roll was called and the Society on motion adjourned. H. Cardozo Jr., Secretary

C.D.S., June 23rd 1851

On the evening of the above date, this Society held its regular Semi monthly meeting. It was called to order by the President, the first [roll] was called, and the minutes of the last meeting were read and approved. The Vice President being absent from the city, Mr. E. G. Beaird was called on to fill his seat. The regular debates now commenced and not one moment had elapsed when the sound of voices were not heard successively on each side of the question, and such was the warmth with which it was supported that time was forgotten in the excitement of debate. but as all things must have an end this had to meet the same fate. when after its close, the President arose and announced his decision—which was in favor of the affirmative side of the question. The committee of Queries now produced their questions, from which the following was chosen "Which is the most responsible for an article the Composer or the Publisher." Mr. S. W. Beaird was read out on the first—and Mr. E. G. Beaird on the latter portion of the question. It was now proposed that the letter of an applicant which was in possession of one of the members be now brought before the Society, but it being found ^that^ the possessor had forgotten to bring it, It was moved by Mr. H. Cardozo Jr. that an extra meeting be called for the consideration of the letter, and that next Monday evening be the appointed time, which was seconded, and carried. According to previous notice Mr. S. W. Beaird brought forward an alteration to the amendment which requires the "Secretary to read the Constitution quarterly for the benefit of the Society" which alteration reads thus—The <u>Reader</u> shall read the Constitution at every <u>installation</u> meeting for the benefit of the Society. the amendment was put to the house and unanimously adopted. All business of importance being now finished, the Reporter made his report, the last roll was called, and the Society on motion adjourned.
H. Cardozo Jr., Secretary

C.D.S., June 30th 1851

An 'extra' meeting of this Society was held on the evening of the above date. being called to order by the President, the first roll was called and the proceedings of the last regular meeting read and approved. The President then received a letter directed to the officers and Members of the Clionian Debating Society, through Mr. W. H. Gaillard which was refferred [*sic*] to the Secretary and upon being opened was found to contain an application for membership from

Mr. Alexander Forrester, concerning whom the committee on general interests made a favorable report. he was then ballotted for, and declared elected. Mr. S. W. Beaird gave due notice that at our next regular meeting he would bring forward some other alterations to the Constitution. The Secretary also gave due notice that our next meeting would be the regular time for the general election of officers for the 12th term. All business of importance being concluded, the reporter made his report, the last roll called, and the Society on motion adjourned.

H. Cardozo Jr., Sec.

C.D.S., July 14th 1851

A regular Semi-monthly meeting of this Society was held on the above date. The first roll was called, and the proceedings of the last (extra) meeting were read and approved. The President and Vice President being absent, their seats were respectively filled by Messrs. Gailliard and Hampton. The regular debates now commenced—was spiritedly carried on—and ended only when it could be no longer continued. The President "Pro-tem" now arose and announced his decision as being in favor of the latter portion of the question. Due notice having been given that this would be the time for the election of officers for the 12th term— The Committee of General Interests accordingly opened the ballot box, and after the votes were deposited—and counted, the following gentlemen were declared elected (See officers list). the next meeting was appointed as the regular installation meeting. No more business appearing to demand attention, the reporter made his report, the last roll was called, and the Society adjourned by motion.

H. Cardozo Jr., Secretary

C.D.S., July 28th 1851

With her usual promptness, this Society assembled on the evening of the above date. It was called to order by the President—the first roll called, and the proceedings of the last meeting read and approved. Mr. Forrester the member elect being present—the reader proceeded to read the Constitution for his hearing— and after the conclusion of which he came forward—signed his name—Paid the 'initial fee' and thereby became a regular and respected member of the Clionian Society. The regular installation now commenced with a few remarks from the retiring President in which he expressed himself highly gratified to know that the utmost harmony of feeling had prevailed during his official term, and that he had the happy consciousness of having done his duty. he then turned to his successor and congratulated [him] on his election to that important post, and being confidant [sic] that he will be fully able to discharge the duties and responsibilities incumbent on such an office, cheerfully resigned to him the chair. The new President now accepted the dignified office, and assured his fellow members that with the constitution as his guide he would discharge the duties of his office to the best of his abilities. nearly all of of [*sic*] the officers elect being present—he proceeded to install them successively—all of whom affirmed that they would faithfully perform the duties incumbent on their respective offices. The installation being now concluded, the President proceeded to make several appointments, the first of which was that of Mr. R. L. Deas, as Chairman of the committee on 'general interests,' and Messrs. S. W. Beaird, R. L. Deas, and I. A. Hyams as the committee to examine the books of the Secretary and Treasurer. Mr. Cardozo having declined serving on the 'Committee of Queries' on account of his many duties as Secretary and Treasurer, and his declination having been accepted, it was moved that an election to fill the vacancy take place at the <u>next</u> meeting, which motion was seconded and carried. The Committee of Queries now handed in their questions from among which the following was chosen, "Which exercises the greatest beneficial influence upon society Intellectual or Moral excellence." Mr. Barrow was read out on the first, and Mr. Cardozo on the latter portion of [the] question. All business of importance being now concluded, the reporter made his report, the last roll was called and the Society on motion adjourned.

H. Cardozo Jr., Sec.

C.D.S., August 11th 1851

A regular meeting of this Society was held on the above date. the President called it to order, the first roll was called, and the proceedings of the last meeting read and approved. The election to fill the vacancy in the committee of Queries now took place, and resulted in the choice of Mr. R. L. Deas. The President then proceeded to install the Vice President (who was absent at the last meeting) and the elected member of the "Committee of Queries" Mr. R. L. Deas, presented to the Society two very valuable pamphlets containing an address from the Hon. W. D. Porter,[8] and a sermon from the Rev. Mr. Miles.[9] this repeated manifestation of his regard for the Society was unanimously accepted by them. The regular debates now commenced, and after every possible moment being used on the subject, it was moved that it be deferred to the next meeting for further discussion. The President having decided in favor of the motion, he gave ^due^ notice to that effect. All business of importance being now concluded, the Reporter made his report, the last roll was called, and the Society on motion adjourned.

H. Cardozo Jr., Secretary

C.D.S., August 25th 1851

The above mentioned date brought together the members of this Society for a regular Semi-Monthly meeting. It was called to order by the President, the first roll was called, and the proceedings of the last meeting read and confirmed. The Vice President being absent Mr. Deas was appointed to fill his seat. The President now gave notice that the floor is opened for the further ^discussion of^ the subject deferred from the last meeting. The chance was embraced, and one after another arose in quick succession each warmly supporting his side, until the last moment allowable had ceased, the President then arose and gave his decision in favor of the latter portion of the question. The 'Committee' now handed in their questions from among which the following was chosen—"Has the Intellect been <u>beneficial</u> or <u>deleterious</u> to man's Happiness?" Mr. J. M. Dereef was appointed on the first and Mr. R. L. Deas on the latter portion of the question. The Chairman on the "Committee to examine the Books of the Secretary and Treasurer" made a favorable report thereon and which was unanimously accepted by the Society. Mr. R. L. Deas "Chairman on the committee of general interests" now presented to the Society a list of such members as he had chosen to serve with him on that committee. All business of importance being now finished, the Reporter made his report, the last roll was called, and the Society on motion adjourned.
H. Cardozo Jr., Secretary

C.D.S., September 8th 1851

Under a sense of advantages enjoyed, the Clionians assembled in their hall on the evening of the above date for a regular meeting—It was called to order by the President, the first roll was called, and the proceedings of the last regular meeting was read and confirmed. The regular debates now commenced and was carried on with increasing vigor even to the close, after which the President arose and gave his decision in favor of the first portion of the question. The 'Committee' now handed in their questions from among which the following was chosen—"Which is the most Advantageous, desirable, and Beneficial—a Married or Single Life." Mr. Forrester was read out on the first, and Mr. Gaillard on the last portion of the question. The President now informed the Society that he had received through Mr. Forrester a letter which he gave to the Secretary to read who upon opening found that it contained an application for membership in the Society from Mr. Henry J. D. Cardozo. The Constitutional two thirds not being present further action on the letter was postponed. All business of importance being now concluded, the reporter made his report, the last roll was called, and the Society on motion adjourned.
H. Cardozo Jr., Secretary

C.D.S., September 22nd 1851

Proving true to the avowed object of the Society its members assembled for another regular meeting,—which was called to order by the President, the first roll called—and the proceedings of the last regular meeting read and confirmed. The time now arrived for the hearing of the regular debates, which was commenced, and was carried on with growing fervor, each side receiving increasing support and proportionately growing in interest, when to the regret of all, it had to cease for want of time, after which the President arose and gave his decision in favor of the first portion of the question. The "Committee" now handed in their questions, from among which the following was chosen—"Was the conduct of Gen. Lopez commendable or condemnable."[10] Mr. Hyams was read out on the first portion of the question, and Mr. Horry on the last. The President now arose and stated that for two meetings the requisite number to act on a letter of application ^was not present^ and for that reason he requested the secretary to summon the members for an extra meeting to be held on Thursday Night. No further business appearing, the Reporter made his report, the last roll was called, and the Society on motion adjourned.

H. Cardozo Jr., Sec.

[The proceedings volume held at the Charleston Library Society ends here. The volume at Duke University begins with a modified version of the minutes of the meeting of September 22, 1851.—Ed.]

Continued Proceedings
of the
Clionian. Debating. Society.
"Clionian Society," September 22nd 1851

Proving true to the avowed object of the Society, its members assembled for a regular meeting, which was called to order by the President, the first roll called, and the proceedings of the last regular meeting read and confirmed. The time having now arrived for the hearing of the regular debates, they were accordingly commenced, and were carried on with increasing fervor—each side receiving a warm support, and growing in interest, even to the close (which was hastened for the want of time) after which the President arose and announced his decision, which was in favor of the first portion of the question. The 'Committee' now handed in their questions from among which the following was chosen—"Was the conduct of Gen. Lopez commendable or condemnable." Mr. Hyams was appointed on the first, and Mr. Horry on the last portion of the question. The President now arose and stated that as two meetings had elapsed, and the

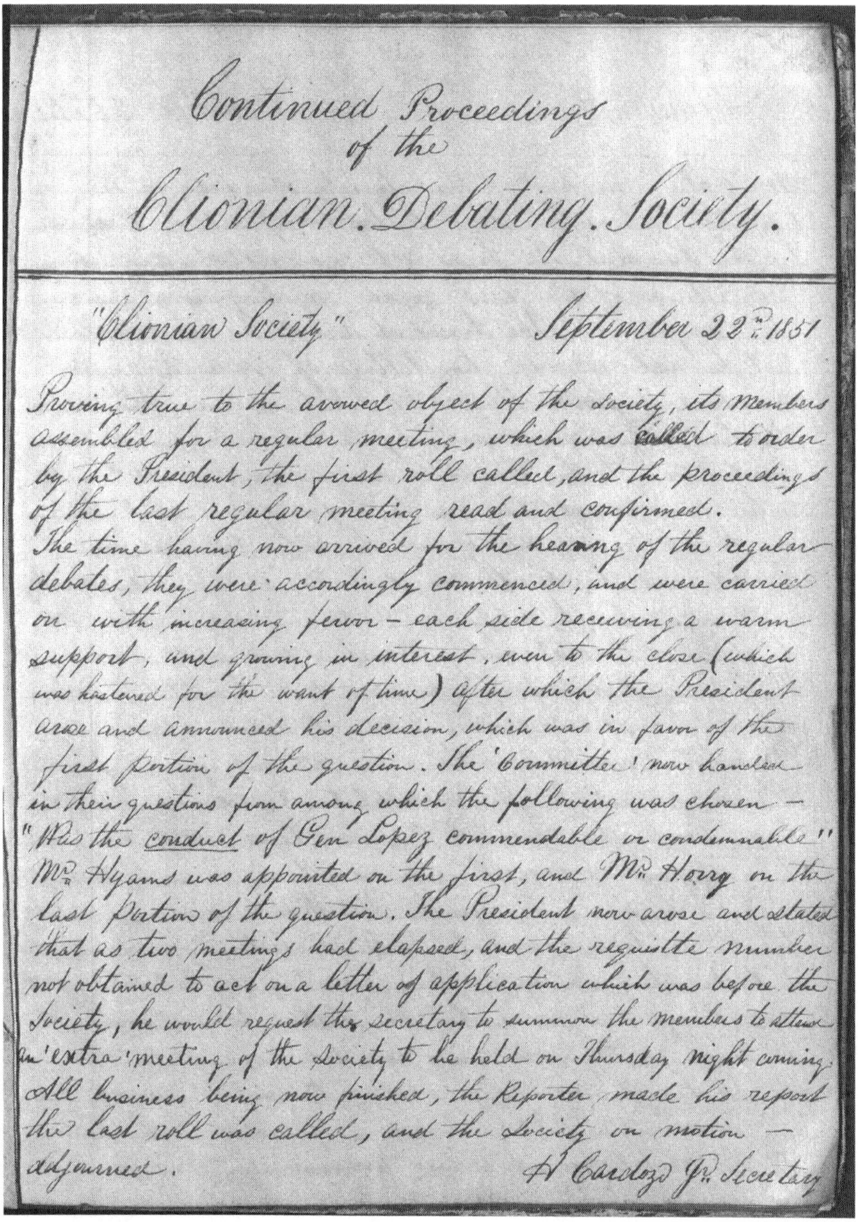

Continued Proceedings of the

Clionian. Debating. Society.

"Clionian Society"   September 22ⁿᵈ 1851

Proving true to the avowed object of the society, its members assembled for a regular meeting, which was called to order by the President, the first roll called, and the proceedings of the last regular meeting read and confirmed.

The time having now arrived for the hearing of the regular debates, they were accordingly commenced, and were carried on with increasing fervor — each side receiving a warm support, and growing in interest, even to the close (which was hastened for the want of time) after which the President arose and announced his decision, which was in favor of the first portion of the question. The Committee now handed in their questions from among which the following was chosen —

"Was the conduct of Genl Lopez commendable or condemnable" Mr. Hyams was appointed on the first, and Mr. Hoeg on the last Portion of the question. The President now arose and stated that as two meetings had elapsed, and the requisite number not obtained to act on a letter of application which was before the Society, he would request the secretary to summon the members to attend an 'extra' meeting of the society to be held on Thursday night coming. All business being now finished, the Reporter made his report the last roll was called, and the society on motion — adjourned.

                                        H Cardozo Jr. Secretary

Figure 5. First page of Clionian Debating Society (Charleston, SC), Proceedings, 1851–1858, David M. Rubenstein Rare Book and Manuscript Library, Duke University, Durham, NC, reprinted by courtesy.

requisite number not obtained to act on a letter of application which was before the Society, he would request the Secretary to summon the members to attend an 'extra' meeting of the Society to be held on Thursday night coming. All business being now finished, the Reporter made his report the last roll was called, and the Society on motion—adjourned.

H. Cardozo Jr., Secretary

Clionian D. Society, September 25th 1851

An "Extra meeting" of this Society was held on the Evening of the above date. After being called to order by the President, the first roll was called, and the proceedings of the last <u>regular</u> meeting were read and confirmed. The President now arose, and stated that he had received two letters of application for membership from Messrs. H. J. D. Cardozo, and Robert Sanders, which were read by the Secretary, and then handed over to the "Committee on General Interests" who after some consultation made a favorable report thereon the Ballot Box was then opened, the votes deposited, and counted, and the Gentlemen declared elected. The Secretary was then requested to notify the Gentlemen, and summon them to appear at the next meeting. According to previous notice— Mr. S. W. Beaird, offered an amendment to the Constitution, which was as follows, Every member failing to debate after being notified, and who shall after a month's indulgence fail to come forward to offer a constitutional excuse, His fine being levied after, shall be known as legal. Absence from the city, and sickness, the only exceptions. The amendment was put to the house, and carried. Mr. W. H. Gaillard now moved that the Society go immediately into an election for Semi-Annual Orator, which was objected to on account of the lateness of the hour, it was then moved that the election be postponed to the next meeting, which was seconded, and carried. Mr. S. W. Beaird now brought before the Society several valuable works, and a beautiful picture, presented to the same by Mr. A. L. Horry, which was unanimously received. Mr. R. L. Deas then moved that a letter of thanks be returned to the kind donor, which motion was carried. A committee of six was then proposed for that purpose. The President accordingly appointed the following gentlemen. R. L. Deas, Chairman, S. W. Beaird, W. H. Gaillard, H. Cardozo Jr., I. A. Hyams, and A. C. Forrester, Committee. The Secretary then presented the invitation which was received by the Society from the Utopian Association, and which was unanimously accepted. All business of importance being now finished, the Reporter made his report, the last roll was called, and the Society on motion adjourned.

H. Cardozo Jr., Secretary

Clionian D. Society, October 6th 1851

Another "Extra meeting" of this Society was held on the evening of the above date, it was called to order by the President, the first roll called, and the proceedings of the last 'extra' meeting were read and approved. The President then arose and after stating the objects of the meeting, requested the Reader to read the Constitution to the members elect, (who were then present) which was done by that officer in a distinct manner, they then expressed their approval in a few neat and appropriate remarks, signed their names, paid the "initial fee" and thereby became regular and respected members of the Clionian Fraternity. Mr. S. W. Beaird now proposed an addition to the 10th Resolution which provides for the election of the Succeeding Orator at the same time that the Semi-Annual Oration is delivered. it was seconded, and carried. He also gave notice that at the next meeting, he would bring forward an addition to the 2nd Amendment of the Constitution. Mr. H. Cardozo Jr. offered the following resolution which was seconded, and carried. Resolved, that as [in] order to preserve the distinctiveness of the Clionian Debating Society that whomsoever shall become a member shall in no wise be a member or apply for membership in other Institutions raised and carried on for the support of the same principles. Resolved—That as Mr. W. E. Marshall has already been, and is a member of another Institution of the same character, previous to the passage of the above resolution—he be considered the only exception. All business of importance being now finished, the Reporter made his report the last roll was called, and the Society on motion adjourned.

H. Cardozo Jr., Secretary

"Clionian D. Society," October 13th 1851

The Society held its regular Semi-Monthly meeting on the evening of the above date, it was called to order by the Vice President, the first roll was called, and the proceedings of the last "extra meeting" were read and approved. The time now arrived for the hearing of the regular debates they were accordingly commenced, and was carried on with much Life and Vigor even to the close, when the President arose, and announced his decision in favor of the first portion of the question. The Committee now handed in their questions from among which the following was chosen—"Whether forms of Government exert any important influence on the growth and character of National Literature." Mr. S. J. Maxwell was appointed on the affirmative, and Mr. W. E. Marshall on the negative of the question. According to previous notice Mr. S. W. Beaird brought forward his Addition to the second Amendment of Constitution which reads thus—No applicant's letter can be acted upon until the meeting following that of the reading of his letter. It was put to the house and unanimously carried. As was previously agreed on the polls were now opened for the election of Semi-Annual Orator, and which resulted in the choice of Mr. B. E. K. Hampton who upon being informed of his election—arose and announced that he would be utterly unable to serve the Society in that capacity, and would therefore decline. Mr. S. W. Beaird then moved that at the next meeting we go into another election, which was seconded, and carried.

All business of importance being now finished, the Reporter made his report, the last roll was called, and the Society on motion adjourned.
H. Cardozo Jr., Secretary

"Clionian D. Society," October 27th 1851

The lapse of two weeks, again brought together the members of this Society for a regular meeting. The President being absent, the Vice President filled his seat and Mr. W. H. Gaillard filled that of the Vice, the meeting was then called to order, the first roll called, and the minutes of the last regular meeting read and approved.

The regular debates now commenced on an interesting question, which was warmly supported on each side until the adjourning hour checked its further continuance. The President then arose, and announced his decision in favor of the affirmative portion of the question. The Committee now handed in their questions, from among which, the following was chosen—"Whether success in difficult Sciences are the results of Genius, or Industry and Perseverance." Mr. Robert Sanders was appointed on the first, and Mr. W. O. Weston on the last portion of the question. Mr. S. W. Beaird gave due notice that at the next meeting he would offer the striking out of several articles of the Constitution rendered unimportant by succeeding ones.

All matters of importance being now attended to, the Reporter made his report, the last roll was called, and the Society on motion adjourned.
H. Cardozo Jr., Secretary

"Clionian D. Society," November 10th 1851

A regular Semi-Monthly meeting of this Society was held on the evening of the above date. The President being absent the Vice President filled his seat, Mr. Hyams filled that of the Vice, the meeting was then called to order, the first roll called, and the proceedings of the last regular meeting read and approved. Mr. S. W. Beaird now arose, and moved that, on account of the lateness of the hour, the regular debates be postponed to the next debating meeting, the motion was seconded, and carried. The general election of officers for the 13th term then took place—and which resulted in the choice of the following gentlemen (See officers list) The election of Semi-Annual Orator also took place, which resulted in favor of Mr. I. A. Hyams who, upon being informed of his election, arose, and announced that he would be unable to serve the Society in that capacity, and therefore declined. It was then moved that the Society go into another election, the motion was carried, the Box was then reopened, the votes deposited and counted, and Mr. A. C. Forrester declared elected. According to previous notice, Mr. S. W. Beaird offered the following resolution which was adopted. Resolved—That as certain portions of the Amendments of the Constitution of this Society have become superfluous and useless, that they be blanked out of the regular order of rules, To wit, the 1st and 6th of the Constitution, The 1st and 3rd of the Bye Laws, and the 1st Resolution. All business of import being now concluded, the reporter made his report, the last roll was called, and the Society on motion adjourned.

H. Cardozo Jr., Secretary

"Clionian D. Society," December 1st 1851

An "extra meeting" of this Society was held on the evening of the above date. The President having called it to order, the first roll was called, and the proceedings of the last regular meeting were read and approved. The Reader then proceeded to read the Constitution for the benefit of the Society, this being done, the regular installation commenced with a few appropriate remarks from the retiring President, who, after expressing his thanks to his fellow members for aiding and sustaining him in his course during his official term; and congratulating his Society on its bright prospects of future eminence: proceeded to install the Vice President (The President being absent) who after accepting the office, then installed the subordinate officers, all of whom manifested such cheerfulness in accepting their respective positions, and expressing such a willingness to serve the Society, as to leave one to infer that they intend to give a practical exemplification of the excellent maxim that "When duty is known duty will be performed," and thus ended the Installation. Mr. S. W. Beaird now arose and offered the following resolution, Resolved—That the thanks of this Society be tendered to its late President Mr. B. E. K. Hampton for the faithful and impartial manner in which he discharged his duties during his official term. it was seconded, and unanimously adopted. The President according to Constitution, appointed a Committee of three, composed of the following gentlemen—R. L. Deas, W. O. Weston, and S. J. Maxwell, to examine the Books of the Secretary and Treasurer, and report thereon at the next meeting.

82   *Free Black Charlestonians in Debate*

All business of importance being now finished, the Reporter made his report, the last roll called, and the Society on motion adjourned.

H. Cardozo Jr., Sec.

"Clionian D. Society," December 8th 1851

On the evening of the above date, this Society held its regular Semi-Monthly meeting, it was called to order by the Vice President, the first roll called, and the proceedings of the last 'extra' meeting were read and approved.

The regular debates now commenced, and was carried on with increasing warmth, until when at its height the adjourning hour arrived, and there being many who had not yet spoken on the question, it was moved that it be postponed until the next meeting for further discussion—the President being favorable to the motion, announced the continuation of the debates to the next meeting. Mr. S. W. Beaird a member of the Committee on General Interests—informed the Society that purchase had been made of a work called "The Book of the World"[11] in two volumes, which was received as information. The President elect being now present was duly installed by the Vice President and after accepting the office offered a few appropriate remarks, in which he expressed his gratification at being made the Head of a Society whose object and aim were among the noblest that could engage the mind of man, and therefore would endeavor to act in accordance with his position. All business of import being now finished, the Reporter made his report, the last roll was called, and the Society on motion adjourned.

H. Cardozo Jr., Secretary

Clionian D. Society, December 22nd 1851

With undeviating punctuality this Society held its regular meeting on the evening of the above date. The President and Vice President being absent, Mr. W. H. Gaillard was chosen President "Pro tem," and Mr. Forrester Vice President. The meeting was then called to order, the first roll called, and the minutes of the last meeting read and approved. Mr. S. W. Beaird now arose, and moved that as the meeting had organized at so late an hour and the debates to be finished being of an interesting nature—they be further postponed 'till the next Monday night, the motion was seconded, and carried. The Committee appointed to examine the Books of the Secretary & Treasurer, made a favorable report thereon, which was received by the Society. Mr. R. L. Deas Chairman of the committee appointed some time since to return the thanks of the Society by letter to Mr. A. L. Horry for his valuable presents—submitted a copy of the same, which was received. Mr. S. W. Beaird a member of the Committee on General Interests laid before the Society several valuable works purchased for the Library, which was received, and the thanks of the Society tendered to the Committee for their excellent choice. Mr. A. C. Forrester now arose and gave notice that under present circumstances he would be unable to serve the Society as Semi-Annual Orator, and therefore declined his declination was accepted. Mr. R. L. Deas then moved that at the next meeting another election be had for Semi-Annual Orator, which was seconded and carried. Upon motion of Mr. S. W. Beaird the Utopian Society was unanimously invited to attend our approaching Anniversary. Mr. E. G. Beaird Chairman of the Committee on General Interests reported to the President the appointment of his committee which was received. All business of importance being now finished the Reporter made his report, the last roll was called, and the Society on motion adjourned. H. Cardozo Jr., Secretary

Clionian. D. Society, December 29th 1851

An "extra meeting" of this Society was held on the evening of the above date. The President being absent, the Vice President filled his seat, and Mr. E. G. Beaird, that of the Vice. The meeting was then called to order, the first roll called, and the proceedings of the last meeting read and approved. The President now arose, and stated that the meeting was called for the purpose of finishing the postponed debates, and therefore the floor remained opened for the members at large. The chance was embraced, and in a short time the heat of the former debates were rekindled and fresh fuel being ^now^ added thereto, created a flame, which would have continued to spread, were it not that that powerful Engine—Time arrived and quenched its its [sic] glowing ardor after which, the President gave his decision in favor of the first portion of the question. Among the questions handed in by the "Committee" the following was chosen "Which is the most conducive to Man's Happiness Mechanical or Agricultural employments." Mr. S. W. Beaird was appointed on the first, and Mr. E. G. Beaird on the last portion of the question.

All business of importance being now finished, the Reporter made his report, the last roll was called, and the Society on motion adjourned. H. Cardozo Jr., Secretary

NOTES

1. *Satiated* was likely intended.
2. This is likely a revisiting of the query about the exile to St. Helena that the Clionians debated in March 1849, with "the allied nations of Europe" referring to those arrayed against Napoleon at the Battle of Waterloo. These forces encompassed the Duke of Wellington's allied army (British, Dutch, Belgian, and German) and the Prussian army commanded by Gebhard Leberecht von Blücher.

3. Multiple editions of the works of the Irish poet Thomas Moore (1779–1852) had been published by 1851. Frances Pinckney Bonneau, a teacher of Black children in the 1850s, was the daughter of the prominent schoolmaster Thomas S. Bonneau, who died in 1831. Frances would marry Richard S. Holloway, who joined the Clionian Debating Society in April 1853. See Amrita Chakrabarti Myers, *Forging Freedom: Black Women and the Pursuit of Liberty in Antebellum Charleston* (Chapel Hill: University of North Carolina Press, 2011), 101–2.

4. A variety of republican uprisings swept Europe in 1848, although revolutionary governments were short-lived, and social and economic issues remained unresolved.

5. *Proximo,* abbreviated *prox.:* "occurring in the following month." That is, the oration was scheduled for April 7. It would be delayed until April 14.

6. *Chance* was likely intended.

7. The Great Exhibition of the Works of Industry of All Nations was held in London's Crystal Palace from May to October 1851.

8. Local white attorney William Dennison Porter (1810–1883), the son of a grocer and an alumnus of the College of Charleston, delivered an address to his fellow alumni in February 1851, which was published as a pamphlet entitled *Self-Cultivation.* See Edmund L. Drago, *Charleston's Avery Center: From Education and Civil Rights to Preserving the African American Experience,* rev. ed., rev. and ed. W. Marvin Dulaney (Charleston, SC: History Press, 2006), 38.

9. James Warley Miles (1818–1875), a white Episcopal minister, missionary, and educator, was a professor of Greek and history at the College of Charleston between 1851 and 1854. A number of his sermons and addresses were published as pamphlets. See William Henry Longton, "Miles, James Warley," in *American National Biography,* ed. John A. Garraty and Mark C. Carnes, vol. 15 (Oxford: Oxford University Press, 1999), 443–44.

10. The Mexican army officer and statesman Antonio López de Santa Anna (1794–1876), victor at the Alamo, was a powerful, controversial leader in the Texas Revolution and the Mexican–American War.

11. Richard Swainson Fisher's two-volume *Book of the World* was published in New York in 1849, with a second edition in 1850–1851.

— 1852 —

[In this year society secretaries minuted nineteen meetings; nine included debates, two included orations.—Ed.]

4th Anniversary Celebration of Clionian. D. Society., January 1st 1852

This day, so fraught with interest to every Clionian and which, serving as a standpoint in the history of the Society, from which they may retrospect the past with pleasing emotions, and feel inspired with bright hopes in looking to the future—was welcomed by them. In the afternoon the Society assembled in her strength in the meeting room; from whence accompanied by the Utopian Society, they marched to the Hall above; where (notwithstanding the inclemency of the weather) a very respectable audience greeted them. After seating themselves; the exercises were commenced with prayer by Honorary Member Jacob Weston. the Annual Oration was then delivered by S. W. Beaird who, in a most logical and convincing manner showed "The Influence of <u>Principle</u> and <u>Action</u> on the future destiny of Man," giving force and beauty to the subject by the most vivid illustrations from Sacred and Profane History and ended in discoursing on the indestructibility of the Mind, in a manner truly sublime, and thus after enchaining the attention of the audience for a considerable length of time, he sat down amidst the greatest applause. the exercises were then closed with the benediction, and the delighted audience dismissed for their homes, leaving the Society doubly encouraged to persevere in their efforts for "Mental Improvement."
H. Cardozo Jr., Secretary

Clionian. D. Society, January 26th 1852

On the evening of the above date, a regular meeting of this society was held. The President and Vice being absent Mr. W. H. Gaillard was appointed President Pro-Tem and Mr. Sanders Vice. The meeting was then called to order, the first roll called, and the proceedings of the last <u>extra</u> and <u>Anniversary</u> meetings

were read and approved. The regular debates now commenced and received a warm support from the respective debatants on both sides of the question, who consumed every moment of time in giving light on the subject, but were stopped in their progress for the want of time, after closing, the President arose and announced his decision in favor of the last portion of the question. From among the questions handed in by the "Committee" the following was chosen "Would the United States be Justifiable in interfering with the present struggles of Europe." Mr. H. Cardozo Jr. was appointed on the affirmative, and Mr. H. J. D. Cardozo, on the negative of the question. Mr. E. G. Beaird now presented a letter to the Society, which upon being read by the Secretary was found to contain an application for membership in the Society from Mr. J. B. Grimball Jr. the Secretary then notified the members that according to Constitution the next meeting would be the time for action on the same providing there be two-thirds present. All business of importance being now attended to, the reporter made his report the last roll was called, and the Society on motion adjourned.
H. Cardozo Jr., Secretary

Clionian. D. Society., February 23rd 1852

This Society assembled for its regular Semi-Monthly meeting on the evening of the above date, the President and Vice President being absent, Mr. Hampton was chosen President "Pro tem," and Mr. Gaillard Vice. The meeting was then called to order, the first roll was called, and the proceedings of the last regular meeting were read and confirmed. Mr. H. Cardozo Jr. now arose, and moved that a copy of the last Annual Oration be requested of the worthy Orator, which ^request^ being made by the President, was willingly complied with. He also moved that the Society go immediately into an election for Annual Orator for 1853. the motion being carried, the Ballot Box was then opened, the votes deposited, and counted, and Mr. W. O. Weston declared elected. The President now received a letter from Mr. W. H. Gaillard which he handed to the Secretary, and upon perusal was found to contain an application for membership from Mr. C. D. Ludeke. the Secretary then notified the Society that action would be had thereon, as soon as the Constitutional two thirds could be obtained. Mr. S. W. Beaird now arose, and stated that as a recommender he was requested by Mr. Grimball to withdraw his letter of application which request was put to the house, and granted. The regular debates now commenced, and received that warm support which the subjects discussed generally receives, every moment of time allowable, was employed by the debatants in building arguments upon arguments which increased in force and power, but its onward course was now checked by the expiration of the time. The President then announced his decision in favor of the last portion of the question. The "Committee" then handed in their questions from among which the following was chosen "Are we to infer from the teachings of History that the <u>Sword</u> has been more <u>destructive,</u> than <u>beneficial</u> to the happiness of Mankind?" Mr. J. M. F. Dereef was appointed on the first, and Mr. R. L. Deas on the last portion of the question. The secretary now gave notice that the next meeting would be the time for the general election of officers for the 14th term. Mr. S. W. Beaird now gave notice that as soon [as] two thirds were present he would offer two augmentations to the Constitution. All business of importance being now finished, the reporter made his report, the last roll was called, and the Society on motion adjourned. H. Cardozo Jr., Secty.

Clionian. D. Society., March 8th 1852

Another fortnight having elapsed, this Society convened for a regular meeting. The seats of the President and Vice President being vacant, Messrs. E. G. Beaird and R. Sanders respectively filled them, the meeting was then called to order, the first roll called, and the minutes of the last regular meeting read and approved. Mr. S. W. Beaird now arose, and moved that as the Society had assembled too late to allow the regular debates to take place, that they be postponed, and the Society go into an election of officers for the 14th term—The motion was seconded, and carried. The "Committee on general Interests" now brought forward the Ballot Box the votes were deposited, and counted, and the following gentlemen declared elected (See officers list). All important matters being now attended to, the Reporter made his report, the last roll was called, and the Society on motion adjourned.
H. Cardozo Jr., Secretary

Clionian. D. Society., March 22nd 1852

With characteristic punctuality the members of this Society assembled for a regular meeting, in the absence of the President, and Vice President, Messrs. E. G. Beaird & S. J. Maxwell filled their seats. The meeting was then called to order, the first roll called, and the proceedings of the last meeting read and confirmed. The regular inauguration now commenced, with the installing of the President elect who upon taking the chair, returned his thanks to the society for having chosen him to fill the highest office in the gift of the Society, and in a few appropriate remarks congratulated the Society on its present advantages for Mental Improvement, which are solely attained by their unyeilding [*sic*] perseverance under the most despairing circumstances which surrounded them in the past. he then signified his acceptance, and ^afterwards^ proceeded to install the subordinate officers, every one of whom seemed willing to bear a part of the burden, and therefore accepted the respective trust committed to them, with a promise to serve to the best of their abilities. and thus ended the interesting ceremony of Installation. It now became the duty of the duty of [*sic*] the President to appoint a Chairman on the "committee on general Interests." Mr. H. Cardozo Jr. was chosen for that office, who signified his acceptance. The President—(According to Constitution) then appointed a Committee to examine the Books of the Secretary and Treasurer which consisted of Messrs. S. W. Beaird, W. H. Gaillard, and E. G. Beaird. Mr. S. W. Beaird now arose, and moved ^that^ the elections for Semi-Annual Orator be continued until the whole list ^of members^ passed through, the motion upon being amended by H. Cardozo Jr. that the election take place at the next meeting which being the first in April would be the regular time, was seconded and carried. Mr. W. H. Gaillard now notified the Society that at the next meeting he would offer Dr. Thomas Dick as a candidate for Honorary Membership in the Society. All business of importance being now finished, the Reporter made his report, the last roll was called, and the Society on motion adjourned.

H. Cardozo Jr., Secretary

Clionian. D. Society, April 12th 1852

True to purpose, the members of this Society assembled for a regular meeting on the ~~above~~ evening of the above date, after being called to order, the first roll was called, and the proceedings of the last meeting read and approved. The regular debates then commenced, which did not fail to prove interesting from the amount of light given on the subject, and would have continued to increase in weight, and interest, were it not for the limited time given, it therefore closed, and upon a motion to postpone it being lost—The President decided in favor of the first portion of the question. The "Committee["] then handed in their questions, from among which the following was chosen—"Emigration; does it tend, or has it ever tended to the advancement of civilization?" Mr. Forrester was appointed on the former, and Mr. W. H. Gaillard on the latter portion of the question. The Committee appointed to examine the Books of the Secretary and Treasurer made a favorable report thereon, which was unanimously received by the Society. The Chairman on the committee on General Interests, made a report of those whom he had chosen to serve with him on that Committee, which was received by the Society. The President now handed over to the Secretary for perusal, two letters which he had received from Mr. I. A. Hyams, and upon opening were found to contain applications for Membership from Messrs. Marion L. Stent & J. F. Lindsay which the President notified the society would be acted on as soon as the Constitutional two thirds could be obtained. The election for Semi-Annual Orator now took place, and resulted in the unanimous choice of Mr. H. J. D. Cardozo. All things else that required attention being attended to, the reporter made his report, the last roll was called, and the Society on motion adjourned.

H. Cardozo Jr., Secretary

Clionian. D. Society, April 26th 1852

Another fortnight having elapsed, the members of this Society were ~~still~~ found assembled for a regular meeting. It ~~being~~ was called to order by the President, the first roll called, and the proceedings of the last meeting read and approved. The regular debates then commenced and with characteristic force was the subject treated, light being given on both sides, by convincing arguments, and truthful references, which rendered the subject interesting even to its close after which, the President with praiseworthy carefulness summed up the arguments, and announced his decision in favor of the latter portion of the question. The "Committee" then handed in their questions from among which, the following was chosen—"Which were the best disciplinarians of Youths—the Athenians, or Spartans." Mr. Hyams was appointed on the former, and Mr. Horry on the latter portion of the question. All business of importance being now attended to, the Reporter made his report, the last roll was called, and the Society on motion adjourned.

H. Cardozo Jr., Secretary

Clionian. D. Society, June 14th 1852

On the evening of the above date the members of this Society assembled for a regular meeting. It was called to order by the President, the vice President being absent Mr. Forrester filled his seat, the first roll was then called, and the proceedings of the last meeting read and approved. The regular debates now had a hearing, and were attended with the usual share of interest that historical questions generally afford, many arguments being adduced from the "records of the past" which served to illustrate the question on both sides, but as all things, must have an end these agreeable exercises shared the general fate. The President then arose, and announced his decision in favor of the former portion of the question. The "Committee" now handed in their questions from among which the following was chosen—"Who was the Greatest and most virtuous General, Caesar or Pompey?"[1] Mr. Hampton was appointed on the former and Mr. Maxwell on the latter portion of the question.

Mr. S. W. Beaird now proposed to the Society the adoption of resolutions in honour of the death of our late Honorary Members—Benjamin Huger, and

90   *Free Black Charlestonians in Debate*

John Mishaw,[2] the President considering it too late to act on the resolutions arose to defer them to the next meeting, a discussion having then arisen as to the constitutionality of his doing so, the matter was then taken up by the body, and a motion made from among them to defer them—which the President hesitated to put to the house, the time of adjournment having now passed, the subject received no further consideration. The Reporter then made his report, the last roll was called, and the Society on motion adjourned.

H. Cardozo Jr., Sec.

"Clionian, D. Society," June 28th/52

The members of this Society gave a full attendance at their regular meeting held on the evening of the above date. It was called to order by the President, the first roll called, and the proceedings of the last meeting read and approved. Now "in order" came the time for the hearing of the regular debates, which was commenced, and continued to rise in vigor and interest, each side receiving considerable support, till from all appearances the characters ~~supported~~ defended ~~on each side,~~ had the superiority over each other, but the case was soon decided by the announcement of the President that the character who constituted the latter portion of the question was superior. The "Committee" now handed in their questions from among which the following was chosen—"Did Wellington in the battle of Waterloo prove himself a greater General than Napoleon Bonaparte?"[3] Mr. Marshall was appointed on the former, and Mr. Sanders on the latter portion of the question. The Secretary notified the body that the next regular meeting would be the time for the general election of officers for the 15th term. He also ~~begged~~ informed them of his unwillingness to be any ^longer^ a candidate for the Secretary and Treasurerships, there being others who should share the honor of serving ^such^ an Institution ~~like this~~. All matters of import being now attended to, the reporter made his report, the last roll was called, and the Society on motion adjourned.

H. Cardozo Jr., Sec.

Clionian Society, July 1st 1852

An "Extra" meeting of this Society was held on the evening of the above date, The President called it to order, the first roll being then called. He announced to the body the intention of the meeting, which was to act on the letters of application which were before the body. The Committee on General Interests accordingly retired to consult upon the character of the respective applicants, which were reported on favorably. The Ballot Box was then opened, and Mr. C. D. Ludeke balloted for, who, upon the report of the "Committee" was declared elected. Next in order was Mr. M. L. Stent who was balloted for, but upon report of the "Committee" ~~was~~ declared <u>rejected</u>. Mr. J. F. Lindsay was then ballotted for, and was also declared <u>rejected</u>.[4] All matters of importance being now attended to, the last roll was then called and the Society on motion adjourned. H. Cardozo Jr., Sec.

"Clionian. D. Society," July 29th 1852

Another "Extra" meeting of this Society was held on the evening of the above date. The President having stated the object of the meeting, the first roll was called, and the proceedings, of the two last meetings (regular and extra) were read and approved. The General election of officers for the 15th Term now engrossed the attention of the meeting, the Ballot Box was accordingly brought forward by the "Committee on General Interests" the votes deposited, and counted and the following Gentlemen declared elected (See Officers list). The President then gave notice that the next meeting would be the time for the Installation of Officers. Mr. S. W. Beaird expecting to be absent from the city, at the time of the Installation meeting, now made known his acceptance of the offices to which he was elected.

The business of the meeting being now attended to, the Reporter made his report, the last roll was called, and the Society on motion adjourned. H. Cardozo Jr., Secretary

"Clionian. D. Society.," September 13th 1852

The members of this Society having been prevented from holding their regular meetings, during the past month—on, account of sickness, absence from the city, and other causes, now assembled for a regular meeting. The President, and Vice-President being absent—Mr. R. L. Deas, was chosen President "Pro-tem" Mr. A. C. Forrester, Vice President. The meeting was then called to order, the first roll called, and the proceedings of the last <u>Extra</u> meeting read and approved.

The ceremony of Installation now commenced with ^the^ President <u>elect</u>— who in accepting the "Chair" seemed aware of the important position he was now about to occupy, and in addressing his fellow members—recurred in feeling language, to the history of ~~our~~ ^their^ past existence as a society, and then urged a quickened exertion, and lofty aim, in ~~our~~ ^their^ present and future movements, having finished, he then proceeded to install the subordinate officers such as were present, all of whom accepted the respective trusts committed to them, and vowed to evince their regard for their society's welfare by a strict performance of the duties incumbent on them, and thus ended the Installation. The President then appointed Mr. Hampton Chairman of the "committee on general interests," and Messrs. E. G. Beaird, A. C. Forrester & R. L. Deas a committee to examine the Books of the Secretary and Treasurer. All business being now attended to, the Reporter made his report, the last roll was called, and the Society on motion adjourned.

H. Cardozo Jr., Secretary

"Clionian. D. Society," October 11th 1852

This association, had its devotees, (In the person of members) out, on the evening of the above date, in large numbers, for the hearing of ^the^ regular Semi-Annual Oration, the Hall was—as usual on such occasions—graced with the presence of several Honorary Members. The meeting was called to order by the President, the first roll, called, and the proceedings, of the last meeting read, and approved. The President then introduced to the audience Mr. H. J. D. Cardozo as the Orator, on the occasion—who modestly opened his subject, and discoursed largely and eloquently on the "Paramount Importance of <u>Timely Mental Culture</u>" frequently illumining his theme with illustrations drawn from the treasures of Ancient Literature nor did he fail to enter the Biographical Department by adducing—as incentives to exertion—some, of the greatest characters; whose every step on the "Ladder of Fame," was constructed of the material of Early Intellectual exertion; and in such a strain ~~did~~ he continue^d^ (for a lengthy period,) to enchain the attention of the audience; while his fluency in the Ancient Classic, as well as the modern Tongue; rendered him peculiarly and pleasingly interesting; but the happy Orator had to check his expansive mind as time would not allow; accordingly he sat down amid the applauses of the whole audience. Mr. R. L. Deas now arose, and moved that a copy of the address be requested of the speaker, which being seconded, and unanimously carried, was carried into effect by the President, who received from the Orator an answer in the affirmative. The time being now far spent, it was moved that all other business be suspended until the next meeting, which was carried. The last roll was then called. The Reporter made his report, and the Society on motion adjourned.

H. Cardozo Jr., Secretary

Clionian. D. Society, October 25th 1852

The evening of the above date assembled the members of this Society for a regular meeting. The President in the chair, and the Vice President's seat filled by Mr. Dereef, the meeting was called to order, the first roll called, and the proceedings of the last meeting read and approved. The President now took occasion to Install a few of the officers elect who were absent at the Installation meeting. Mr. Ludeke, the member elect being now present The Constitution was read for his benefit, upon his approval of which, he came forward, signed his name, paid the "Initial Fee," and thereby became a regular and respected member of the Clionian Fraternity.

The regular debates, now commenced, and as usual was carried on with considerable warmth and vigor, to the close, upon which, the President gave his decision in favor of the former portion of the question. A letter was now handed to the Society by Mr. W. H. Gaillard from Mr. W. S. Lord, which, upon opening, was found to contain an application for membership, from that Gentleman, notice was then given that it would be acted on at the next meeting should the Constitutional Two thirds be present. Mr. S. W. Beaird now handed to the President a letter received by him for the Society, the reading of which was postponed to the next meeting on account of the lateness of the hour. The election of Semi-Annual [orator] then took place which resulted in the choice of Mr. W. E. Marshall. The Committee of Queries now handed in their questions from among which, the following was chosen "Which is more likely to injure the prosperity of a Country, Foreign Broils or Intestine Commotions." Mr. W. O. Weston was appointed on the former, and Mr. S. W. Beaird, on the latter portion of the question. The Secretary notified the Society ^that^ the next meeting would be the time for the general election of officers for the 16th term. All matters being now attended to, the Reporter made his report, the last roll was called, and the Society on motion adjourned.

H. Cardozo Jr., Secretary

Clionian, D. Society, November 8th/52

With steadiness of purpose the members of this Society assembled on the evening of the above date for a regular meeting. The President in the Chair, Mr. Sanders, filling that of the Vice President—The meeting was called to order, the first roll called, and the proceedings of the last meeting read and approved.

The regular debates, now had a hearing, which continued with increasing ardor, even beyond the time allotted, having then closed the President gave his decision in favor of the latter portion of the question. The general election of officers for the 16th term now took place, which resulted in the choice of the following gentlemen (See officers list). There being a tie in the votes for President, Vice President, and Librarian, The President gave his casting vote in favor of Mr. W. H. Gaillard for the first, Mr. S. W. Beaird for the second, and Mr. W. O. Weston for the third office. All business being now attended to that time would allow for, The Reporter made his report, the last roll was called, and the Society on motion adjourned.

H. Cardozo Jr., Secretary

Clionian. D. Society, November 29th/52

An <u>Extra</u> meeting of this Society was held on the evening of the above date. It was called to order by [the] President, Mr. Forrester filled the seat of the Vice President, Mr. E. G. Beaird that of the Reporter. The first ^roll^ was ^then^ called and the proceedings of the last regular meeting were read and approved. The regular Installation of Officers now commenced with the President elect, who, after a few encouraging and enlivening remarks, again accepted the high and important trust recommitted to him. He then proceeded to install the other officers, nearly all of whom being present, accepted the respective offices chosen for them, and declared their intention to fulfil their duties to the best of their abilities. The President then appointed Mr. E. G. Beaird Chairman of the "Committee on general Interests," and Messrs. S. W. Beaird, S. J. Maxwell, and E. G. Beaird the Committee to examine the Books of the Secretary & Treasurer. The Committee of Queries now handed in their questions from among which the following was chosen—"Would the increase of Territory prove an advantage to the United States?"[5] Mr. E. G. Beaird was appointed on the affirmative, and Mr. G. B. [G. F.] Barrow on the negative of the question. All business (for which there was time) being now attended to, the Reporter made his report, the last roll was called, and the Society on motion adjourned.

H. Cardozo Jr., Secretary

Clionian. D. Society., December 13th 1852

The members of this Institution assembled on the evening of the above date, for a regular meeting, which being called to order, the first roll was called, and the proceedings of the last meeting read and approved. The regular debates then commenced—and were supported for a length of time with considerable strength of argument, and warmth of spirit. After their conclusion, the President gave his decision in favor of the negative portion of the question. The "Committee" then handed in their questions, from among which the following was chosen—"Was Charlemagne a great man."[6] Mr. H. Cardozo Jr. was appointed on the affirmative, and Mr. H. J. D. Cardozo on the negative of the question. The President then notified the Body that as the Constitutional Two thirds were present, the letter of application before them from Mr. W. S. Lord, would now be acted on. The Chairman of the "Committee on general Interests" accordingly brought forward the Ballot Box, the votes were deposited, and counted, and the Gentleman declared unanimously elected. The President now took occasion to Install such Officers elect, as were absent at the regular Installation meeting, who accepted the respective trusts committed to them. A letter was then received from Mr. W. O. Weston (who expected to be unavoidably absent from the meeting) Assuring the Society of his regret to inform them "that circumstances have rendered it such, that he will not be able to take that prominent position in the exercises of their expected Anniversary, which they elected him to fill. That nothing but a sad affliction, and, a sense of propriety connected with it, could have established such a conclusion; as the production had already been written; and required but little application for readiness at the call. He therefore left it to the judgement of the Society to postpone it or act as they think correct."[7] Upon this a discussion arose, which, extending over the adjourning hour, was checked by a motion from Mr. R. L. Deas that an adjourned meeting be held on next Thursday evening for further deliberation, which was seconded, and carried. Mr. S. W. Beaird now took occasion to offer two amendments to the Constitution, which reads thus: 1st "All motions for the adjournment of any meeting, after being seconded, must be put to the house and carried by a majority." 2nd Every Officer, Orator, &c. elect, shall be expected to serve in that capacity—if he has not served in the same the preceding term, and for the refusal so to do, shall be fined in a sum not less than 50 cents, they were put to the house, and carried. The meeting according to Mr. Deas' motion was then dismissed.

Thursday Evening, December 16th [1852]

Consistent with agreement, the members of the Society assembled on the evening of the above date. The meeting was called to order by the President, the first roll called. Mr. H. Cardozo Jr. then arose, and moved, that the House be resolved into a "Committee of the whole" for the further consideration of the unfinished business of the last meeting, and that Mr. R. L. Deas fill the chair, the motion being seconded, and carried. Mr. Deas accordingly acted as Chairman, Mr. W. H. Gaillard then arose, and, after a few preliminary remarks in favor of the nonpostponement of the Anniversary—Offered a Preamble and Resolutions to the effect, that While we deeply sympathise with our fellow member in his sad affliction, and are willing to pay to pay [sic] all due deference to the respected deceased. Yet being anxious to celebrate the Anniversary at the usual time would earnestly request him to lay aside his feelings and yeild to the wishes of the Society. the resolutions were seconded, and unanimously adopted.

The Secretary then notified the Body that a letter from their fellow member Augustus L. Horry had been received by the Penny Post, from "Philadelphia Pa," which being addressed to the "Clionian Debating Society"[8]—was now opened, and read, and found to contain the information that as he had ^left^

the State "probably for life" it behooved him <u>unwillingly</u> to resign his existing connection with the Society as a member, assuring them of his love for the Institution, quickened by the recollection of past benefits, and the Interesting associations connected therewith; ~~and~~ that his warmest wishes are for its welfare; and that he would as a token of regard; forward at as early a day as possible; a "Gilt Frame Mythological Picture." The letter was favorably received, and according to a motion of Mr. W. H. Gaillard, which was seconded, and carried—a committee of nine were appointed to correspond with Mr. Horry, composed of the following gentlemen—W. H. Gaillard, Chairman, S. W. Beaird, H. Cardozo Jr., W. O. Weston, E. G. Beaird, S. J. Maxwell, C. D. Ludeke, R. L. Deas, and R. Sanders, Committee. Mr. E. G. Beaird then moved that the answer to Mr. Horry be prepared by the next meeting, which was seconded, and carried. All business being now attended to, the Reporter made his report, the last roll was called, and the Society on motion adjourned.

H. Cardozo Jr., Secretary

Clionian. D. Society., December 30th 1852

An <u>extra</u> meeting of this society was held on the evening of the above date, which being called to order, the first roll was called, and upon the reading of the proceedings of the last <u>regular</u> and <u>adjourned</u> meetings, Mr. W. O. Weston expressed his disapproval of that portion of them that contained an account of the resolutions then adopted, and sent to him, which—(although found to be a true statement) were, upon motion altered to his wishes.* Mr. Weston then informed the Society that upon further deliberation he concluded to yeild to their anxious wishes to serve them on the regular annual day, which information was gladly received. Mr. W. S. Lord, the member elect being now present, the Constitution was read to his hearing, upon his approval of which, he came forward, signed his name, paid the "Initial fee," and thereby became a regular and respected member of the Clionian. Debating. Society. Mr. W. H. Gaillard, Chairman of the Committee appointed to correspond with Mr. Horry, now brought forward his answer to that Gentleman's letter, which, upon reading was favorably received. Mr. S. W. Beaird then arose, and proposed Mr. Horry as a candidate for Honorary Membership, he was accordingly balloted for, and declared unanimously elected. The information of his election were—upon motion—to be given him in the answer about to be sent ~~him~~. A motion was made by Mr. W. O. Weston that the "Utopian Society" be invited to attend the celebration of our fifth anniversary, which was seconded, and unanimously carried. Mr. S. W. Beaird now moved that as the first of January would fall on Saturday—a very inconvenient day—that the celebration be postponed to Monday the third of the month, the motion was seconded, and unanimously carried. All business of importance being now finished, the Reporter made his report the last roll was called, and the Society upon motion adjourned.

H. Cardozo Jr., Secretary

*The proceedings were then put to the house, and approved of.

NOTES

1. Pompey the Great (106–48 BCE), Roman general and statesman, was an ally and then a rival of Julius Caesar.
2. Benjamin T. Huger (ca. 1796–1852), a free Black tailor and enslaver, died of typhus in Charleston on May 5, 1852, and was interred in the cemetery of the Brown Fellowship Society; he was also a member of the Friendly Union Society. See "South Carolina, U.S., Death Records, 1821–1971," Ancestry.com (online database), 2008, https://www.ancestry.com/search/collections/8741/; Larry Koger, *Black Slaveowners: Free Black Slave Masters in South Carolina, 1790–1860* (Jefferson, NC: McFarland, 1985), 99, 147, 149; and *Constitution and By-Laws of the Friendly Union Society of Charleston, S.C., Organized May 4th 1813* (Charleston, SC: Karrs and Welch, 1889), 22.

   John Mishaw (ca. 1797–1852), a free Black shoemaker and enslaver, had been one of the eight founders of the Friendly Union Society in 1813, along with William W. Seymour, later an honorary Clionian. Daniel A. Payne long remembered Mishaw's kindness to him prior to his departure from Charleston in 1835. See *Constitution and By-Laws of the Friendly Union Society*, 22; Koger, *Black Slaveowners*, 149; Daniel Alexander Payne, *Recollections of Seventy Years* (Nashville, TN: A.M.E. Sunday School Union, 1888), 39–40.
3. The Irish-born British soldier and statesman Arthur Wellesley, first Duke of Wellington (1769–1852), commanded the allied army that, along with Prussian forces, defeated Napoleon's French army at Waterloo in 1815.
4. The rationale for the rejection of Stent and Lindsay is unknown. Both men were active members in the Friendly Association at least from 1853; Lindsay resigned in July 1856, as he planned to leave the state, and Stent resigned in September 1860. On December 15, 1856, Stent was fined by the Friendlies for "Smoking a Segar while the Society was in cession," contrary to the association's rules and in defiance of the president's calling him to order three times. See Friendly Association Records, 1853–1869, South Carolina Historical Society, Charleston, SC.
5. US territory had expanded significantly across the North American continent during the 1840s, owing to the annexation of Texas (1845), the acquisition of the Oregon Country (1846), and the Mexican Cession (1848). In 1853 the United States would acquire another portion of northern Mexican territory, now southern Arizona and New Mexico, via the Gadsden Purchase.
6. Charlemagne (ca. 747–814) was king of the Franks, king of the Lombards, and emperor of the Romans, ruling what was later called the Holy Roman Empire.
7. William O. Weston was mourning the death of his mother, Hannah Clark Weston. She died in childbirth on November 24, 1852, at age forty-two, and was interred in the cemetery of the Brown Fellowship Society; "South Carolina, U.S., Death

Records, 1821–1971," Ancestry.com (online database), 2008, https://www.ancestry
.com/search/collections/8741/.

8. Horry's letter traveled by up-to-date methods, with costs paid by the sender rather than the recipient. The US Congress's postal reform acts of 1845 and 1851 had made letter-writing more affordable; see David M. Henkin, *The Postal Age: The Emergence of Modern Communications in Nineteenth-Century America* (Chicago: University of Chicago Press, 2006), 22.

— 1853 —

[In this year society secretaries minuted twenty-three meetings; thirteen included debates, three included orations.—Ed.]

"5th Anniversary Celebration" of Clionian. D. Society, January 10th 1853

The above ^event^ now took place, after a second postponement (on account of the inclemency of the weather). But "Nature," as if to encourage, bestowed upon us her "Sunny" smiles, and a bright day greeted our eyes. The Members assembled in their strength in the afternoon, in their "Meeting room," whence they marched to the Hall above, where one of the largest audiences awaited them. After being seated, the Exercises were commenced with prayer by Honorary Member Jacob Weston. The President then introduced to the audience W. O. Weston Esq., the speaker on the occasion[1]—Who, after a few preliminary remarks, gracefully and effectively—addressed his hearers on the all-important subject of—"Influence," adducing for his basis the scriptural affirmation that "No man liveth to himself,"[2] he thereupon enlarged with much force of argument, tracing the operations of that Principle from the Creation of the World—The Fall of Man by the Influence of Woman—then gliding along the course of time, and plucking from the paths of "Science and Literature,["] "Church and State" those flowers of illustration which the Lives of the <u>Great</u> and <u>Good</u>, the <u>Wicked</u> and <u>Base</u>—afford, who, though long passed away, have left their Influences behind them whether in recorded thoughts, or acts; to bless, or curse posterity. He then entered the precincts of the Domestic circle, and touchingly alluded to the all-pervading Influence of Parents over offspring, whose Examples, whether Good or Evil, must be read in the future destinies of their children. And of Woman in general—while reminding ^them^ of their responsibilities—he acceded the <u>palm</u> of their acknowledged Influence. And in such a strain did the happy Orator rivet the attention of the audience for a reasonable length of time, he then (after an affecting and inspiring address to his fellow members) concluded, amidst great and prolonged applause. The fair

assemblage was then dismissed with the "Benediction" and after a visit to the Society's "meeting room" below, they dispersed for their homes, well pleased with the Intellectual, and Moral entertainment just enjoyed, but not without imparting their joyousness of feelings to the "Clionians" who, seemed inspired with fresh zeal and courage, in their aspirations after Intellectual culture.
H. Cardozo Jr., Secretary

Clionian. D. Society., January 12th/53

A "deferred" meeting of this Society was held on the evening of the above date, for regular business, after being called to order, the first roll was called, and the proceedings of the last <u>Extra</u> and <u>Anniversary</u> meetings were read and approved. The regular debates now had a hearing, and were vigorously supported, on either side, with well founded arguments, warmly laid down, which told out <u>for</u> and <u>against</u> the character discussed. after their conclusion, the President arose, and gave his decision, in favor of the negative side of the question. The "Committee" then handed in their questions from among which the following was chosen—"Are the late improvements of decided advantage to Mankind." Mr. J. M. F. Dereef was appointed on the affirmative, and Mr. R. L. Deas on the negative of the question. Mr. H. Cardozo Jr. now arose and moved that a copy of the instructive and impressive address delivered on the Annual day by W. O. Weston, Esq., be requested of him, which was seconded and unanimously carried. According to Constitution, the election of Annual Orator for 1854 now took place.—The Ballot box was brought forward, the votes deposited, and counted, and Mr. H. Cardozo Jr. declared duly elected upon which that gentleman arose, and after expressing his thanks to the society for their appreciation of his feeble attainments, consented to serve them—more from considerations of duty than a knowledge of personal abilities, which was favorably received. All matters being now attended to, the Reporter made his report, the last roll was called, and the Society on motion adjourned.
H. Cardozo Jr., Secretary

Clionian. D. Society, February 14th/53

On the evening of this date the members of the Society, assembled for a regular meeting which was called to order by the President. Mr. Hampton filling the chair of the Vice President, and Mr. Ludeke, that of the Reporter. The first roll was called, and the proceedings of the last "deferred" meeting read and approved. Mr. H. Cardozo Jr. now arose and moved, that on account of the lateness of the hour the regular debates be postponed to the next meeting, which was seconded, and carried. The President then handed to the Secretary a letter directed to the Clionian. Debating Society, which upon reading was found to contain an application for membership from—Mr. Richard. S. Holloway, which the Secretary gave notice, would be acted on as soon as two thirds could be obtained. Mr. H. Cardozo Jr. now arose and moved that as several members who fill important offices in the Society—now have unavoidable engagements on Monday evenings—that that portion of the Constitution which requires us to meet on the 2nd and 4th <u>Monday</u> evenings of every month; be suspended for a while; and that we meet on the 2nd and 4th <u>Wednesday</u> evenings; the motion was seconded and <u>unanimously</u> carried. The Reporter then made his report, the last roll was called, and the Society on motion adjourned.

H. Cardozo Jr., Secretary

Clionian. D. Society, February 23rd/53

In accordance with convictions of duty—the members assembled on the evening of the above date. The President called the meeting to order with Mr. Hyams in the chair of the Vice President, and Mr. E. G. Beaird filling that of the Reporter. The first roll was then called, and the proceedings of the last regular meeting were read and approved. Next in order came the hearing of the debates, which were commenced and carried on with increasing animation, argument after argument were added with fresh ardor on both sides until the ^subject^ seemed exhausted, the debates then closed, and the President gave his decision in favor of the affirmative of the question. The "Committee" then handed in their questions from among which the following was chosen—"Does the distance of a Country's dominions weaken the force of its Laws therein?" Mr. Forrester was appointed on the affirmative, and Mr. Hyams on the negative of the question. The Secretary then notified the Society that the next meeting would be the regular time for the general election of officers for the 17th term. All matters being now attended to the Reporter made his report, the last roll was called, and the Society on motion adjourned.

H. Cardozo Jr., Secretary

Clionian. D. Society., March 9th 1853

The lapse of two weeks again brought together the members of this Society for a regular meeting, which after being called to order, the first roll was called, and the proceedings of the last meeting, read and approved. Then in course came the most interesting and profiting part—The regular debates—which were opened, and sustained with the best founded arguments; whose depth and weight gave new light on the subject; and increasing interest ^were^ added thereto from the many illustrations adduced from the past and the present in

102   *Free Black Charlestonians in Debate*

their support; In this strain did they continue—until inexorable "Time" decreed their close; when the President arose, and gave his decision in favor of the affirmative portion of the question. According to Constitution, the General election of Officers for the 17th term now took place. The Ballot Box was accordingly brought forward; the votes deposited and counted; and the following gentlemen declared duly elected (see Officers list). No questions were handed in by the "Committee" the next meeting being Installation meeting. All business being now attended to the Reporter made his report, the last roll was called, and the Society on motion adjourned.

H. Cardozo Jr., Secretary

Clionian. D Society., March 23d/53.

The members of this body assembled in large numbers to witness that impressive ceremony, the installation of the officers elected for the succeeding term. The retiring President arose, and while delineating the importance of the trust conferred upon his successor, and his best wishes that his career might be marked with unmitigated prosperity; in an elegance of style depicted the duty of every one to avail himself of the opportunity of improving his mind, and of adding incessantly to his store-house of Knowledge. The President elect after thanking the Society for their repeated manifestations of favour in electing him to such important positions, proceeded to solicit their each and every exertion in the grand scheme, not only of intellectual progression, but in a continual discharge of duties, and a regular attendance at every meeting when possible. He then showed the importance of & Reading, & the peculiar adaptness of the debating Society in impressing such ideas upon the mind not only of the individual, but of his hearers. After continuing for some time in such a delightful strain, he proceeded amid rapturous applause to the installation of the subordinate officers, who after receiving a full statement of their respective duties, accompanied with the solemn injunction that Clio "expects every man to do his duty,"[3] acknowledged their thanks to their fellow members, and promised in glowing terms that their allegiance to the "ship of many storms" would be exhibited not only in words but by their <u>actions</u>. The President according to the Constitution appointed a Chairman of the committee on general interests: Mr. Robert Sanders the gentleman chosen, not being present, the Secretary was requested to inform him of the same. The President also selected a committee of three, consisting of Messrs. S. W. & E. G. Beaird & W. O. Weston, to examine the books of the Secretary for the past term, and report on the same to the Society at its next meeting.

    The Committee of Queries then presented their questions, from which was selected the following "Does the prosperity and progress of a nation depend more upon the observance of its laws by its subjects, or the strict execution of the same by those empowered." Mr. B. K. Hampton was appointed on the former, and Mr. C. Ludeke on the negative of the question. The Secretary was also requested to inform Mr. Wm. Marshall Orator elect, that the ~~first~~ Second Wednesday in April is the regular time for the hearing of the Semi-annual oration: and that in case of the said gentleman consenting to serve at said time, to inform the members that their[4] would be no debates; but if he is not prepared at that time that their would be a discussion on question chosen for that evening. At this stage of the meeting the President was requested to retire; whereupon the house formed itself on motion of Mr. W. Gailliard, into a committee of the whole, (Mr. B. K. Hampton in the chair) and offered the following resolutions "Resolved 1st that the thanks of the Society be unanimously tendered to Mr. H. J. Cardozo jr. for the able, consistent and dignified manner with which he has for a series of terms, discharged the duties of Secretary and Treasurer of the Clionian Society. Resolved 2dly That his elevation to the office of President, be but considered as a feeble token, of that high regard, which we entertain for his administrative abilities; and that in his retirement from the one, to the more dignified position of the other, he carries along with him our best wishes for his success and prosperity." The appointed committee, then returned from their mission, accompanied by the President, who being informed of the resolutions adopted unanimously by the Society, gave vent to a strain of thought and feeling which was responded to by enchanted Clio in such a burst of applause as made the "welkin ring."[5] No more business demanding the attention of the Society the roll was called, the reporter made his report, and the Society on motion adjourned.

W. O. Weston, Secretary

Clionian Society, April 14th 1853.

A regular meeting of this association was held at the usual time & place. The members as if eager to show their allegiance to Clio, assembled in large numbers, and manifested their increasing interest in it, by participating extensively in its operations. The Chairman of the Committee on general interests, being in attendance, the President after reading from the Constitution the prescribed duties of the same, in an impressive manner warned him of the responsibility about being incurred, & the necessity of a proper selection of his assistants. Having consented as such, to serve, he was then duly qualified. The regular debatants were then named for the evening ~~was then named~~ and upon the conclusion of the remarks of the member present, the house was opened for any to speak of the interesting theme of discussion; the time was most voraciou[s]ly seized upon, & only ceased in consequence of the "President's hat" announcing "that time was now no more."[6] The decision was then given by the President in favour of the affirmative of the question. The question chosen for the next meeting reads as follows "Is Louis Napoleon an usurper or not."[7] Mr. W. S. Lord on the affirmative and Mr. Stephen J. Maxwell on the negative. On motion of Mr. Gailliard and seconded by Mr. S. Beaird it was determined that the President be requested to give orders to the Secretary to summon the members for an extra meeting on tomorrow evening, (Thursday). Mr. S. Beaird also gave notice, that he would at any time that a sufficient number be present, offer a resolution for the changing of the time of meeting from the second and fourth Wednesdays of the month to every alternate Wednesday. He in addition to this, gave notice that under such circumstances he would move that the President be empowered to appoint a committee for the purpose of combining the multiplicity of articles of the Constitution, into a few essential and compact rules, that may be impressed distinctly upon the minds of all the members.

According to Constitution Mr. Sanders reported the following gentlemen, as selected for his assistants as regards his appointment as chairman committee on "general interests." No more business demanding the attention of the Society, the reporter made his report, the last roll was called & the Society was on motion adjourned.

W. O. Weston, Sec.

Erratum. The following are Mr. Sanders' assistants Messrs. R. L. Deas, I. Hyams, & W. S. Lord.

Clionian Society, April 15th 1853.

According to the orders of the President, the members of the Clionian Society assembled en-masse to an extra meeting, for the transaction of important business. The first roll being called ^&c.^, a letter of application was received through his recommenders from Mr. Richard Holloway jr. His character having been favourably reported upon, by the "Committee on general interests," the Society proceeded to ballot on said letter, & who on report of the committee on polls was declared duly elected: whereupon the Secretary was instructed to inform him of his election & request his presence at the next general meeting. Mr. Simeon W. Beaird according to previous notice, introduced the following Resolutions which being seconded, they were unanimously adopted "Resolved that after the passage of this resolution, that clause of the Constitution which requires the meetings of this Society ^to^ be held on the second and fourth Wednesdays of every month, be so altered as to require a meeting on every alternate week throughout the year."

"Whereas the greater portion of the membership of this Society, having discovered by experience, that our Constitution as it now stands is composed of many parts that may be condensed and many other clauses that may be struck off, and desiring to have a Constitution that will approximate a little more to perfection in the order of the arrangements of its several Articles, and that also will be less bulky and more comprehensible and retainable by the membership and which in the end will tend to the better observance of the same. Therefore be it resolved 'That the President be empowered to appoint a Committe[e] of Six members, whose duty it shall be to revise the Constitution of the Clionian Debating Society in accordance to the above Preamble, and report the result of their labours as early as they can make it convenient.'" On motion of Mr. W. O. Weston seconded by Mr. S. Beaird it was resolved unanimously that the Society do add the President as one to said Committee. The President stated to the meeting that the importance of the Committee would induce him to state his appointments, after more mature reflection. Mr. Gailliard gave notice that at the first meeting that the Constitutional number were present, he would offer as Honorary members Dr. Thomas Dick, & Messrs. Henry Frost & Wm. McKinney. The committe[e] on the books of the late Secretary & Treasurer reported that their examination had resulted in their accordance to the faithfulness of the same. No more business appearing to demand the attention of the Society, the reporter made his report, the last roll was called, and this Society of mutual & orderly intellectual aspirants, was on motion adjourned. S. W. Weston, Sec.

NB. The letter of Mr. Holloway was received at a previous meeting, & only acted on at the present time.

Clionian Society, April 27th/53.

A meeting of old Clio at the regular time was again held at the usual place. This being the regular period for the hearing of the semi-annual oration, Mr. W. E. Marshall orator elect arose and for a considerable space enchained the attention of the Society in a most masterly effort; commencing with the beauties of nature, he took a cursory glance at the fall of man, and concluded amid bursts of applause, with a truthful dissertation on the evil effects of intemperance. Mr. W. O. Weston seconded by Mr. S. Beaird ^moved^ that the society request a copy of the same, which being done by the President & unanimously approved of by the Society, the original was kindly presented.

The President stated the following gentlemen as the committee on Revision of Rules: Messrs. S. W. Beaird, W. O. Weston, W. H. Gailliard, R. L. Deas, B. E. K. Hampton, E. G. Beaird, & the President ex officio.[8] No more business

106   *Free Black Charlestonians in Debate*

demanding the attention of the Society, the reporter made his report & the society on motion adjourned.

W. O. Weston, Sec.

Erratum: Mr. Richard Holloway member elect appeared and upon his hearing & approving of the rules was declared a legal member of the Society.

Clionian Society, May 11th 1853.

A regular meeting of the above association was held at the usual time & place. The proceedings of the last meeting being read (after the first roll was called) was approved. The regular debatants being read out, the subject for discussion was announced; Indeed it was well sustained on both sides with great enthusiasm, & was only concluded by that most unpleasant of all obstacles on certain occasions, "the president's hat" warning us, that the sands of time had slipped from under us & we could plead no more. The question was decided finally in the negative. The president in giving his decision spoke in the most complimentary manner of the effort of one of the members, who though but a stripling in the advantages of the Society, had determined to obey that injunction which has accomplished wonders, "I will try," & concluded with the hope that every member would represent the grand principles which gave birth to the institution, that in the time of trial, they may withstand the "flashing of the guns," & successfully batter every stronghold of ignorance. The question for the next meeting's reflection reads as follows "Is it right to remove the Indians from Florida?"[9] Mr. W. E. Marshall on the affirmative & Mr. Robert Sanders on the negative. No more business appearing to demand the attention of the Society, the reporter made his report & the Society on motion adjourned.

W. O. Weston, Sec.

~~Clionian~~ June 8th 1853. Clionian Society.

True to purpose, true to duty, the devoted desciples [*sic*] of Clio, though prevented by fortuitous circumstances, from exhibiting their devotion to her exalted shrine, at the time for the last regular meeting, determined that their preparation for debates, as well as business should answer for both; at this meeting. The vice president being absent, also the Secretary, Messrs. Deas & S. W. Beaird were requested to act in their capacities. At this stage of the proceedings Mr. S. W. Beaird arose & stated that the cause of his rising was sufficient of itself, to sanction his action. Which was "death." The death of a fellow member: and the very first in the "Clionian Phalanx." he then proceeded to eulogise his character & to impress upon the minds of his fellows the suddenness & consequently the need of a preparation for death, & concluded by offering the following preamble & resolutions:

1853 107

Whereas, it is with the deepest regret & sorrow that we, the membership of the Clionian Debating Society have received the sad intelligence, that on the 18th Day of May 1853, the all powerful and inevitable hand of death, was laid upon our fellow member, Alexander C. For[r]ester;[10] And in order that we as a body of young men, should join in paying a last tribute of respect to his memory, do unanimously adopt the following Resolves:

Resolved—That we as a Body do deeply sympathize with the relatives and friends of our deceased brother member Alexander C. For[r]ester; in his being almost suddenly snatched from their circle, as well as the first among the membership of this Institution, whose death we have to notice and record.

Resolved—That a blank page on the minute book of our institution, be dedicated to his memory.[11]

Resolved. That the Secretary be required to transmit a copy of this preamble & resolutions to the bereaved family of our deceased brother member.

Mr. W. H. Gailliard then arose to second the resolutions, accompanied by a few appropriate remarks in support of the virtues of the deceased. The President before offering the same, for the concurrence of the members, also expressed himself deeply solemnized by the occasion & the increased effect of his conviction of the vanity of earthly things. The preamble & resolutions were then put to the house & unanimously adopted. The regular debates were then commenced & carried on with great animation untill that unappealing judge & sometimes annoying visitor: the President hat warned one and all that the intellectual repast must cease. but willing as a dying man clinging to a strand, to have one breath longer, they took hold of the compromise of the Constitution & to their universal satisfaction, had it postponed for continued discussion at the next meeting. The President notified the members that [as] the time for the election of a semi-annual orator had long passed by, they should enter into an election for the same. the result of which was the declaration that Mr. R. L. Deas was chosen. The result being announced Mr. Deas signified his acceptance of the call. No more business demanding the attention of the Society, it was on motion adjourned.

W. O. Weston, Sec.

Erratum. The proceeding of the last meeting, as well as the first roll were called & approved before Mr. Beaird arose to offer his resolutions.

Clionian Society, June 22d 1853.

A regular meeting of the above named Society was held at the usual time & place. The first roll being called, the proceedings of the last meeting were read and approved. The continued question for debate was then announced; whereupon the members seized upon it with a firm grasp, & the avidity ~~with~~ which they displayed, showed that neither the fact of its being argued already, nor the lapse of time, had daunted them in the least. The time when their trumpet tongues must cease,[12] having arrived, the president arose & with a few preliminary remarks decided that they were not ^right^ in removing the Indians from Florida. The question for the next meeting reads as follows: "Was Lafayette right in assisting the colonies in their revolt against the mother country?["][13] Mr. W. O. Weston on the former & Mr. S. W. Beaird on the latter portion of the question. Many unimportant transactions being disposed of that are attendant upon meetings, the reporter made his report, the last roll was called & the Society on motion adjourned.

W. O. Weston, Sec.

Clionian Society, July 6th 1853.

A regular & enthusiastic gathering graced the Clionian Hall at the appointed time: the roll being called, the proceedings of the last meeting were read and approved. The subject of debate was then announced, & was kept up with great animations by the appointed debatants and members untill the time for adjournment. The President then arose and decided the question in the affirmative. The Election for officers then took place which resulted in the choice of the present administration for another term. The next meeting being the installation time no question for debate was chosen. No more business demanding the attention of the Society the last roll was called & the society on motion adjourned.

W. O. Weston, Secretary

Erratum Mr. A. L. Horry honorary member of the Society & formerly a member, was on motion of Mr. Gailliard invited through the Secretary as the especial guest of the Society at next meeting.

Clionian Society, July 20th/53.

Actuated by the noble design of "improving the mind" the devotees of old Clio assembled in large numbers at their Hall. The first roll being called, the proceedings of the last meeting were read and approved. According to previous notice, the installation of officers was about to occupy the attention of the Society, when the President arose, and, in the unanimous voice of Clio welcomed, yea "thrice welcomed"[14] Mr. A. L. Horry as the invited guest of the Society. Proceeding to call his attention to his past connection & usefulness among us, he concluded with extending to him the privilege allowed to all Honorary members of attending every meeting during his sojourn among us. Mr. Horry responded in words & expressions that not only "breathe but burn,"[15] & concluded by telling us that words could convey no adequate expression of his thoughts, when he told ~~them~~ ^us^ that he was grateful for ~~their~~ ^our^ kindness, & that this memorable scene would be one that he would be able to point out as being ~~one of the~~ a green oasis in the history of his life. Enchaining the attention of his hearers in a strain like this, he sat down amid the repeated plaudits of his brother members. The Installation of such officers as were present then took place. Mr. C. Ludeke having been appointed "chairman committe[e] of general interests" the president informed him that he must notify him of his appointed assistants at next meeting. The question adopted for discussion at the next meeting reads as follows. "Is the Maine liquor law conducive to the happiness of American citizens, and in accordance with her free institutions."[16] Mr. E. G. Beaird on the affirmative & Mr. G. F. Barrow on the negative. No more business demanding the attention of the Society, the reporter made his report & the society on motion adjourned.

W. O. Weston, Secretary

Erratum: The President appointed Messrs. S. W. Beaird, E. G. Beaird & W. H. Gailliard a committee to examine the books of Secretary & Treasurer.

Clionian Society, August 3d/53

The members of this Society again assembled at the usual time and place. The first roll was called, & the proceedings of the last meeting were read and approved. The question for discussion was then announced, and upon Mr. E. G. Beaird participating as ^a^ regular debatant, the president stated that Mr. G. F. Barrow being absent, the floor was now opened for any member who wished to take a part. The query being an interesting one, the animation continued without abatement untill the "President's hat" warned them that for this time at least they must desist. The question was then decided in the affirmative. The question for next evening[']s discussion reads as follows: "Did the games and oracles of the ancient Greeks produce many salutary effects upon their national character." Mr. H. J. D. Cardozo on the affirmative and Mr. J. M. F. Dereef on the negative. The arrears and last roll being called, the reporter made his report, and the Society on motion adjourned.

W. O. Weston, Secretary

Clionian Society, September 14th 1853.

A regular meeting was held at the usual time and place. The proceedings of the last meeting were read and approved after the calling of the first roll. The President then called upon the regular debatants, none of whom being present, the floor was opened to any gentleman desiring to participate. Most eagerly did they avail themselves of the opportunity, for they occupied every inch of ground. The president then decided the question in the negative. The question for the next regular evening's discussion reads as follows: "Was Caesar a great man." The Society then agreed by motion, to adjourn over to Friday evening. The reporter also made his report, the last roll was called & the Society on motion adjourned.

W. O. Weston, Secretary

NB. Mr. Robert Deas on the affirmative & Mr. Gailliard on the negative ~~of question~~ of question.

Charleston, September 16th/53.

A^n^ ~~regular~~ extra meeting of the Clionian Society or in other words an adjourned meeting was held at the usual place at the time above specified. The President having called the meeting to order, the roll was called, and the proceedings of the last meeting read and approved. A letter of application was then read from Mr. Benjamain Roberts as a member which letter after being favourably reported on by the Committee was balloted for & upon report was found duly elected. The Secretary was then ordered to inform him of the same. No more business appearing to demand the attention of the Society, it was on motion adjourned.

W. O. Weston, Secretary

Clionian Society, September 28th/53.

A regular meeting of the sons of Clio was held at their Hall at the usual time. The first roll being called the proceedings of the last meeting were read and approved. The regular debates for the evening then commenced & was carried on with animation untill the hour of adjournment when it was postponed untill the next meeting. Mr. Benjamain Roberts member elect was present, and upon hearing and approving of the rules & constitution paid the initial fee & was declared a member of the same. At this stage of the proceedings Mr. S. W. Beaird gave notice of his intention to introduce several augmentations to Constitution, viz. One in regard to restricting debatants to a limited time for argument; another to govern the President in his allot[t]ing time to debatants occupying the floor at the hour of adjournment; and another to alter the article in regard to general elections taking place twice a year instead of three times; last roll was then called and the Society on motion adjourned.

W. O. Weston, Sec. & Treasurer

Clionian Society, October 12th 1853.

True to purpose, true to duty the desciples of old Clio met at her shrine at the usual time. The first roll being called, the proceedings of the last meeting was read and approved. The deferred debate was then recommenced & carried on with considerable animation untill the hour when the President's hat announced a conclusion to all discussion. The question was then decided in the negative. The question for the next evening reads as follows: Is a rude state of Society favourable to patriotism? Mr. Hyams on the affirmative; Mr. Hampton on the negative. No more business demanding the attention of the Society, it was on motion adjourned after the reporter made his report & the last roll was called.

W. O. Weston, Sec. & Treasurer

Clionian Society, November 9th/53.

This Association though prevented from gathering at their last regular meeting in consequence of the inclemency of the weather, assembled in numbers at this more favourable period. The first roll being called the proceedings of the last meeting were read and approved. By advice of the President the debates for this evening[']s discussion were postponed and the polls for election of officers was opened; which resulted in the choice of the following gentlemen: (See Roll of officers book). In the mean time Mr. Gailliard arose and moved that a committee of three be appointed to consult with the other institutions of our city, of renting the Hall used for such purposes as meetings, anniversary occasions &c. & thus secure the permanent use of the same. Prefacing the same with a few remarks, he endeavoured to impress upon them that the time for action had come, and if delayed, might be inevitably lost. There being a difference of opinion among the members in regard to further consultation; the motion not being seconded was rendered powerless. The President gave notice that if no adverse circumstances occurred the ~~Quarterly or~~ semi-annual oration would be delivered. It was also made known that it was the regular time for the Installation of Officers elect. No more business appearing to demand the attention of the Society the Reporter made his report, the last roll called and the Society on motion adjourned.

W. O. Weston, Sec.

Clionian Society, November 23d 1853.

A meeting of the above named Society was held at the usual time and place. The first roll being called the proceedings of the last meeting were read and approved. The interesting scene of installation ^was^ then commenced: The

112   *Free Black Charlestonians in Debate*

retiring President after returning thanks to his fellow members for their urbanity and courtesy during his administration; ~~and~~ welcomed his successor as a fit representative of Clio, and concluded with the hope that peace and harmony may crown his efforts as chief magistrate of the fraternity. The President elect after expressing his gratitude, declared himself ready at all times to maintain the Constitution and acknowledged the acceptance of the same.[17] He then proceeded to install all the officers elect who were present; the countenances of whom were irradiated with cheerfulness, and evinced by their actions that they were doubly nerved to fight the battles of Clio and lead her sons on to glorious victory. The President gave notice that the address that was somewhat expected that evening, would take place at the next regular meeting. The Secretary was therefore notified to acquaint the honorary members of the same. He also appointed Mr. S. W. Beaird Chairman of Committee of general interests for the present term. Mr. Gailliard then renewed his motion of a past meeting, that a committee be appointed to wait on the other societies and if possible, secure through their cooperation the Hall used for meetings, anniversary occasions &c. (which he thought would be a benefit to the community.) Accepting of a few modifications, Mr. Cardozo seconded his motion, which was when put to the house unanimously adopted. The President then appointed the Committee at the head of which Mr. Gailliard was appointed; but he refusing to serve as a member of the committee in any capacity in consequence of other pressing engagements Mr. S. W. Beaird was appointed in his place. The committee now consists of the following gentlemen Messrs. S. W. Beaird, H. Cardozo Jr. R. S. Holloway & H. J. D. Cardozo.[18] No more business appearing to demand the attention of the Society, the reporter made his report, ^the last roll was called,^ and the Society was on motion adjourned.

W. O. Weston, Secretary

Clionian Society, December 7th/53

A regular meeting of the above named Society was held at the usual time and place; The first roll being called, the proceedings of the last meeting were read and approved. The President then arose from his chair and in the capacity of Semi annual Orator, delivered a thrilling address on the subject of Ambition in its different phases. Applying his remarks to the Clionians he marked out the happy results of a well directed ambition. Suffice it to say, every one left the hall, with a new infusion of determination to let their good works so shine as to be an example to others.[19] A copy of the same on motion was requested, which was freely complied with. The deferred debate was made the order of the next meeting; The Society then proceeded to elect an orator for the ensuing six months.

On report of Managers Mr. J. F. M. [J. M. F.][20] Dereef was declared elected. The orator elect then signified his acceptance of the call. Several of the officers elect having appeared, were qualified. No more business demanding the attention of the Society, it was on motion adjourned.

W. O. Weston, Secretary.

Clionian Society, Decbr 21st 1853.

A meeting of the above Society was held at the usual place. The first roll being called; the proceedings of the last meeting were confirmed, after being read. The question on being read for the evening's discussion, Mr. Reporter announced, that the regular debatants were absent, whereupon the house was opened, for all desirous of participating. The question was ably argued on both sides untill the hour for adjournment. The President decided it in the affirmative. The question for the next meeting reads as follows: "Is a nation strictly justifiable in compelling another nation by force of arms to open her port for trade."[21] Mr. Holloway on the affirmative Mr. C. Ludeke on the negative. No more business demanding the attention of the Society, the reporter made his report & the Society was on motion adjourned.

W. O. Weston, Secretary

Erratum: The President being absent, Vice President E. G. Beaird presided.

NOTES

1. Honorary member Jacob Weston, who delivered the invocation, was the uncle of William O. Weston, the orator at the anniversary event.
2. Weston cites Romans 14:7 (KJV).
3. During the Napoleonic Wars, the Battle of Trafalgar in October 1805 decisively affirmed British naval supremacy. Just before the battle, Admiral Horatio Nelson signaled from his flagship *Victory* to the British fleet: "England expects that every man will do his duty."
4. *There* was intended.
5. *Welkin:* "the vault of heaven," "the firmament," "the sky."
6. Possibly the Clionians followed a practice like that of the Society of United Irishmen, founded in 1791. The president of this society could command the members' silence and attention by "rising from his Chair and taking off his hat"; *Society of United Irishmen of Dublin, Established November IX. MDCCXCI* (Dublin, 1794), 201.
7. Louis-Napoléon Bonaparte, or Napoleon III (1808–1873), was president of the Second Republic of France from 1850 to 1852 and then French emperor from 1852 to 1870. He was the nephew of Napoleon I.
8. *Ex officio:* "because of an office held."
9. Based on the Indian Removal Act of 1830, the US government attempted forcibly to relocate members of the Seminole Nation from Florida to Indian Territory (Oklahoma), meeting strong and sustained resistance from Seminole people. The

Clionians owned a memoir of the Second Seminole War written by a US Army lieutenant; see the entry for December 26, 1849. Questions about displacing Indigenous people were common in nineteenth-century debating societies; see Angela G. Ray, "The Permeable Public: Rituals of Citizenship in Antebellum Men's Debating Clubs," *Argumentation and Advocacy* 41, no. 1 (2004): 17.

10. Alexander Forrester died of tetanus at age twenty-two on May 18, 1853, and was interred in the cemetery of the Brown Fellowship Society. He had paid state capitation taxes as a "free Negro" for several years; the 1851 tax records show his address as 15 Pitt Street. In early 1854 Forrester's estate was valued at $476.00, all in the form of financial assets. See "South Carolina, U.S., Death Records, 1821–1971," Ancestry.com (online database), 2008, https://www.ancestry.com/search/collections/8741/; "South Carolina, Charleston, Free Negro Capitation Books, 1811–1860," FamilySearch.org (online database), last modified June 15, 2024, https://www.familysearch.org/search/collection/3405101; and "South Carolina, Charleston District, Estate Inventories, 1732–1844," FamilySearch.org (online database), last modified June 15, 2024, https://www.familysearch.org/search/collection/3460989.

11. In the minute book, two blank facing pages follow the minutes of this meeting. For comparison, a memorial page for Robert L. Deas can be seen following the minutes of April 28, 1865, in the Friendly Association Records, 1853–1869, South Carolina Historical Society, Charleston, SC.

12. Weston adapts language from act 1, scene 7, of Shakespeare's *Macbeth* and from 1 Corinthians 13:8 (KJV).

13. The Marquis de Lafayette (1757–1834), as a young French aristocrat, fought with the American colonists against Britain during the American Revolution. In 1825 he visited Charleston while touring the United States.

14. Weston may have adapted this phrase from act 5, scene 1, of Shakespeare's *Twelfth Night*.

15. The English poet Thomas Gray referred to "thoughts that breathe, and words that burn" in his Pindaric ode "The Progress of Poesy" (1757). The commonly quoted phrase also appears in the address by Francis Withers Capers that Robert L. Deas donated in pamphlet form to the Clionian library on April 17, 1850; F[rancis] W[ithers] Capers, *State Military Academies: An Address Delivered before the Calliopean Society of the Citadel Academy, Charleston* (Charleston, SC: Tenhet and Corley, 1846), 16.

16. Long a bastion of temperance activism, Maine outlawed the manufacture and sale of liquor in 1851.

17. Robert L. Deas was president for the society's nineteenth term. Elected semiannual orator on June 8, he delivered his oration on ambition on December 7.

18. The minutes of the Friendly Association on December 19, 1853, report: "A letter were handed in by Mr. J. E. Barreau from the Clionian D Society the Purport of the letter were to know if we the members of the Friendly Association would assist them in hireing Mr. Holloway's Hall in Beaufain St. as it would be very convenient for meetings[.] after the letter was read The President directed the Secry to inform them that the body could not take any action on it whatever, for our Rules compel the Stewarts [Stewards] to furnish A Place for our meetings"; Friendly Association Records, 1853–1869. Active members of the Friendly Association at this time included Gabriel F. Barrow, Robert L. Deas, and Isadore A. Hyames, all of

whom were also active Clionians, as well as J. F. Lindsay and Marion L. Stent, who
had been rejected for Clionian membership in July 1852.

19. Weston's language alludes to Christian scripture: "Let your light so shine before
men, that they may see your good works, and glorify your Father which is in heaven"
(Matthew 5:16, KJV).

20. Dereef's forenames were Joseph Moulton Francis.

21. In debating this query, the Clionians likely discussed the US naval expedition of
Commodore Matthew Perry's squadron to Japan's Edo Bay in the summer of 1853.

— 1854 —

[In this year society secretaries minuted thirteen meetings; six included debates, two included orations.—Ed.]

Sixth anniversary celebration of Clionian Debating Society., January 2d 1854.

Animated by a sincere love of their fostering parent the desciples of Clio assembled <u>en masse</u> in their Hall to celebrate their Sixth anniversary. Nature as if sanctioning their praiseworthy efforts smiled on them propitiously; rendering every assistance to make it one of the loveliest days that the eyes of man ever beheld. The time of preparation having been absorbed, the members preceded by the Honorary ones moved in phalanx to the Hall above; where a brilliant assemblage of both sexes greeted their arrival.[1] Harmony being restored the exercises were commenced by a prayer from Honorary member S. Weston. The President then arose and introduced Mr. Henry Cardozo jr. the orator of the day to the audience.—who after a short introductory directed their attention to the rewards and results of a well directed ~~attention~~ ambition. Sketching the effects which both the extremes of the subject have exerted upon the world, he drew a masterly conclusion from the premises deduced, & left an enchained auditory doubly convinced that an ambition well directed, is propitious of the grandest results. But the members were not left thirsting for intellectual & moral advice, for they received also a full share. Applying the subject to an interest which they should always manifest in the Society, he showed them conclusively that by so doing Clio may point at no distant day to some of the brightest stars of the intellectual firmament and claim them as her jewels. Enchaining their attention in such a strain for a reasonable period, he ceased amid the unbounded applause of the vast assemblage. The audience being invited to the Hall below to examine the Society's Library. The benediction was pronounced & this vast gathering retired benefited; no doubt with the firmest resolutions to direct hereafter their ambition not to the destruction, but to the good of the human family.
W. O. Weston, Secretary

Clionian Society, February 1st 1854

Circumstances of an unavoidable nature having interfered with the last meeting, the desciples of Clio came out in strength on this occasion. The first roll being called, the proceedings of the last meetings were put to the house by Vice President E. G. Beaird. (the President being absent) & unanimously adopted. The question for the evening was then discussed, & most warmly was it argued untill the President's hat stopped the debate. It was decided in the negative by the President. The question for the next meeting reads as follows: "Which is more condemnable at the bar of Public Opinion Slander or Flattery." Mr. W. S. Lord on the affirmative, Mr. S. J. Maxwell on the negative. In consequence of the lateness of the hour the Election of Annual Orator was postponed untill next meeting.* No more business demanding the attention of the Society, it was on motion adjourned.

W. O. Weston, Sec.

*The last roll was called & reporter made his report.

Clionian Society, February 14th/54.

A meeting of the above named Society was held at the usual time and place. The first roll being called, and the proceedings of the last meeting read and approved, it was on motion resolved that the time being far spent, the debates be deferred untill the next meeting. The election for annual orator then took place for January 1855, & on counting the votes Mr. B. E. K. Hampton was found unanimously elected. The Secretary was ordered to notify him of the same. No more business demanding the attention of the body, the reporter made his report, the last roll was called & the society on motion adjourned.

W. O. Weston, Sec.

Errata The committee also reported on the correctness of Treasurer's account. Mr. S. W. Beaird arose and in an impressive strain moved that a copy of Mr. H. Cardozo Jr. oration be requested by the Society; which being seconded was put to the house, and unanimously carried. The speaker then thanked the members for their good feelings & promised them to comply with their request.

Clionian Society, March 14th 1854.

A meeting of the above society was held at the usual time and place. The first roll being called, the proceedings of the last meeting were read and approved. The Orator elect being absent, & having given no answer to the letter informing him of his election, a Committee was appointed to wait on him & procure if possible a decisive answer from the gentleman. During this interval, the regular debatants for the evening were read out; & upon the Reporter announcing their absence, the floor was opened to any member who wished to take a part. The excitement was kept up untill the hour of ceasing presented itself, when the President decided it, in the negative. The Committee having discharged their duty, were relieved from further action. Mr. Hampton arose and after thanking the Society, for their partiality to him, stated that engagements would prevent his acceptance of the honour conferred on him. His resignation being accepted & another election held, Mr. R. L. Deas was declared elected;—who ~~declared~~ stated that he ^would^ give a positive answer of his acceptance at the next meeting. The question for the next meeting reads as follows: "Is France & England right in interfering in the present struggle between Russia & Turkey."[2] Mr. W. G. Marshall on the affirmative. Mr. Roberts on the negative. No more business appearing to demand the attention of the Society, the reporter made his report & the Society on motion adjourned.

W. O. Weston, Secretary

Clionian Society, March 28th 1854.

A meeting of the above named Society, was held at the usual time and place. The first roll being called, the proceedings of the last meeting were read and adopted. The regular debatant on the affirmative being absent & the gentleman on the negative having concluded, the floor was opened to any member. The excitement continued untill the very moment of ceasing arrived; the question was then decided in the negative. Mr. Deas who was elected annual orator stated that circumstances of an unavoidable nature compelled him to decline serving in said capacity; which resignation being accepted, the election of another was postponed in consequence of the lateness of the hour, to the next meeting. The question for the next meeting reads as follows: "Was England right in banishing Obrien, Meagher & their coadjutors?"[3] Mr. Robert Sanders on the affirmative, Mr. W. O. Weston on the negative. Mr. Dereef semi-annual orator elect, being notified that the fulfil~~ling~~^ment^ of his engagement, was nigh at hand, he informed the Society, that the press of engagements, had caused a delay of preparation & that he would when ready, notify them. No more business appearing to demand the attention of the Society, the reporter made his report & the Society on motion was adjourned.

W. O. Weston, Secretary.

Clionian Society, April 25th 1854.

A meeting of the Clionian Society was held at the usual time & place. The first roll being called, the proceedings of the previous meeting were read and approved. The debatant on the affirmative being absent & the one on the negative having concluded the floor was opened to any one who desired to take part in the discussion. The time was occupied untill the President's hat signified that all debate must now cease. The question was decided in the negative. The question for the next meeting reads as follows: "Have the various fairs that have been held tended to excite among the people a spirit of industry and improvement?" Mr. S. Beaird on the affirmative & Mr. E. G. Beaird on the negative. Mr. R. S. Holloway was also elected annual orator for January 1st 1855, & Mr. Robert Sanders semiannual orator. No more business demanding the attention of the Society, it was on motion adjourned.

W. O. Weston, Secretary

Clionian Society, May 11th/54.

A regular meeting of the above Society was held at the usual time & place. The first roll being called & the proceedings of the last meeting read and approved, the regular debatants discussed the questions for the meeting's debate: which was decided in the affirmative. The question for the next meeting reads as follows: Is absolute religious toleration conducive to the stability of a government & the moral excellence of a people. Mr. G. F. Barrow on the affirmative; Mr. H. Cardozo Jr. on the negative. A Book was handed over to the Society purporting to be information in reference to Rio De Jenario [sic] as a present from A. L. Horry formerly a member: for which the thanks of the Society was immediately volunteered. No more business demanding the attention of the Society it was on motion adjourned.

W. O. Weston, Sec.

Clionian Society, July 12th 1854

A meeting of this Society having been prevented for some time by unavoidable circumstances, an extra meeting was held at the above time. The President & Secretary being absent Mr. C. Ludeke was called to the Chair & Mr. H. Cardozo Jr. was appointed Secretary. The first roll being called & the proceedings of the last meeting read and approved, a general election of officers took place. (See List of Same). Mr. R. Holloway Orator Elect declined serving in said capacity, & on his resignation being accepted, an election was ordered for next meeting. The President notified the Society that the semi-annual oration will be heard on next meeting, & the Secretary who was absent ordered to be acquainted with the same, that his business on such occasions, might be attended to. No more business demanding the attention of the Society, the reporter made his report, the last roll was called & the Society on motion adjourned.

W. O. Weston, Secretary

Clionian Society, July 19th 1854

A regular meeting of this Society was held at the usual time & place. The first roll being called, the proceedings of the last meeting were read and approved. The President then arose & informed the body that the Semi Annual Oration will not be delivered this meeting as was announced. Mr. S. W. Beaird then arose and moved that an extra meeting be called on the ensuing Wednesday Evening for the hearing of said oration & Installation of Officers, which being put to the house was carried. The President then extended orders for the summoning of Honorary & regular members, as is customary on said occasions.

An Election was again held for the vacant office of Orator (annual) for January /55 & Mr. R. L. Deas elected; who deferred an answer untill the next meeting. The first[4] roll was then called, reporter made his report, & society on motion adjourned.

W. O. Weston, Secretary

Clionian Society, July 26th/54

An extra meeting of this institution was held at the usual place. The first roll being called, the proceedings of the last meeting were read and approved. The President then introduced to the audience the orator elect Mr. J. F. M. F. [J. M. F.] Dereef, who for a considerable time enchained the attention of the assemblage on the advantages of reading standard works, showed that men of the first rank in science were indebted solely to this medium, for their superiority; that such a course improves the habits & tempers as well as the mind of a man, and concluded with a glowing application of the same to his fellow members.

Mr. S. W. Beaird introduced several additions and alterations to the Constitution; the requisite number being present it was on being seconded adopted. Mr. B. E. K. Hampton arose and stated that in his opinion the gentleman and the signer of the said additions and alterations had assumed the power invested in the Committee on "revision of rules" & that if the gentleman wished such to be done, that it should have been placed for action, before said Committee & that he would move that the Committee be discharged from further action. The gentlemen then explained their position, by stating that the necessity of the same together with the fact of 2/3 being expected to be present, together with the good of the Society had induced them to press it immediately before the attention of the Society; The motion being seconded was put to the house and lost. Mr. R. L. Deas Orator elect, having declined, an election was ordered for next meeting. The regular debates and installation of officers was postponed also untill next meeting. No more business demanding the attention of the Society, the last roll was called and the Society on motion adjourned.

W. O. Weston, Secretary

NB Mr. W. O. Weston seconded by Mr. H. Cardozo Jr. moved a copy of the orator's address which being carried into effect by the President was heartily responded to by the orator.

Clionian Society, August 30th/54

A regular meeting of this Society was held on the evening of the above date, the first roll was called, The President in the chair—Mr. Roberts filling that of the Vice President—the proceedings of the last ^meeting^ were read, upon which there arose a discussion—which being settled—the proceedings were then put to the house and approved of. Mr. S. W. Beaird then arose and moved that as the time had much elapsed and but few of the members [were] present— several being out of the City—and some indisposed—that the regular debates be postponed to the next meeting—which was seconded, and carried. The election for Annual Orator for 1855. now took place—which resulted in the choice of Mr. B. L. Roberts—upon which he returned his thanks to his fellow members—and informed them that he would give an answer at next meeting as to his acceptance. Mr. H. Cardozo Jr. then arose and moved that as but a short time remained for the preparation of the Annual address—that the rule requiring the celebration on the 1st of January, be for this time suspended—and that the Orator be allowed to choose any period between ~~that~~ then, and the first Monday in April—which was seconded, and unanimously carried. Mr. S. W. Beaird then moved that as the Secretary would be absent from the city for a while—that some one fill his place which being carried—the President accordingly appointed Mr. H. Cardozo Jr. Secretary "pro tem." The business of the meeting having been concluded, the Reporter made his report, the last roll was called, and the Society on motion adjourned.

H. Cardozo Jr., Secretary Pro-tem.

Clionian. D. Society., Decr 6th 1854

A regular meeting of this Society was held on the evening of the above date. The President and Vice President being absent—Mr. Dereef was chosen Chairman— and Mr. ^Roberts^ filled the Chair of the Vice, and Mr. H. Cardozo Jr. Secretary "pro-tem." The first roll was then called, and the proceedings of the last meeting read and approved. The regular debates then commenced—and were spiritedly carried on up to the latest possible period—after which a decision was pronounced in favor of the affirmative of the question. Mr. S. W. Beaird now offered a resolution—that the rule requiring meetings every alternate Wednesday evening—be suspended for a while—and that the Society meet every second and fourth Monday evenings of the month, which was seconded—and unanimously adopted. Mr. Roberts now informed the body that he had accepted the office of Annual Orator—to which he was chosen at the last meeting. Mr. Dereef now laid before the body a letter directed to the President and members of the Clionian. D. Society—which was opened—and found to contain an application for membership from Mr. A. Bonneau Lee, which letter was accepted by the Society—and ordered to a second reading at the next meeting. Mr. H. Cardozo now presented as a gift to the Society—"Bachman's Unity of the Human race"[5] which was received—and upon motion of S. W. Beaird the thanks of the body were returned to the donor. Mr. H. Cardozo now arose and moved that as the delivery of the Semi-Annual Oration by Mr. Sanders did not take place at the regular time—being the first meeting in September last—The absence from the City of several members—the then prevailing sickness[6]—and since— the pressure of business—these together preventing a meeting down to the present time—that he be informed that the Society was now ready for the hearing of said—Oration—which motion was seconded, and carried, and the Secretary directed to inform Mr. Sanders by letter of the same. The business being now concluded—The reporter made his [report]—the last roll was called and the Society on motion adjourned.

H. Cardozo Jr., Secretary-pro-tem

"Omitted"—The question adopted for the next meeting's discussion—read— "Would it have been criminal in Socrates to have attempted to escape prison upon the suggestion of his friend Crito?"[7] Mr. H. J. D. Cardozo was appointed on the affirmative—and Mr. Dereef on the negative of the question.

[The following indented entries, for December 29, 1854, and January 1, 1855, appear on two facing pages in the proceedings volume. At one time these pages were attached to each other with four drops of red adhesive along the outer edges. The subsequent entries, for the same dates, offer a clearer account of an officer installation.—Ed.]

Clionian Society, December 29th/54

This society was summoned on the above date to attend an extra meeting.

The first roll being called & the proceedings of the last meeting read and approved, a notice was received from Mr. Benjamain Roberts stating that he would serve the Society on their regular anniversary; which being put to the house was received. Mr. W. S. Lord Vice-President elect being present was installed by Mr. E. G. Beaird the acting President; who in his turn installed the other officers who were present. The following gentlemen received appointments as Committee on general interests from Mr. H. Cardozo Jr. after his selection as Chairman of the same by the President. Messrs. I. A. Hyams, B. L. Roberts, S. W. Beaird & E. G. Beaird. The meeting was then adjourned over till first day of January 1855.

Erratum: Mr. W. S. Lord acted as President ^(he as _vice_ being installed by Mr. E. G. Beaird:)^ on this occasion: Mr. R. Holloway being not installed till the adjourned meeting on Monday 1st January 1855.

Clionian D Society., Seventh anniversary, January 1st 1855

An adjourned meeting was held in the Hall at four O'clock P.M. according to previous notice. A letter of Application from Mr. Arthur Lee & which had passed through the constitutional process was then acted on, & he declared unanimously elected. The Secretary was then ordered to inform him of the same. Mr. R. S. Holloway President elect, who was not present among the other installed officers at the last meeting, was appropriately addressed on the duties of the same. He then on accepting the same was declared legal President of the Society.

Clionian Society, December 29th/54

An extra meeting of this Society was held at the usual _time_ and _place_. The first roll being called & the proceedings of the last meeting read and approved, a letter of notification was received from Mr. Benjamain Roberts that he would serve the society on their approaching anniversary, which was received as information. Mr. W. S. Lord Vice President elect was then installed by Mr. E. G. Beaird the acting President; he upon accepting the same position, proceeded to qualify those officers who were present. Mr. H. Cardozo was appointed Chairman on Committee of general interests, who made selection of the following gentlemen: Messrs. E. G. Beaird, I. A. Hyams, B. L. Roberts & S. W. Beaird. The meeting then adjourned to meet on important business January 1st 1855.
W. O. Weston, Secretary

NOTES

1. Although language earlier in the minutes implies that women attended the anniversary meetings (e.g., "lovely smiles" on January 1, 1850, and "the fair assemblage" on January 10, 1853), this is the first time that a mixed-sex audience is unambiguous.
2. This query pertains to the ongoing Crimean War.
3. William Smith O'Brien (1803–1864) and Thomas Francis Meagher (1823–1867) were Irish nationalist leaders exiled to Van Diemen's Land (now Tasmania) owing to their involvement in an abortive, armed insurrection against English rule in

County Tipperary in 1848. Arriving in Hobart in 1849, Meagher escaped in 1852, and O'Brien was released in February 1854, shortly before the Clionians debated the exile. See G. Rudé, "Meagher, Thomas Francis," and "O'Brien, William Smith," both in *Australian Dictionary of Biography*, vol. 2 (Melbourne, Australia: Melbourne University Press, 1967).

4. *Last* was intended.

5. John Bachman (1790–1874), a white Lutheran minister and, from 1848 to 1853, a professor of natural history at the College of Charleston, published *The Doctrine of the Unity of the Human Race Examined on the Principles of Science* in Charleston in 1850.

6. The Charleston City Council reported that between April and November 1854, 675 people died from fever in Charleston, about 60 percent of them in September. Most of the deaths were attributed to yellow fever. See *Report of the Committee of the City Council of Charleston, upon the Epidemic Yellow Fever, of 1858* (Charleston: Walker, Evans, 1859), 63; the report presents comparable data from 1821 through 1858.

7. Plato's dialogue *Crito* describes a conversation between Socrates and Crito occurring in the prison cell of Socrates while the philosopher awaits execution. The character Crito pleads with Socrates to escape.

— 1855 —

[In this year the society minuted its final library acquisition and elected its last member. Secretaries minuted five meetings; two included debates, one included an oration.—Ed.]

Seventh Anniversary., Clionian D Society, January 1st 1855

According to previous notice an adjourned meeting of this Society took place at four O'clock PM. Mr. R. S. Holloway President elect being present was duly installed. The letter of application from Mr. Arthur Lee which had passed through the Constitutional process was then balloted for & he declared unanimously elected.

The Society then proceeded into the Hall, where a brilliant assemblage of the fairer & sterner sex greeted their presence. The exercises being opened with prayer by Mr. H. Cardozo Jr. the annual oration was delivered by Mr. Benjamain Roberts. For twenty or thirty minutes did he enchain an enlightened auditory on the various phases of Education. The Press, the Pulpit, the College as well as the achievements of Watt, a Newton & the other channels & instruments of the onward march of Education, were dilated on by the Master touch of the Orator.[1] The ascendant star in the galaxy of Palestine's hopes was bu^r^nished with a sun-like aspect by this son of Clio & the not far distant day when Ethiopia too shall shall stretch forth her hands,[2] appeared but as the 'morrow before the phrophetic [sic] touch of the speaker. Concluding with an exhorting appeal to his fellow members, he took his seat amidst the plaudits of surrounding friends. The benediction being pronounced, the Society as well as the audience, dispersed with the solemn conviction, that they were well repaid for leaving their homes & firesides.
W. O. Weston, Secretary

Clionian Society, January 22nd/55.

A regular meeting of the above named Society was held at the usual time and place.

The first roll being called, the proceedings of the two last meetings were read and approved. The Vice President being absent, Mr. Cardozo was appointed in his place. Mr. C. Ludeke was appointed Reporter the incumbent being absent. The evening being far advanced the only important business transacted, was the election of Mr. R. S. Holloway as Annual Orator. The reporter made his report & the last roll being called, the Society on motion adjourned.

W. O. Weston, Secretary

Clionian Society, June 18th/55

A regular meeting of the above named Society was held at the usual time & place; The first roll being called the proceedings of the last meeting were read and approved. At this time a present of "Josephus works"[3] to the Society was announced & a vote of thanks unanimously tendered the munificent donor. The gift was still more highly cherished when it was known, that it came from an Honorary Member Mr. Richard Dereef who has ever been ready in time of need to subscribe liberally to Clio's funds.[4] Mr. Sanders Orator elect having declined, that & the debates were postponed untill next meeting. ~~A letter of thanks was ordered to be written to Mr. Dereef for his kindness.~~ The Society on motion after the report & roll was called adjourned.

W. O. Weston, Sec.

Clionian Society, July 9th/55

A regular meeting of the above named Society was held at the usual time & place. The first roll being called, the proceedings of the last meeting were read & approved. The long postponed debate then took place. Mr. H. J. D. Cardozo the affirmative debatant being absent & the gentleman of the negative Mr. J. M. F. Dereef having pleaded from a variety of reasons non compulsion to debate, the floor was opened to any disputants. The discussion was warm & ceased not untill the President gave notice that what was not said, could not again be said—at least publicly. It was decided in the affirmative.

The vacant Semi Annual Oratorship was then filled by the election of Mr. W. H. Gaillard; notice was also given that an election for general officers would be held at the next meeting. No more business appearing to demand the attention of the Society, it was on motion after reporter made report, adjourned.

W. O. Weston, Secretary

Erratum. The President being absent Mr. E. G. Beaird was called to the Chair.

The question adopted for the next meeting read thus—"Is the occurrence of great events indicative of a progressive spirit"—Mr. R. L. Deas was appointed on the affirmative, and Mr. W. H. Gaillard on the negative of the question.

Clionian Society, July 23rd/55

A regular meeting of this Society was held on the evening of the above date. The first roll was called, the proceedings of the last meeting read and approved. The regular debates were now opened and were spiritedly carried on even beyond the time for closing, after which the President announced his decision in favor of the affirmative.

The question adopted for next meeting's discussion read thus "Do the consequences of <u>Success</u> tend to Good or Evil." Mr. I. A. Hyams'[5] was appointed on the former, and Mr. B. E. K. Hampton on the latter portion of the question. The general election of officers now took place, which resulted as follows (see Officers list). At the opening of the meeting Mr. H. Cardozo Jr. was appointed Secretary pro-tem. All business being now concluded, the Reporter made his report, the last roll was called, and the Society on motion adjourned.
H. Cardozo Jr., Sec. pro-tem

NOTES

1. Roberts refers to the Scottish inventor James Watt (1736–1819), best known for his steam engine, which contributed to the Industrial Revolution, and to Sir Isaac Newton (1642–1727), the English physicist and mathematician whose laws of motion prompted the law of universal gravitation.

2. The biblical phrase "Ethiopia shall soon stretch out her hands unto God" (Psalm 68:31, KJV) was commonly used among nineteenth-century advocates of African evangelization.

3. Several editions of the works of the first-century CE Jewish historian Flavius Josephus were available in 1855.

4. Richard E. Dereef (1798–1876) was a wealthy wood factor, an enslaver, a member of the Brown Fellowship and Friendly Union Societies, and the father of Clionian regular member J. M. F. Dereef. See Eric Foner, *Freedom's Lawmakers: A Directory of Black Officeholders during Reconstruction,* rev. ed. (Baton Rouge: Louisiana State University Press, 1996), 62; Bernard E. Powers Jr., *Black Charlestonians: A Social History, 1822–1885* (Fayetteville: University of Arkansas Press, 1994), 43; Larry Koger, *Black Slaveowners: Free Black Slave Masters in South Carolina, 1790–1860* (Jefferson, NC: McFarland, 1985), 16; and *List of the Tax Payers of the City of Charleston for 1860* (Charleston, SC: Evans and Cogswell, 1861), 319.

5. This is the last mention of Isadore A. Hyames (1829–1901) in the Clionian minutes. Hyames was also a member of the Friendly Association; on August 27, 1856, that group recorded receipt of a letter from Hyames declaring his intention to leave South Carolina permanently. In 1861 he served as a corporal in the New York State Militia for three months. For the remainder of the century, census records and city directories listed him as a tailor in Manhattan. At his death in 1901, he was interred in Brooklyn's Green-Wood Cemetery, where former Clionian honorary member Job G. Bass was buried earlier that year. See Friendly Association Records, 1853–1869, South Carolina Historical Society, Charleston, SC; Isadore A. Hyames, Co. D, Eighth New York State Militia, in Records of the Adjutant General's

Office, 1780s–1917, Record Group 94, National Archives and Records Administration, Washington, DC; "New York, New York, U.S., Death Index, 1892–1898, 1900–1902," Ancestry.com (online database), 2003, https://www.ancestry.com/search/collections/6492/; and Green-Wood Historic Fund, "Burial and Vital Records, 1840–1937," Brooklyn, NY, 2024, https://www.green-wood.com/burial-and-vital-records/.

— 1856 —

[In this year the society minuted its final officer election and held its last debate. Secretaries minuted five meetings; three included debates, one included an oration.—Ed.]

Eighth Anniversary celebration of Clionian D. Society, January 7th 1856

On account of inclement weather the annual celebration was postponed to the above date. The Members and Honorary Members gathered in their Hall at the usual hour, and found a fair audience of respectable numbers to greet their arrival, after ~~repairing to~~ which, the exercises were commenced with prayer by Honorary Member Sam[ue]l Weston, the President then announced Mr. R. S. Holloway as the Orator ~~on~~ for the occasion, who, after expressions of congratulations upon the recurrence of the happy event, then with becoming grace, and modesty, addressed his audience on the "advantages accruing from a cultivated mind"—the proper conceptions it gave Mankind of himself—his wonderful physical organization, his capability of comprehending, and appreciating the revelations, and operations of Nature, and the qualifications it imparted for extended, and increasing Usefulness, enforcing his position with illustrations at once striking and forcible—thus giving fresh impetus to the March of Mind. He then specially addressed his fellow members invoking them to renewed efforts in the cause they have espoused, exciting their ambition by a bright array of blessings consequent thereon, and thus he closed amidst the applauses of a delighted assembly. The exercises ^were^ then concluded with the benediction, and the audience dispersed ~~for their~~ but not without expressions of their gratification and pleasure.

A^n^ ~~regular~~ extra meeting of the Society was afterward held, which was called to order by the President. Mr. H. Cardozo Jr. then arose and offered a resolution that in order to a better attendance the Society meet hereafter monthly—on the first Monday evening of every month, which was seconded by Mr. S. W. Beaird with the amendment that the members be summoned, and thus unanimously carried. Mr. Cardozo also offered a resolution that the "Committee on general Interests" be empowered to examine the books of the Secretary & Treasurer at the end of every Term, and any Two of that committee when all cannot be procured, also seconded, and carried. Mr. S. W. Beaird then offered a resolution that the arrears of such members whose (probably unavoidable) absence had increased to a heavy amount, be so lightened as to require ^payment^ only to the first of May/54, inclusive the time to ^which^ the regularly attending members had ^last^ paid—and that from that time the Semiannual contributions be ^also^ altogether discontinued, and the monthly contribution only kept up, these were also seconded, and unanimously carried. Mr. H. Cardozo now ~~moved that~~ ^arose and said that^—from a sense of duty, and not simply a compliance with custom—he would move that a copy of the speaker's address just delivered be requested of him for the benefit of the Society, which was seconded, and unanimously carried. All business of importance being now concluded, the Society on motion adjourned.

H. Cardozo Jr., Secretary

Clionian. D. Society, February 4th/56

A regular meeting of this Society was held on the evening of the above date. In the absence of the President and Vice—Mr. B. E. K. Hampton was called to the Chair—the meeting was then called to order, the first roll called, and the proceedings of the last meetings read and approved. Mr. R. L. Deas now arose and moved that in consequence of the lateness of the hour, and other reasons together with the general desire to participate in the interesting question—that it therefore be postponed to the next meeting, which was seconded by S. W. Beaird and carried.

The Society now proceeded to the election of Annual Orator for 1857— which resulted in the unanimous choice of Mr. R. L. Deas—and which ^office^ was accepted by the gentleman—declaring—his inducement to yield to the wishes of his fellow members—as the result of a sincere desire to contribute his best endeavors for the advancement of an Institution he so much loved. Business being concluded, the last roll was called, and the Society on motion adjourned.

H. Cardozo Jr., Secretary

Clionian D. Society, April 7th/56

A regular meeting of this Society was held on the evening of the above date. In the absence of the President and Vice—Mr. E. G. Beaird was called to the Chair—the meeting was then called to order, the first roll called, ^and^ the

pro[ceedings] of the last meeting read and approved. The regular debates were then opened by B. E. K. Hampton one of the appointed, and spiritedly carried on beyond the allotted time—after closing—the President announced his decision in favor of the ~~negative~~ latter portion of the question. The "Committee" then handed [in] their questions from among which the following was adopted—"Is a rude state of Society favorable to Patriotism?" Mr. R. S. Holloway was appointed on the affirmative, and Mr. C. D. Ludeke on the negative of the question. All business being now concluded, the Reporter made his report, the last Roll called. (The Society was notified that the next meeting would be the regular time for the general election of Officers.) The meeting then on motion adjourned.
H. Cardozo Jr., Secretary

Clionian. D. Society, May 5th/56

At this date a regular meeting was held, and organized by E. G. Beaird, filling the chair of the absent President. The first Roll was then called, and the proceedings of the last meeting read and approved. Next in order came the debates— the regular appointees being absent—the floor was opened to the members at large—which opportunity was embraced—and the question received on both sides good ~~and~~ fair and forcible arguments in its elucidation, and support. after their conclusion—the President announced his decision in favor of the affirmative of the question. The Committee then handed in their questions—from among which the following was chosen—"Is increase of Territory injurious to the permanency of a Government."[1] Mr. W. S. Lord was appointed on the affirmative, and Mr. S. J. Maxwell on the negative of the question. The general election of Officers now took place and resulted in the choice of the following gentlemen—(See officers list). Business being now concluded, the Reporter made his report, the last Roll called, and the Society on motion adjourned.
H. Cardozo Jr., Secretary

Clionian. D. Society, June 2nd/56

Another month having elapsed—the members of this Society convened for a regular meeting—which was organised by Mr. E. G. Beaird filling the chair of the absent President, after being called to order, the first Roll was called, and the proceedings of the last meeting read and approved.[2] The regular debates now opened (the appointees being absent from the city) the floor was opened to the members at large—the opportunity was embraced—the question taken up and discussed until the time had expired. The President now arose, and announced his decision in favor of the affirmative of the question.[3] The Installation of Officers now took place—the President "pro-tem" now turned to the cheif [sic]

Officer-elect—and invited him to the Chair—requesting his acceptance of the office to which he had been called by his fellow members—who—from reasons given—expressed his reluctance to accept—but ~~with~~ overcomed [*sic*] by a strong desire to serve the Society—he would yeild to their wishes—and endeavor to fulfil the trust committed to him. The President then installed the subordinate ~~that~~ officers that were present—all of whom signified their acceptance of the positions assigned them. The Committee now handed in their questions—of which—the following was adopted—"Which is more conducive to Individual improvement—Solitude or Society?" Mr. W. E. Marshall was appointed on the former and Mr. B. L. Roberts on the latter portion of the question. The last roll was then called, and the Society on motion adjourned.

H. Cardozo Jr., Sec.

NOTES

1. The Clionians debated a similar question in December 1852.
2. This is the last minuted reference to Enoch G. Beaird, a founding member of the society and brother of Simeon W. Beaird. By 1861 Enoch Beaird was in Washington, DC, employed as a messenger for the Quartermaster's Department of the US Department of War. He lived in the national capital, where he worked as a tailor, until his death in 1903. Beaird bequeathed his financial assets and other property to Sarah E. Washington, a Virginia-born Black woman in whose lodging house Beaird lived for decades. See US Department of the Interior, *Register of Officers and Agents, Civil, Military, and Naval, in the Service of the United States, on the Thirtieth September, 1861* . . . (Washington, DC: GPO, 1862), 108; "District of Columbia, U.S., Wills and Probate Records, 1737–1952," Ancestry.com (online database), 2015, https://www.ancestry.com/search/collections/9083/.
3. This is the last minuted debate and verdict.

— 1857 —

[In this year the society held its last anniversary event, which included its last minuted oration. Secretaries minuted two meetings.—Ed.]

Clionian. D. Society, February ^2nd^ 1857

A regular meeting of this Society was held on the evening of the above date, was called to order by the President; and in the unavoidable absence of the Secretary's books—the Society proceeded to other business—the matter of the Annual celebration (which was unavoidably postponed) was now taken up; a committee was by unanimous motion—appointed to confer with Mr. Rich[ar]d Dereef on the proffered use of his House for the place of celebration;[1] it was then moved and carried that the third Monday in the present ^month^ be the time for that event.

The Society now entered into a discussion concerning the propriety and necessity of a change in the object and purposes of the same—from a <u>debating</u> to a <u>reading</u> association; ~~which was thought would be more suitable~~ and of meeting quarterly, instead of monthly—which was thought would be more favorable to the circumstances of the members—who found it difficult to meet the present requirements: but it was agreed upon by a majority of those present that it should continue as heretofore; with the exception of a motion by Mr. S. W. Beaird that the "legal quorum be reduced from five to three members"—which was thought would ~~be~~ result in more regular meetings—this motion was seconded, and unanimously carried. All business being now concluded; the Society by motion adjourned.
H. Cardozo Jr.

Ninth Anniversary Celebration of Clionian. Debating Society, February 16th 1857

Uncontrollable ~~circums~~ ^causes^ preventing the observance at the usual time; it was accordingly had on the above date, at the residence of Mr. R. E. Dereef, where a respectable audience of the fair and sterner sex assembled—awaiting the exercises—At a few minutes before 5 o clock the Members—with their Honorary Member appeared in the Hall, and commenced the regular exercises with prayer by Honorary Member Jacob Weston; after this it was announced by the Acting President W. O. Weston that the Ninth Annual Oration would now be delivered by R. L. Deas Esq. a Member, who now arose, and after a fitting exordium; proceeded to show the advantages of Intellectual and Moral culture—combined—its tendency to ameliorate the condition; improve the circumstances; and elevate the views of Mankind; illustrating his position with forcible and striking instances adduced from the History of Individuals and Nations; and in such a strain ^the modest speaker^ enchained the attention of his audience for the space of thirty minutes; and then closed with a happy application of the foregoing truths—obtaining ~~during~~ from beginning to end, loud demonstrations of approval and delight at the successfulness of the effort.

The exercises were then closed with the benediction and the audience retired with countenances and expressions that told of the instructiveness as well as pleasantness of the afternoon's entertainment. The members then exchanged their mutual joys and pleasure on the refreshing and encouraging influences of the occasion, and then finally dispersed for their respective homes.

H. Cardozo Jr., Sec.

NOTE

1. Dereef lived on Washington Street, not far from his wood factorage on Dereef's Wharf. See J. H. Bagget, *Directory of the City of Charleston, for the Year 1852* (Charleston, SC: Edward C. Councell, 1851), 33; and Frederick A. Ford, *Census of the City of Charleston, South Carolina, for the Year 1861* (Charleston, SC: Evans and Cogswell, 1861), 215.

— 1858 —

[In this year the society dissolved. A society secretary minuted one meeting. —Ed.]

Clionian. D. Society, Jany 14th/58

A special meeting of this Society was called on the evening of the above date. In the absence of the President and Vice the meeting was called to order by the next table Officer—Secretary H. Cardozo Jr. Upon motion of S. W. Beaird, Esq., Mr. Wm. E. Marshall was unanimously called to the Chair. Mr. Beaird now arose and spoke of the object that called us together—he alluded to the many difficulties and discouragements under which the Society labors, and which has so greatly crippled her efforts, and retarded her progress as to bring its members to the reluctant conclusion that her existence had better be discontinued: he also alluded in feeling terms to the matter of a dissolution—which would cause a severance of ties that had been so pleasant and profitable. After he took his seat other members in succession arose and followed in the same strain of remarks—giving expression to the solemnity and grief that pervaded their minds while considering the impossibility of continuing the existence of our much loved, and highly cherished Institution under present <u>political</u> disadvantages. After a full interchange of opinions and feelings a motion from H. Cardozo Jr. was unanimously adopted that the Society do now discontinue its existence.

Mr. S. W. Beaird then moved that a Committee of five be appointed to consider the best mode of effecting a dissolution—which was unanimously carried, the Chair then appointed Messrs. S. W. Beaird, R. L. Deas, C. D. Ludeke, W. O. Weston, and H. Cardozo Jr. for this purpose, who will make a report at the next meeting of the Society.[1]

All business being now concluded, the Society on motion adjourned.
Hy. Cardozo Jr.

NOTE

1. Simeon W. Beaird (1826–1894), who had been reared in the family of Samuel Weston after his own father died, taught a clandestine school for Black children in Charleston in the 1850s. Beaird moved to Augusta, Georgia, during the Civil War. A schoolteacher, Methodist minister, and Republican political leader, Beaird was elected to Georgia's state constitutional convention in 1867–1868. Returning to South Carolina in the 1870s, Beaird served as county treasurer of Aiken County. He remained committed to education and religion throughout his life. See B. F. Witherspoon, "The Rev. T. [sic] W. Beaird," *Southwestern Christian Advocate*, January 24, 1895, 5; and Angela G. Ray, "Warriors and Statesmen: Debate Education among Free African American Men in Antebellum Charleston," in *Speech and Debate as Civic Education*, ed. J. Michael Hogan, Jessica A. Kurr, Michael J. Bergmaier, and Jeremy D. Johnson (University Park: Pennsylvania State University Press, 2017), 25–28.

Robert L. Deas remained in Charleston until his death of typhoid fever on April 27, 1865, at age thirty; death records listed his occupation as porter. At the time Deas was president of the Friendly Association. In 1860 he had paid tax on $1,600 worth of real estate, and he bequeathed a life interest in a house on Charlotte Street to his mother and the residue of his estate to his wife, Hannah G. Deas. He was interred in the cemetery of the Brown Fellowship Society. See "South Carolina, U.S., Death Records, 1821–1971," Ancestry.com (online database), 2008, https://www.ancestry.com/search/collections/8741/; Friendly Association Records, 1853–1869, South Carolina Historical Society, Charleston, SC; Robert L. Deas, last will and testament, Will Books for Charleston County, 1790–1860, vol. 50 (1862–68), 334, South Carolina Department of Archives and History, Columbia, SC.

Conrad D. Ludeke (1835–1895), who was an active member and sometime officer of the Friendly Association, resigned from that group in June 1860, stating his plan to leave the state and appointing Robert L. Deas to act as his agent to receive the financial allotment due him from the group's treasury. In April 1861 Ludeke, then living in New York City, enlisted in the Union Army. During the war he served in Company B, 82nd Regiment, New York Infantry (1861), Company C, 90th Regiment, New York Infantry (1861–1863), and Company C, 1st Regiment, New Orleans Infantry (1863–1866), attaining the rank of captain and adjutant. He then worked as a clerk for the Metropolitan Police of New Orleans; in 1871 he returned to Charleston. Ludeke was married twice, first to Elizabeth Chloe Sparrow Wrigley Esmond Ludeke (m. 1864, div. 1873) and then to Julia Brennan Ludeke (m. 1874). His and Julia's daughter, Ada L. Ludeke (1877–1932), was a schoolteacher in Charleston. Conrad D. Ludeke died on March 14, 1895. Friendly Association Records, 1853–1869; Conrad D. Ludeke, Pension Application File, Records of the Department of Veterans Affairs, 1773–1985, Record Group 15, National Archives and Records Administration, Washington, DC; Angela G. Ray, "Rhetoric and the Archive," *Review of Communication* 16, no. 1 (2016): 51–56.

William O. Weston (1832–1907), son of Methodist tailor Samuel Weston and Hannah Clark Weston, was a teacher in freedmen's schools in postwar Charleston, along with his wife, Monimia Weston. In the late 1860s he served on Charleston's board of aldermen and was an associate pastor at Centenary Methodist Episcopal Church, where he was remembered as "a clear and strong preacher." See American

Missionary Association Archives, 1839–1882, Amistad Research Center, Tulane University, New Orleans, LA; Centenary Methodist Episcopal Church Records, Avery Research Center for African American History and Culture, College of Charleston, Charleston, SC; Eric Foner, *Freedom's Lawmakers: A Directory of Black Officeholders during Reconstruction,* rev. ed. (Baton Rouge: Louisiana State University Press, 1996), 226; and William H. Lawrence, "A Sketch of the History of the Reorganization of the South Carolina Conference, and of Centenary Church," in *The Centenary Souvenir, Containing a History of Centenary Church, Charleston, and an Account of the Life and Labors of Rev. R. V. Lawrence, Father of the Pastor of Centenary Church* (Charleston, SC, 1885), xvi.

Henry Cardozo (1830–1886) was the eldest son of Lydia Weston, who was enslaved at the time of her birth, and the Jewish merchant Isaac N. Cardozo. Married to Catherine F. McKinney Cardozo, he worked as a tailor in Cleveland, Ohio, from 1858 to 1868. Cardozo was elected to the South Carolina state senate from Kershaw County in 1870 and later presided over the board of Claflin University. He served for many years in the Methodist Episcopal Church and was pastor of Charleston's Old Bethel in the mid-1880s. See *Minutes of the Annual Conferences of the Methodist Episcopal Church: Spring Conferences of 1887* (New York: Phillips and Hunt, 1887), 84; *Claflin University and South Carolina Agricultural College and Mechanics' Institute, Orangeburg, S.C., 1876-77* [Orangeburg, SC, 1877]; and Foner, *Freedom's Lawmakers,* 40. Please note that two individuals in the Clionian minutes are named Henry Cardozo; one joined the society in 1849, the other in 1851.

APPENDIX A
Members, Honorary Members, and Supporters

Alternate spellings of surnames appear in brackets. For members and honorary members, initial dates given are dates of election to membership unless otherwise noted; founding members are indicated by "1847" only. For supporters, dates indicate the first mention. Death dates are provided for individuals whose deaths are noted in the proceedings.

Members

Barrow, Gabriel F., December 8, 1847

Beaird, Enoch G., 1847

Beaird, Simeon W., 1847

Cardozo, Henry J. D., September 25, 1851

Cardozo, Henry, Jr., February 28, 1849

Deas, Robert L., September 27, 1849

Dereef, Joseph Moulton Francis, December 1, 1847

Forrester, Alexander C., June 30, 1851; died May 18, 1853

Gailliard [Gaillard], William H., 1847

Greene [Green], G. C., 1847; resigned February 23, 1848

Greene [Green], Jacob J., Jr., 1847; resigned February 23, 1848

Grimball, John B., Jr., applied January 26, 1852; withdrew application February 23

Hampton, Benjamin E. K., October 4, 1849

Holloway, Richard S., April 15, 1853

Horry, Augustus L., February 28, 1849; resigned December 16, 1852 (see Honorary
Members)

Hyames [Hyams], Isadore A., February 2, 1848; resigned March 1, 1848; reelected
March 5, 1849

Lee, Arthur Bonneau, January 1, 1855

Legare, R. F., February 2, 1848; resigned March 1, 1848

Lindsay, J. F., application for membership rejected July 1, 1852

Lord, W. S., December 13, 1852

Ludeke, Conrad D., July 1, 1852

Marshall, William E., November 23, 1847

Maxwell, Stephen J., 1847

Oliver, F. H., 1847; resigned February 23, 1848

Roberts, Benjamain L., September 16, 1853

Sanders, Robert, September 25, 1851
Stent, Marion L., application for membership rejected July 1, 1852
Weston, Samuel W., 1847; resigned February 23, 1848
Weston, William O., 1847

Honorary Members

Bass, Job G., January 5, 1848
Bland, A. M. (Philadelphia), December 22, 1847
Clark, William B., September 13, 1849
Dereef, Richard E., December 26, 1848
Dick, Thomas, nomination projected, March 22, 1852, April 15, 1853
Frost, Henry, nomination projected, April 15, 1853
Greene [Green], Jacob, Sr., December 22, 1847
Holloway, Charles H., March 15, 1848
Horry, Augustus L. (Philadelphia), December 30, 1852 (see Members)
Huger, Benjamin T., December 22, 1847; died May 5, 1852
Johnson, J., January 5, 1848
Long, Florian H., December 22, 1847
McKinlay, William, December 19, 1848
McKinney, William, nomination projected, April 15, 1853
Mishaw, John, December 22, 1847; died 1852
Parker, John S., December 22, 1847
Payne, Daniel A. (Baltimore), December 22, 1847
Seymour, William W., December 22, 1847
Weston, Jacob, December 22, 1847
Weston, Samuel, December 22, 1847

Supporters

Bonneau, Frances Pinckney, March 10, 1851
Farbeaux, Emma K., September 13, 1849
Farbeaux, Jacob, December 26, 1849
Mood, Francis Asbury, December 15, 1847
Mood, John Amos, December 15, 1847
Mood, William, December 15, 1847

APPENDIX B
Debating Questions and Decisions

Dates given are dates that debates occurred; questions were selected earlier. Some questions include minor alterations of punctuation to ensure clarity. The minutes are ambiguous about whether decisions were rendered based on the judge's opinion of the merits of the question or the quality of the debaters' performance, but evidence of debaters' comparative success suggests that decisions were likely based at least in part on proficiency.

1847
November 16: [Question unstated], Affirmative
November 23: Whether the present War with Mexico, will be of any advantage to the United States of America, Negative
December 1: Whether the (United States) was right in declaring her Independence, Negative
December 8, 22: Which is the most desirable, Literary or Military glory? Literary

1848
January 5: Whether a Republican or Monarchial government tends most to the happiness of a people, Republican
January 12: Which is the happier, civilized or savage life? Civilized
January 19: Which excelled the more in literary pursuits, the Moderns or Ancients? Moderns
January 26: Whether the liberty of the press should be restrained or not, Negative
February 2: Which is the most useful, literary or romance reading? Literary
February 9: Whether the application of steam to machinery has been of any disadvantage to mankind or not, Advantage
February 23: Which was the greatest and most virtuous general, Washington or Alexander? Washington
March 1: Which was the most skilful general, Hannibal or Napoleon? Napoleon
March 22: Which is of the most service to man, those machines that ply upon the water or land? Water
April 5, June 7: Was it ambition that led Napoleon to battle or not? Affirmative
September 18: Which nation fought on the most just side, the United [States] or Mexico? United States

141

142 *Appendix B*

December 26: Will the acquisition of California be of any great use to the U.S.?
Affirmative

1849

February 7, March 14: Which country presents the brightest prospects for future happiness and permanency, the U.S. or Great Britain? U.S.

March 21: Was England right in banishing Napoleon Bonaparte to the Island of St. Helena? Affirmative

March 28: Are there any benefits derived from riches? Affirmative

April 4: Is the Republic of France likely to remain permanent? Negative

April 11: Has the Pope's banishment been or is likely to be of any advantage to Rome? Negative

May 21: Was Brutus right or wrong in condemning his sons to execution, when tried before him for conspiring against the government? Right

June 6: Which will a man hear first, the prayer of his wife or mother? Wife

June 20: Were the Athenians right in condemning Socrates to death? Negative

June 27, July 5: Which tends most to the diminution of murders, "capital" punishment or "life-time" imprisonment? Capital punishment

July 10, 12: Which tends most to the ruin of the human race, Dishonesty or Intemperance? Dishonesty

August 1: Which the more useful, Telegraphic or Steam power? Telegraphic

August 8: Was the treatment of the English to the Irish tyrannical? Affirmative

August 22: Which the better, a Mechanical or Professional pursuit? Professional

August 29: Were the French right in interfering with the late affairs at Rome? Negative

September 6, 13: Which the greater protection against a foreign foe, a nation's Military or Naval force? Naval

September 27: Which the greater incentive to exertion, punishment or rewards? Rewards

October 4, November 5: Which the more interesting, Ancient or Modern history? Ancient

1850

January 7: Is war the proper means for the gratification of national revenge? Affirmative

February 4: Which tends most to a nation's benefit, its agricultural or commercial advantages? Agricultural

March 4: Who was the most patriotic, Demosthenes or Socrates? Socrates

April 3: Whether a man condemned to die, though unjustly, can without a crime escape from justice & the laws, Negative

April 10: By whom has the most good been effected, Martin Luther or George Washington? Luther

April 17: Which [is] the more conducive to moral purity, a Country or City life? Country

May 1, 22: Who deserves the greater meed of praise, the Inventor or Improver of a project? Inventor

May 29, June 12: Was Caesar right, in usurping the government of the Roman Empire? Affirmative

Appendix B **143**

June 19, July 1: Whose learned men have contributed most to the advancement of civilization, those of the Greeks or Romans? Greeks

July 24: Was Themistocles right in committing suicide rather than assist an enemy of his country? Negative

July 31: Who accomplished the greatest good for his country, Demosthenes or Cicero? Demosthenes

September 4: Which was calculated to shed the brightest lustre and influence on Grecian manners and character, the laws of Solon or Lycurgus? Solon

September 11: Was Cromwell right in usurping the reins of Government in England? Negative

September 18: Are afflictions in any manner beneficial to humanity? Affirmative

October 2: Who has the greatest chance to show forth his patriotism in time of war, the statesman in the hall of power, or the soldier on the field of battle? Soldier

October 14: Was Caesar right in crossing the Rubicon or not? Negative

November 4: Was the conduct of the Roman General Regulus commendable or condemnable? Commendable

1851

January 6: Is education beneficial to society? Affirmative

February 3: Which had the greatest influence on Grecian character, their Poetry or Philosophy? Philosophy

March 31: Were the allied nations of Europe justifiable in banishing Napoleon? Negative

June 9: Have the late Revolutions of Europe tended much to benefit the condition of the people of that Continent? Affirmative

June 23: Will the World's Fair bring about the contemplated union of intercourse among the nations of the earth? Affirmative

July 14: Which is the most responsible for an article, the Composer or the Publisher? Publisher

August 11, 25: Which exercises the greatest beneficial influence upon society, Intellectual or Moral excellence? Moral

September 8: Has the Intellect been *beneficial* or *deleterious* to man's Happiness? Beneficial

September 22: Which is the most Advantageous, desirable, and Beneficial—a Married or Single Life? Married

October 13: Was the conduct of Gen. Lopez commendable or condemnable? Commendable

October 27: Whether forms of Government exert any important influence on the growth and character of National Literature, Affirmative

December 8, 29: Whether success[es] in difficult Sciences are the results of Genius, or Industry and Perseverance, Genius

1852

January 26: Which is the most conducive to Man's Happiness, Mechanical or Agricultural employments? Agricultural

February 23: Would the United States be Justifiable in interfering with the present struggles of Europe? Negative

144 *Appendix B*

April 12: Are we to infer from the teachings of History that the *Sword* has been more *destructive,* than *beneficial* to the happiness of Mankind? Destructive

April 26: Emigration; does it tend, or has it ever tended to the advancement of civilization? Negative

June 14: Which were the best disciplinarians of Youths—the Athenians, or Spartans? Athenians

June 28: Who was the Greatest and most virtuous General, Caesar or Pompey? Pompey

October 25: Did Wellington in the battle of Waterloo prove himself a greater General than Napoleon Bonaparte? Affirmative

November 8: Which is more likely to injure the prosperity of a Country, Foreign Broils or Intestine Commotions? Intestine Commotions

December 13: Would the increase of Territory prove an advantage to the United States? Negative

1853

January 12: Was Charlemagne a great man? Negative

February 23: Are the late improvements of decided advantage to Mankind? Affirmative

March 9: Does the distance of a Country's dominions weaken the force of its Laws therein? Affirmative

April 14: Does the prosperity and progress of a nation depend more upon the observance of its laws by its subjects, or the strict execution of the same by those empowered? Observance of the Laws

May 11: Is Louis Napoleon an usurper or not? Negative

June 8, 22: Is it right to remove the Indians from Florida? Negative

July 6: Was Lafayette right in assisting the colonies in their revolt against the mother country? Affirmative

August 3: Is the Maine liquor law conducive to the happiness of American citizens, and in accordance with her free institutions? Affirmative

September 14: Did the games and oracles of the ancient Greeks produce many salutary effects upon their national character? Negative

September 28, October 12: Was Caesar a great man? Negative

December 21: Is a rude state of Society favourable to patriotism? Affirmative

1854

February 1: Is a nation strictly justifiable in compelling another nation by force of arms to open her port for trade? Negative

March 14: Which is more condemnable at the bar of Public Opinion, Slander or Flattery? Flattery

March 28: Is [sic] France & England right in interfering in the present struggle between Russia & Turkey? Negative

April 25: Was England right in banishing Obrien, Meagher & their coadjutors? Negative

May 11: Have the various fairs that have been held tended to excite among the people a spirit of industry and improvement? Affirmative

December 6: Is absolute religious toleration conducive to the stability of a government & the moral excellence of a people? Affirmative

1855

July 9: Would it have been criminal in Socrates to have attempted to escape prison upon the suggestion of his friend Crito? Affirmative

July 23: Is the occurrence of *great events* indicative of a progressive spirit? Affirmative

1856

April 7: Do the consequences of *Success* tend to Good or Evil? Evil

May 5: Is a rude state of Society favorable to Patriotism? Affirmative

June 2: Is increase of Territory injurious to the permanency of a Government? Affirmative

Question selected on June 2 but never debated: Which is more conducive to Individual improvement—Solitude or Society?

APPENDIX C
Orations

Dates of delivery are listed; the society elected orators in advance. Many titles are generated from descriptive text.

Annual
January 1, 1849: Job G. Bass, topic unstated
January 1, 1850: Enoch G. Beaird, "An Energetic and Persevering Mind"
January 1, 1851: William H. Gailliard, "Knowledge"
January 1, 1852: Simeon W. Beaird, "The Influence of *Principle* and *Action* on the Future Destiny of Man"
January 10, 1853: William O. Weston, "Influence"
January 2, 1854: Henry Cardozo Jr., "Rewards and Results of a Well-Directed Ambition"
January 1, 1855: Benjamain L. Roberts, "The Phases of Education"
January 7, 1856: Richard S. Holloway, "The Advantages Accruing from a Cultivated Mind"
February 16, 1857: Robert L. Deas, "The Advantages of Intellectual and Moral Culture"

Quarterly, Regular, and Semiannual
February 16, 1848: Samuel W. Weston, topic unstated
December 26, 1848: Enoch G. Beaird, "The Advantages Derived from Good and Careful Reading"
May 30, 1849: William H. Gailliard, "Neglected Genius"
August 15, 1849: William O. Weston, "Education"
December 26, 1849: Simeon W. Beaird, "Industry, Perseverance, and Patience"
March 27, 1850: Henry Cardozo Jr., "The True Happiness of Man"
August 14, 1850: Augustus L. Horry, "Perseverance"
April 14, 1851: Stephen J. Maxwell, "Education"
October 11, 1852: Henry J. D. Cardozo, "Paramount Importance of *Timely Mental Culture*"
April 27, 1853: William E. Marshall, "Nature, the Fall of Man, Intemperance"
December 7, 1853: Robert L. Deas, "Ambition"
July 26, 1854: Joseph Moulton Francis Dereef, "The Advantages of Reading Standard Works"

APPENDIX D
Publications Acquired for Society Library

Dates indicate minuted references to acquisitions of print publications. Books and pamphlets are listed as described in the minutes; where possible, a plausible citation follows.

1849
January 1: Bible, donated by honorary member Job G. Bass.

October 8: "Two volumes of Macaulay's history of England," donated by supporter Francis Asbury Mood. Thomas Babington Macaulay, *The History of England from the Accession of James the Second,* Vols. 1–2 (London: Longman, Brown, Green, and Longmans, 1849); Macaulay would publish a total of five volumes by 1861.

December 26: "Webster's unabridged Dictionary," donated by supporter Jacob Farbeaux. Several Webster's dictionaries were in circulation; the Clionians may have received *Webster's Dictionary, Unabridged, in One Volume* (Springfield, MA: G. and C. Merriam, 1846).

December 26: "Scenes in Spain," donated by honorary member Job G. Bass. *Scenes in Spain* (New York: George Dearborn, 1837).

December 26: "Paulding Works," donated by honorary member Job G. Bass. A volume of James Kirke Paulding, *Paulding's Works,* 15 vols. (New York: Harper, 1835–1839).

December 26: "Sketches of the Seminole War," donated by honorary member Job G. Bass. Lieutenant of the Left Wing [William Wragg Smith?], *Sketch of the Seminole War and Sketches during a Campaign* (Charleston, SC: Dan J. Dowling, 1836).

December 26: "2 Vols Carlyle French Revolution," donated by honorary member Job G. Bass. Possibly volumes of Thomas Carlyle, *The French Revolution: A History,* 3 vols. (London: Chapman and Hall, 1837); or the "three volumes in two" published in Boston in 1838 by Charles C. Little and James Brown.

December 26: "Grimshaw's France," donated by honorary member Job G. Bass. Possibly an edition of William Grimshaw's *History of France, from the Foundation of the Monarchy, by Clovis, to the Final Abdication of Napoleon,* first published in 1828.

1850
January 7: "2 Volumes of Rollins Ancient history," purchased with money donated by supporter Emma K. Farbeaux. Charles Rollin's eighteenth-century French text was translated in English-language multivolume editions as *The Ancient History*

150 *Appendix D*

of the Egyptians, Carthaginians, Assyrians, Babylonians, Medes and Persians, Macedonians, and Grecians.

April 10: "Three pamphlets of good speeches & valuable letters," donated by member William O. Weston.

April 10: "Five political speeches recently delivered in the Senate and now published," planned society purchase.

April 17: "An address of Professor F. W. Capers before the Citadel Cadets," donated by member Robert L. Deas. F[rancis] W[ithers] Capers, *State Military Academies: An Address Delivered before the Calliopean Society of the Citadel Academy, Charleston* (Charleston, SC: Tenhet and Corley, 1846).

May 1: "Professor B[r]umby's address on geology," donated by member William H. Gailliard. R[ichard] T[rapier] Brumby, *An Address on the Sphere, Interest and Importance of Geology, Delivered December 8, 1749 [sic], in the Hall of the House of Representatives* (Columbia, SC: A. S. Johnston, 1849).

May 22: "Mr. N. Mitchell's address before the 4th of July Association," donated by member Robert L. Deas. Nelson Mitchell, *Oration Delivered before the Fourth of July Association, on the Fourth of July, 1848* (Charleston, SC: J. S. Burges, 1849).

July 31: "Certain valuable books," planned society purchase; August 14: "the valuable works," society purchase.

August 14: "Three very valuable books written by distinguished Authoresses," donated by supporter Emma K. Farbeaux.

December 2: "Hawks Egypt," society purchase. Francis L. Hawks, *The Monuments of Egypt; or, Egypt a Witness for the Bible* (New York: G. P. Putnam, 1850).

December 2: "Noble deeds of Women," society purchase. An edition of Elizabeth Starling's *Noble Deeds of Woman*, first published in London in 1835.

December 2: "Franklin's Life," society purchase. An edition of the autobiography of Benjamin Franklin.

1851

March 10: "Moore's Poetical Works," donated by supporter Frances Pinckney Bonneau. An edition of *The Poetical Works* of the Irish poet Thomas Moore.

March 31: "Two very valuable pamphlets," donated by member Robert L. Deas.

August 11: "An address from the Hon. W. D. Porter," donated by member Robert L. Deas. W[illiam] D[ennison] Porter, *Self-Cultivation: An Address, Delivered before the Society of the Alumni of the College of Charleston at Their Anniversary, February 25th 1851* (Charleston, SC: E. C. Councell, 1851).

August 11: "A sermon from the Rev. Mr. Miles," donated by member Robert L. Deas. Possibly James Warley Miles, *Farewell Sermon, Preached by the Rev. James W. Miles, (Missionary of the Prot. Epis. Church in Mesopotamia,) in St. Michael's Church, Charleston, on the Evening of August 20th, 1843* (Charleston, SC: B. B. Hussey, 1843).

September 25: "Several valuable works," donated by member Augustus L. Horry.

December 8: "'The Book of the World,' in two volumes," society purchase. Richard S[wainson] Fisher, *The Book of the World, Being an Account of All Republics, Empires, Kingdoms, and Nations, in Reference to Their Geography, Statistics, Commerce, &c., Together with a Brief Historical Outline of Their Rise, Progress and Present Condition, &c., &c., &c., with an Index to All the Countries, Cities,*

Appendix D 151

Towns, Islands, Oceans, Seas, Lakes, Rivers, &c., Mentioned on Colton's Illustrated Map of the World, 2 vols. (New York: J. H. Colton, 1849; 2nd ed., 1850–1851). December 22: "Several valuable works," society purchase.

1854

May 11: "A Book . . . purporting to be information in reference to Rio De Jenario," donated by honorary member Augustus L. Horry.

December 6: "Bachman's Unity of the Human race," donated by member Henry Cardozo Jr. John Bachman, *The Doctrine of the Unity of the Human Race Examined on the Principles of Science* (Charleston, SC: C. Canning, 1850).

1855

June 18: "Josephus works," donated by honorary member Richard E. Dereef. An edition of the works of the first-century Jewish historian Flavius Josephus.

FURTHER READING

Selected scholarly resources for the study of free Black Charlestonians and cultures of popular learning in the nineteenth-century United States

Free Blacks in Pre-Civil War Charleston

Birnie, C. W. "Education of the Negro in Charleston, South Carolina, Prior to the Civil War." *Journal of Negro History* 12, no. 1 (January 1927): 13–21.

Browning, James B. "The Beginnings of Insurance Enterprise among Negroes." *Journal of Negro History* 22, no. 4 (October 1937): 417–32.

Curry, Leonard P. *The Free Black in Urban America, 1800–1850: The Shadow of the Dream*. Chicago: University of Chicago Press, 1981.

Curry, Leonard P. "Free Blacks in the Urban South: 1800–1850." *Southern Quarterly* 43, no. 2 (Winter 2006): 35–51.

Drago, Edmund L. *Charleston's Avery Center: From Education and Civil Rights to Preserving the African American Experience*. Rev. ed. Revised and edited by W. Marvin Dulaney. Charleston, SC: History Press, 2006.

Fielder, Brigitte. *Relative Races: Genealogies of Interracial Kinship in Nineteenth-Century America*. Durham, NC: Duke University Press, 2020.

Fitchett, E. Horace. "The Free Negro in Charleston, South Carolina." PhD diss., University of Chicago, 1950.

Foner, Eric. *Freedom's Lawmakers: A Directory of Black Officeholders during Reconstruction*. Rev. ed. Baton Rouge: Louisiana State University Press, 1996.

Gatewood, Willard B., Jr. "'The Remarkable Misses Rollin': Black Women in Reconstruction South Carolina." *South Carolina Historical Magazine* 92, no. 3 (July 1991): 172–88.

Greene, Harlan, and Jessica Lancia. "The Holloway Scrapbook: The Legacy of a Charleston Family." *South Carolina Historical Magazine* 111, no. 1–2 (January–April 2010): 5–33.

Greenidge, Kerri K. *The Grimkés: The Legacy of Slavery in an American Family*. New York: Norton/Liveright, 2022.

Harris, Robert L., Jr. "Charleston's Free Afro-American Elite: The Brown Fellowship Society and the Humane Brotherhood." *South Carolina Historical Magazine* 82, no. 4 (October 1981): 289–310.

Hine, Darlene Clark, and Earnestine Jenkins, eds. *A Question of Manhood: A Reader in U.S. Black Men's History and Masculinity*. Vol. 1, *"Manhood Rights": The*

154 *Further Reading*

Construction of Black Male History and Manhood, 1750–1870. Bloomington: Indiana University Press, 1999.

Hine, William C. "Black Politicians in Reconstruction Charleston, South Carolina: A Collective Study." *Journal of Southern History* 49, no. 4 (November 1983): 555–84.

Jenkins, Wilbert L. *Seizing the New Day: African Americans in Post–Civil War Charleston*. Bloomington: Indiana University Press, 1998.

Johnson, Michael P., and James L. Roark. *Black Masters: A Free Family of Color in the Old South*. New York: Norton, 1984.

Johnson, Michael P., and James L. Roark. "'A Middle Ground': Free Mulattoes and the Friendly Moralist Society of Antebellum Charleston." *Southern Studies* 21, no. 3 (1982): 246–65.

Johnson, Michael P., and James L. Roark, eds. *No Chariot Let Down: Charleston's Free People of Color on the Eve of the Civil War*. Chapel Hill: University of North Carolina Press, 1984.

Kinghan, Neil. *A Brief Moment in the Sun: Francis Cardozo and Reconstruction in South Carolina*. Baton Rouge: Louisiana State University Press, 2023.

Koger, Larry. *Black Slaveowners: Free Black Slave Masters in South Carolina, 1790–1860*. Jefferson, NC: McFarland, 1985.

Krebsbach, Suzanne. "Black Catholics in Antebellum Charleston." *South Carolina Historical Magazine* 108, no. 2 (April 2007): 143–59.

Marks, John Garrison. *Black Freedom in the Age of Slavery: Race, Status, and Identity in the Urban Americas*. Columbia: University of South Carolina Press, 2020.

Milteer, Warren Eugene, Jr. *Beyond Slavery's Shadow: Free People of Color in the South*. Chapel Hill: University of North Carolina Press, 2021.

Myers, Amrita Chakrabarti. *Forging Freedom: Black Women and the Pursuit of Liberty in Antebellum Charleston*. Chapel Hill: University of North Carolina Press, 2011.

Powers, Bernard E., Jr. *Black Charlestonians: A Social History, 1822–1885*. Fayetteville: University of Arkansas Press, 1994.

Thomas, Rhondda Robinson, and Susanna Ashton, eds. *The South Carolina Roots of African American Thought: A Reader*. Columbia: University of South Carolina Press, 2014.

Welch, Kimberly M. *Black Litigants in the Antebellum American South*. Chapel Hill: University of North Carolina Press, 2018.

Wikramanayake, Marina. *A World in Shadow: The Free Black in Antebellum South Carolina*. Columbia: University of South Carolina Press, 1973.

Williams, Heather Andrea. *Self-Taught: African American Education in Slavery and Freedom*. Chapel Hill: University of North Carolina Press, 2005.

US Cultures of Nineteenth-Century Popular Learning

Augst, Thomas, and Kenneth Carpenter, eds. *Institutions of Reading: The Social Life of Libraries in the United States*. Amherst: University of Massachusetts Press, 2007.

Brown, Richard D. *Knowledge Is Power: The Diffusion of Information in Early America, 1700–1865*. New York: Oxford University Press, 1989.

Cobb, Jasmine Nichole. *Picture Freedom: Remaking Black Visuality in the Early Nineteenth Century*. New York: New York University Press, 2015.

Further Reading

Favors, Jelani M. *Shelter in a Time of Storm: How Black Colleges Fostered Generations of Leadership and Activism.* Chapel Hill: University of North Carolina Press, 2019.

Foster, Frances Smith. "A Narrative of the Interesting Origins and (Somewhat) Surprising Developments of African-American Print Culture." *American Literary History* 17, no. 4 (Winter 2005): 714–40.

Hairston, Eric Ashley. *The Ebony Column: Classics, Civilization, and the African American Reclamation of the West.* Knoxville: University of Tennessee Press, 2013.

Harding, Thomas S. *College Literary Societies: Their Contribution to Higher Education in the United States, 1815–1876.* New York: Pageant, 1971.

Kelley, Mary. *Learning to Stand and Speak: Women, Education, and Public Life in America's Republic.* Chapel Hill: University of North Carolina Press, 2006.

Kett, Joseph F. *The Pursuit of Knowledge under Difficulties: From Self-Improvement to Adult Education in America, 1750–1990.* Stanford, CA: Stanford University Press, 1994.

Lapsansky, Emma Jones. "'Discipline to the Mind': Philadelphia's Banneker Institute, 1854–1872." In *A Question of Manhood: A Reader in U.S. Black Men's History and Masculinity,* edited by Darlene Clark Hine and Earnestine Jenkins, vol. 1, 399–414. Bloomington: Indiana University Press, 1999.

Logan, Shirley Wilson. *Liberating Language: Sites of Rhetorical Education in Nineteenth-Century Black America.* Carbondale: Southern Illinois University Press, 2008.

Malamud, Margaret. *African Americans and the Classics: Antiquity, Abolition and Activism.* London: I. B. Tauris, 2016.

McHenry, Elizabeth. *Forgotten Readers: Recovering the Lost History of African American Literary Societies.* Durham, NC: Duke University Press, 2002.

McHenry, Elizabeth. "Rereading Literary Legacy: New Considerations of the 19th-Century African-American Reader and Writer." *Callaloo* 22, no. 2 (Spring 1999): 477–82.

O'Brien, Michael. *Conjectures of Order: Intellectual Life and the American South.* 2 vols. Chapel Hill: University of North Carolina Press, 2004.

Porter, Dorothy B., ed. *Early Negro Writing, 1760–1837.* Boston: Beacon, 1971.

Porter, Dorothy B. "The Organized Educational Activities of Negro Literary Societies, 1828–1846." *Journal of Negro Education* 5, no. 4 (October 1936): 555–76.

Potter, David. "The Literary Society." In *History of Speech Education in America: Background Studies,* edited by Karl R. Wallace, 238–58. New York: Appleton-Century-Crofts, 1954.

Ray, Angela G. *The Lyceum and Public Culture in the Nineteenth-Century United States.* East Lansing: Michigan State University Press, 2005.

Ray, Angela G., and Paul Stob, eds. *Thinking Together: Lecturing, Learning, and Difference in the Long Nineteenth Century.* University Park: Pennsylvania State University Press, 2018.

Woods, Carly S. *Debating Women: Gender, Education, and Spaces for Argument, 1835–1945.* East Lansing: Michigan State University Press, 2018.

Wright, Tom F., ed. *The Cosmopolitan Lyceum: Lecture Culture and the Globe in Nineteenth-Century America.* Amherst: University of Massachusetts Press, 2013.

Wright, Tom F. *Lecturing the Atlantic: Speech, Print, and an Anglo-American Commons, 1830–1870.* Oxford: Oxford University Press, 2017.

Zboray, Ronald J., and Mary Saracino Zboray. *Everyday Ideas: Socioliterary Experience among Antebellum New Englanders*. Knoxville: University of Tennessee Press, 2006.

Zboray, Ronald J., and Mary Saracino Zboray, eds. *US Popular Print Culture to 1860*. Vol. 5 of *The Oxford History of Popular Print Culture*, edited by Gary Kelly. Oxford: Oxford University Press, 2019.

INDEX

Page numbers in italic refer to illustrations.

action, in annual oration, 85
afflictions, debate question about, xi, 59–60, 61
African Methodist Episcopal Church, xvii, 9n15
agricultural employment, debate question about, 83, 86
agriculture, debate question about, 47, 48
Alexander the Great, debate question about, 14, 23n8
ambition: in annual oration, xxv, 116; debate question about, xxii, 16, 17, 18; in semiannual oration, 112
American Antiquarian Society, xxxviin70
The American Debater (McElligott), xxi
American Whig Society (College of New Jersey), xvi
ancient history, debate question about, xxii, 40
The Ancient History of the Egyptians . . . (Rollin), 47, 63n1
ancient literature, debate question about, 10–11
anniversary celebrations: at the 1848–1849 meetings, 21, 22, 24, 39, 43; at the 1850–1852 meetings, 46–47, 66, 85; at the 1853–1854 meetings, 99–100, 116–17; at the 1855–1857 meetings, 125, 129, 133–34
annual orations, deliveries: at the 1849 meetings, 24, 44n9; at the 1850–1853 meetings, 46, 66, 67, 85, 99–100; at the 1854–1857 meetings, 116, 125, 129, 134
annual orations, overview, xxiv–xxv, 147

annual orator, deferrals and declines, 20, 32, 68, 95, 118
annual orator, elections: at the 1848–1849 meetings, 18, 21, 29, 32, 41, 44n9; at the 1850–1853 meetings, 48, 68, 86, 100; at the 1854 meetings, 117, 118, 119, 120, 121, 122; at the 1855–1857 meetings, 126, 129, 130, 133–34
archive creation, xxvii–xxviii
armed force, debate question about, 113, 117
arrears list, discussion, 20
Athenians, debate question about, 89

Bachman, John, xxvi–xxvii, xxx, 122, 124n5
banishment, debate questions about: at the 1849 meetings, 30, 31, 44n7; at the 1854 meetings, 118, 123n3
Barreau, J. E., 114n18
Barrow, Gabriel F.: debate question proposal, 20; diploma proposal, 56; donations, 6, 12; in Friendly Association, 114n18; meeting date proposal, 17; membership admission, 5; membership expulsion motion, 19–20; in membership list, 9n13; motion seconds by, 19, 25, 32–33, 43; office positions, 12, 61; request for debate presentation, 20
Barrow, Gabriel F. (committee appointments): at the 1848–1849 meetings, 16, 19, 26, 31, 43; at the 1850 meetings, 47, 58
Barrow, Gabriel F. (debater appointments): at the 1848 meetings, 11, 14,

157

16, 20; at the 1849 meetings, 30, 31, 37, 42; at the 1850 meetings, 51, 57, 62; at the 1851–1854 meetings, 74, 94, 109, 119

Bass, Ellen, 64n11

Bass, Job G.: at anniversary celebration, 24, 46; as annual orator, xxiv, 21, 24, 25; biographical highlights, 44n3, 64n11, 127n5; donations, xxvi, 25, 43, 48; honorary membership admission, 10, 13; letter with oration copy, 53, 54, 58

Battle of Waterloo, 83n2, 90, 97n3

Beaird, Enoch G.: as annual orator, xxiv, 32, 46; death, 132n2; donor's gift presentation, 68; in founding members list, 8n2; honorary members proposal, 8; meeting date proposal, 17; membership discussions, 86; in membership list, 9n13; motion seconds by, 31, 34, 37, 39, 40, 41, 71; praise for departing members, 15–16; as quarterly orator, xxiv, 14; in Washington, DC, 132n2

Beaird, Enoch G. (committee appointments): at the 1849 meetings, 31, 39, 40, 43; at the 1850–1851 meetings, 47, 68, 83; at the 1852 meetings, 88, 92, 94, 96; at the 1853–1854 meetings, 102, 105, 109, 123

Beaird, Enoch G. (debater appointments): win pattern, xxi; at the 1847–1848 meetings, 5, 11, 14, 16; at the 1849 meetings, 29, 31, 33, 37, 40; at the 1850–1851 meetings, 57, 62, 72, 83; at the 1852–1854 meetings, 94, 109, 119

Beaird, Enoch G. (office positions): at the 1847–1848 meetings, 3, 12, 16, 19, 23n15, n20, 33; at the 1850–1852 meetings, 49, 72, 83, 87, 94; at the 1853–1854 meetings, 101, 113, 117, 122–23; at the 1855–1856 meetings, 126, 130–31

Beaird, Simeon W.: after dissolution of society, xiii, 136n; as annual orator, xxiv, 68, 69, 85; biographical highlights, xviii, xxxi, xxxvn27, 136n; dissolution speech, 135; donor's gift

presentations, 43, 58, 78; eulogy for member, 106–7; in founding members list, 8n2; letter from Payne, 54; library purchase presentations, 58, 63, 82–83; membership discussions, 19–20, 28, 39, 96; in membership list, 9n13; minutes dispute, 49; office positions, 8n1, 16, 19, 56, 64n13, 65n19, 71, 91, 93, 106; as quarterly orator, xxiv, 32, 43; request for debate presentation, xxvii, 20; resignation from office, 23n15; thank you recipient, xi, 57, 60–61

Beaird, Simeon W. (committee appointments): at the 1848–1849 meetings, 19, 26, 31, 39–40, 41, 43; at the 1850 meetings, 47, 51, 54, 63; at the 1851 meetings, 68, 74, 78; at the 1852 meetings, 88, 94, 96; at the 1853 meetings, 102, 105, 109, 112; at the 1854–1858 meetings, 123, 135

Beaird, Simeon W. (debater appointments): at the 1849 meetings, 20, 29, 30, 33, 36, 40; at the 1851–1852 meetings, 72, 83, 93; at the 1853–1854 meetings, 108, 119

Beaird, Simeon W. (motions about constitution): at the 1849 meetings, 28; at the 1851 meetings, 69, 73, 78, 79–80, 81; at the 1852 meetings, 87, 94; at the 1853–1854 meetings, 104–5, 110, 120

Beaird, Simeon W. (motions/proposals): bylaws alteration, 71–72; committee formations, 26, 31, 39, 41, 47, 135; debate deferrals, 71, 80–81, 82, 87, 121; dissolution procedures, 135; finances, 21, 25, 130; honorary members, 39, 96; honoring deceased members, 89–90, 106–7; invitations, 21, 43, 63, 83; library development, 21, 25, 26, 28, 36, 37; meeting dates, 20, 34, 40, 50, 71, 96–97, 104, 120, 121–22; office positions, 49, 68, 91, 121, 135; oration copy requests, xxvii, 22, 25, 32–33, 37, 105, 117; oration delivery dates, 55, 79; quorum numbers, 133; seconds by, 35, 51, 53, 54, 56, 70, 104, 105, 129, 130; semiannual orator election, 88; thank

Index

159

you actions, 39, 41, 43, 47, 52, 68, 70, 81, 122; withdrawal of membership application, 86

benefits for humanity, debate question about, 59–60, 61

benefits from riches, debate question about, 29, 30

Bible donation, xxvi, 25, 44n2

Bingham, Caleb, xviii

Bland, A. M., 8

Blücher, Gebhard Leberecht von, 83n2

Bonaparte, Louis-Napoléon, 44n6, n12, 104, 113n7

Bonaparte, Napoleon. *See* Napoleon, debate questions about

Bonneau, Frances Pinckney (later Holloway), xviii, xxvi, 68, 70, 84n3

Bonneau, Thomas S., xviii, 84n3

Book Committee, 8. *See also* library collection

The Book of the World (Fisher), xxvi, 82

Boyd, William Kenneth, xii

brackets, meaning in text, xli–xlii

break-bone fever, 65n17

"breathe but burn" phrase, 109, 114n15

Brown Fellowship Society: cemetery, 97n2, n7, 114n10, 136n; invitation to, 43; mayoral query, xxxviiin50; members, 9n15, 127n4; recordkeeping, xxvii

Brumby, Richard Trapier, xxvi, 53, 64n8

Brutus, Lucius Junius (debate question about), 31, 44n8

bylaws: at the 1847–1849 meetings, 6, 14, 15, 40, 41; at the 1851 meetings: 71–72, 81

Cadet Riflemen Band, 43

Caesar, Julius (debate questions about): as persistent topic, xxii; at the 1850 meetings, 53, 61, 64n9, 65n21; at the 1852–1853 meetings, 89, 97n1, 110

Calhoun, John C., 64n7

California acquisition, debate question about, xxii, 20, 22, 23n17

Calliopean Society, 64n6

candles donation, 12

Capers, Francis Withers, xxvi, 52, 64n6, 114n15

capital punishment question, 33, 34, 44n11

Cardozo, Catherine F. McKinney, 137n

Cardozo, Henry J. D.: committee appointment, 112; debater appointments, 86, 94, 109, 122, 126; identification, xxxivn24; membership admission, 75, 78; as semiannual orator, 89, 92

Cardozo, Henry, Jr.: at anniversary celebration, 125; as annual orator, xxiv–xxv, 67, 100, 116, 117; biographical highlights, xviii, xxxi, 137n; donation, xxvi, 122; identification, xxxivn24; membership admission, 26; office positions, xii, 42, 103, 119, 121, 126, 127; photograph of, *27;* as quarterly orator, xxiv, 42, 50–51; thank you recipient, 103

Cardozo, Henry, Jr. (committee appointments): at the 1849 meetings, 31, 39–40, 41; at the 1850 meetings, 49, 50, 51, 56; at the 1851 meetings, 68, 74, 78; at the 1852–1853 meetings, 88, 96, 112; at the 1854–1858 meetings, 123, 135

Cardozo, Henry, Jr. (debater appointments): at the 1849 meetings, 29, 33, 38, 42; at the 1850 meetings, 52, 59, 63; at the 1851–1854 meetings, 74, 86, 94, 119

Cardozo, Henry, Jr. (motions/proposals): debate deferrals, 53, 55, 100; dissolution of society, 135; finances, 130; meeting dates, 34, 35, 61–62, 101, 129; membership application procedure, 72, 79; oration copy requests, 67, 86, 100, 130; oration delivery procedures, 51, 55, 58, 59, 88, 121, 122; reading of Bass and Payne letters, 58; seconds by, 52, 112, 121; unfinished business, 95

Cardozo, Isaac N., 137n

Cardozo, Lydia Weston, 137n

carets, meaning in text, xli

Carlyle, Thomas, xxvi, 43, 45n19

Charlemagne, debate question about, xxii, 94, 97n6, 100

160   Index

Charleston Library Society, xii, xiv, xxvii
Chrestomathic Literary Society (College of Charleston), xxi, xxii, xxxvin39
Christian Benevolent Society, 25
Christianity: in annual oration, xxv; scripture uses, xxv, 23n14, 65n20, 113n2, 114n12, 115n19, 127n2
churches, in free Black community, xvii–xviii
Cicero, debate question about, 57, 65n15
Citadel cadets, 52, 64n6
city life, debate question about, 52
civilization advancement, debate questions about, xxiii, 54, 55, 88, 89
civilized life, debate question about, 10
Civil War military service, xxx–xxxi, 64n11, 127n5, 136n
Clark, William B., 39
Clio, in Greek mythology, 44n4, 102, 103, 106, 116
Clionian Debating Society, overview: archive creation, xxvii–xxviii; debating procedures and questions, xx–xxiv, 141–45; library collection, xxv–xxvii, 149–51; membership characterized, xi–xii, xvi–xvii; members listed, 139–40; national context, xiii–xiv; orations, xxiv–xxv, 147; origins of bound minutes, xii–xiii; regional context, xvii–xix, xxxviin50; as safe social space, xvi–xvii, xxviii–xxxii; self-governance principle, xvi–xvii, xix–xx; significance of minutes for history, xiv–xv. See also specific topics, e.g., Beaird entries; library collection; membership decisions
Cliosophic Literary Society (College of Charleston), xxi, xxxvin39
Cliosophic Society (College of New Jersey), xvi
College of Charleston, xxi, xxvi, 9n12, 84nn8–9
College of New Jersey, xvi
Columbian Orator (Bingham), xviii
commerce, debate question about, 47, 48
Committee of Queries, purpose, xx. See also debating activity, overview

Committee on Contracts and Building, 37–38
Committee on General Interests: purpose, 23n16; at the 1848–1849 meetings, 21, 24, 25, 26, 36, 38, 40; at the 1850 meetings, 50, 51, 63; at the 1851 meetings, 69–70, 73, 74, 75, 78, 82–83; at the 1852 meetings, 87, 88, 90, 91–92, 94; at the 1853–1856 meetings, 102–4, 109, 112, 123, 130
Committee on Revision of Rules, 105, 120
committees for thank yous. See thank you actions
composer responsibility, debate question about, 72, 73
constitution, new member readings and signings: at the 1848–1849 meetings, 12, 13, 41; at the 1851 meetings, 73, 79; at the 1852 meetings, 92–93, 96
constitution, original approval, 3
constitution, proposed changes: at the 1847–1849 meetings, 6, 14–15, 16, 17, 18, 28, 41; at the 1851 meetings, 71, 73, 80, 81; at the 1852–1854 meetings, 95, 104–5, 120
Cotarae, 43
country life, debate question about, 52
Crimean War, xxii, 123n2
Crito, debate question about, 122, 124n7, 126
Cromwell, debate question about, 59, 65n18
cultivated mind, in annual oration, xxv, 129
curfews, Black community, xxiv
current events, as debate question theme, xxi–xxii

Deas, Hannah G., 136n
Deas, Robert L.: as annual orator, 118, 120, 130, 134; biographical highlights, 136n; death, 136n; debater appointments, 52, 59, 67, 75, 87, 100, 110, 126; donations, 52, 53, 69, 74, 114n15; in Friendly Association, 114n18; membership admission, 40, 41; memorial

page, 114n11; office positions, 49, 57, 75, 91, 106, 114n17; as semiannual orator, 71, 107, 112

Deas, Robert L. (committee appointments): at the 1849 meetings, 41, 43; at the 1850 meetings, 47, 50, 51, 58, 63; at the 1851 meetings, 68, 74, 78, 81, 82; at the 1852 meetings, 92, 95, 96; at the 1853–1858 meetings, 104, 105, 135

Deas, Robert L. (motions/proposals): debate deferral, 130; meeting dates, 58, 59, 61, 95; oration copy request, 92; semiannual orator election, 83; thank you actions, 57, 58, 61, 78

death penalty, debate question about, xxiii, 33, 48

The Debater (Rowton), xxi

debating activity, overview: procedures, xx–xxi; questions and decisions listed, 141–45; questions characterized, xxi–xxiv

debating traditions, history overview, xv–xvii

Dellquest, Augustus Wilfrid, xii

Dellquest, Augustus William, xii, xiii

Dellquest, Grace Gruber, xii

Demosthenes, debate questions about, 48, 57, 63n2, 65n15

Dereef, Joseph Moulton Francis: committee appointments, 31; letter presentation, 122; membership admission, 5; in membership list, 9n13; office positions, 16, 92, 121; as semiannual orator, xxiv, 113, 118, 120

Dereef, Joseph Moulton Francis (debater appointments): at the 1849 meetings, 42; at the 1850–1852 meetings, 52, 59, 63, 75, 87; at the 1853–1855 meetings, 100, 109, 122, 126

Dereef, Richard E., xviii, 22, 126, 127n4, 133, 134n

destiny of man, in annual oration, 85

Dick, Thomas, 88, 105

diploma proposal, xxiii, 56

dishonesty, debate question about, 34, 35

dissolution, committee for, xx, xxxvn33, 135

distance of dominions, debate question about, xxxi, 101–2

The Doctrine of the Unity of the Human Race . . . (Bachman), xxvi–xxvii, 122, 124n5

donations, 6, 12, 23n5, 35, 39. *See also* library collection, donations

Drago, Edmund L., xiv, xxiii, xxxvin39

Du Bois, W. E. B., xxix–xxx

Duke of Wellington, 83n2, 90, 97n3

Duke University, xii

education: debate question about, 63; in orations, xxv, 37, 70, 125; in pamphlet speech, xxvi; restrictions for free Blacks, xiii, xviii, 9n12; value in Black community, xviii, xxviii–xxx

Egypt a Witness for the Bible (Hawks), 63, 65n23

elections, rules about, 21, 41, 110. *See also* annual orator; membership decisions; office positions; quarterly orator; semiannual orator

emigration, debate question about, xxiii, 88, 89

enforcement clause, constitution proposal, 15

England, debate questions about: at the 1848–1849 meetings, 22, 29, 36, 44n5; at the 1850 meetings, 59, 65n18; at the 1854 meetings, xxii, 118–19, 123n3

Enterpean Debating Society, xvii, 21, 25

epidemic, 59, 65n17

Ethiopia, in annual oration, xxv, 125, 127n2

Europe, debate questions about, 67, 69, 83n2, 84n4, 86–87. *See also* England; France; Napoleon

evil or good, debate question about, 127, 131

expiration clause, constitution proposal, 15

fairs, debate questions about, 71, 72, 119

Farbeaux, Emma K.: biographical highlights, 44n13; donations, xxvi, 47,

162   *Index*

58; letter from Payne, 54; thank you recipient, 39, 40, 48, 61

Farbeaux, Jacob, 43, 44n13, 48

finances: at the 1847–1849 meetings, 6, 25, 26, 28, 32, 37, 42, 43; at the 1850 meetings, 47, 50, 51, 56, 62, 63; at the 1851 meetings, 67, 68, 69, 71, 74, 75, 79, 81, 82; at the 1852 meetings, 88, 89, 92, 93, 94, 96; at the 1853 meetings, 102, 105, 109, 110; at the 1854–1856 meetings, 117, 130

fire in Charleston, 54, 64n12

Fisher, Richard Swainson, xxvi, 84n11

Fitchett, E. Horace, xiv

flattery, debate question about, 117–18

Florida, debate question about, 106, 107–8, 113n9

Flowers Collection, xii–xiii

foreign broils, debate question about, 93

Forgotten Readers (McHenry), xvi

Forrester, Alexander C.: committee appointments, 78, 92; death, xxxi, 107, 114n10; debater appointments, 75, 88, 101; letter presentation, 75; membership admission, 73; office positions, 82, 89, 91, 94; as semiannual orator, 81, 83

founding members, 8n2

Fourth of July oration, Mitchell's, 53, 64n10

France, debate questions about: at the 1849 meetings, 30, 38, 44n6, n12; at the 1854 meetings, xxii, 118–19

Franklin, Benjamin, xvi, 63, 65n23

Franklin, William Temple, 63, 65n23

free Black community, xvi–xix, xxvii, xxix

The French Revolution (Carlyle), xxvi, 43, 45n19

Friendly Association, xxvii, 23n4, 97n4, 114n18, 127n5, 136n

Friendly Moralist Society, xxvii, 44n3

Friendly Union Society, 9n15, 43, 97n2, 127n4

Frost, Henry, 105

Fugitive Slave Act, xv

furniture donation, 35

Gadsden Purchase, 97n5

Gailliard/Gaillard, William H.: as annual orator, xxiv, 48, 50, 66; conflict with Jacob Greene, xix, xxxvn32, 11; deliveries of membership applications, 86, 93; donation, 53; eulogy for member, 107; in founding members list, 8n2; honorary member vote, 8; letter presentations, 72, 86, 93; in members list, 9n13; praise for departing members, 15–16; as quarterly orator, xxiv, 22, 32; as semiannual orator, 126

Gailliard/Gaillard, William H. (committee appointments): at the 1848–1849 meetings, 16, 19, 26, 31, 43; at the 1850 meetings, 48, 56, 58; at the 1851 meetings, 68, 78; at the 1852 meetings, 88, 96; at the 1853 meetings, 105, 109, 112

Gailliard/Gaillard, William H. (debater appointments): at the 1847–1849 meetings, 8, 11, 15, 18, 29, 33; at the 1850 meetings, 47, 52, 59; at the 1851–1852 meetings, 67, 75, 88; at the 1853–1855 meetings, 110, 126

Gailliard/Gaillard, William H. (motions/proposals): about constitution, 28, 69; building rental, 111, 112; committee formations, 8, 96; honorary members, 10, 22, 88, 105, 108; library purchase, 52; meeting dates, 95, 104; oration copy requests, 43, 70; reading of Bass and Payne letters, 54; second by, 107; thank you actions, 61, 103; semiannual orator election, 78; timing of annual orator election, 47

Gailliard/Gaillard, William H. (office positions): at the 1848 meetings, 13, 19; at the 1850 meetings, 49; at the 1851 meetings, 67, 68, 73, 80, 82; at the 1852 meetings, 85, 86, 93

games, debate question about, 109–10, 111

Garibaldi, Giuseppe, 44n12

genius: in annual oration, 32–33; debate question about, xxii, 80, 82, 83

geology speech, Brumby's, xxvi, 53, 64n8

Index

George Washington Flowers Collection, xii–xiii

"the good fight" term, 17, 23n14

good or evil, debate question about, 127, 131

government forms, debate questions about, 8, 10, 79, 80

government stability, debate question about, 119, 121–22

grammar differences, treatment in text, xli

Gray, Thomas, 114n15

Great Britain. *See* England, debate questions about

great events, debate question about, 126, 127

Greeks, debate questions about: at the 1850 meetings, 54, 55, 58–59, 65n16; at the 1851–1853 meetings, 67, 89, 109–10

Greene/Green, G. C.: bylaws proposal, 6, 7–8; in founding members list, 8n2; letter to honorary members elect, 10; in members list, 9n13; secretarial style, 9n10, n16; resignation, 14

Greene/Green, Jacob J., Jr.: conflict with Gailliard, xix, xxxvn32, 11; debater appointments, 4, 11; in founding members list, 8n2; honorary member vote, 8; in membership list, 9n13; membership proposals, 5; resignation, 14

Greene/Green, Jacob, Sr., 8

green oasis metaphor, xxviii–xxxii

Green-Wood Cemetery, 127n5

Greer, John Mayne, xii

Grimball, John B., Jr., 86

Grimshaw, William, xxvi, 43, 45n19

A Guide to Forming and Conducting Lyceums . . . (Morley), xxi

Hampton, Benjamin E. K.: as annual orator, 117, 118; constitution discussion, 120; debater appointments, 48, 54, 61, 69, 89, 103, 111, 127, 131; membership admission, 40, 41; motion, 41; motion second by, 43; office positions, 49, 60, 73, 86, 100, 130; as semiannual orator, 80; thank you recipient, 81

Hampton, Benjamin E. K. (committee appointments): at the 1849 meetings, 41, 43; at the 1850 meetings, 47, 50, 63; at the 1852–1853 meetings, 91–92, 103, 105

handwritten text, examples, *4, 77*

Hannibal, debate question about, xxii, 14, 15, 23n10

happiness: debate questions about, 22, 75, 83, 86, 109; in quarterly oration, 50

Harvard, xvi

Hawks, Francis L., xxvi, 63, 65n23

Hayne, Robert Y., xxxviin50

Hine, Darlene Clark, xxix, xxx

history, as debate question theme, xxii, xxxvin43, 40

History of England . . . (Macaulay), xxvi, 41, 45n16

History of France (Grimshaw), xxvi, 43, 45n19

Holbrook, Josiah, xvi, xxxiiin13

Holloway, Charles H., xviii, 16, 23n13, 66, 114n18

Holloway, Elizabeth Mitchell, 23n13

Holloway, Frances Pinckney (earlier Bonneau), xviii, xxvi, 68, 70, 84n3

Holloway, Richard S.: as annual orator, xxv, 119, 126, 129; biographical highlights, 84n3; committee appointments, 112; debater appointments, 113, 131; membership admission, 84n3, 101, 104–5, 106; office positions, 123, 125

honorary members: function of, 9n15; listed, 140

Horry, Augustus L.: committee appointments, 31, 39, 43, 58; donations, 35, 78, 82, 119; as honorary member, 96, 108–9; membership admission, 26; office positions, 67, 70, 71; participation summarized, xxviii; as quarterly orator, xxiv–xxv, 51, 58; resignation, 95–96

Horry, Augustus L. (debater appointments): at the 1849 meetings, 30, 34, 38; at the 1850 meetings, 48, 53, 60; at the 1851–1852 meetings, 68, 76, 89

Index

Huger, Benjamin T., xviii, 8, 29, 32, 44n9, 89–90, 97n2

Hyames/Hyams, Isadore A.: committee appointments, 31, 43, 51, 74, 78, 104, 123; death, 127n5; departure letter, 127n5; in Friendly Association, 23n4, 114n18, 127n5; letter presentations, 40, 88; membership admissions, 12, 23n9, 26, 28; office positions, 14, 40, 62, 80, 101; resignation, 15–16, 88; as semiannual orator, 81

Hyames/Hyams, Isadore A. (debater appointments): at the 1848–1849 meetings, 14, 30, 34, 38; at the 1850–1851 meetings, 47, 53, 60, 67–68, 76; at the 1852–1855 meetings, 89, 101, 111, 127

improvement of individual, debate question about, xxii, 132

improvements, debate question about, 100, 101

improvement spirit, debate question about, 119

improver praise, debate question about, 52–53

independence declaration, debate question about, xxi, 5

Indians, debate question about, 106, 107–8, 113n9

industry, debate question about, xxii, 80, 82, 83

industry spirit, debate question about, 119

influence, in annual oration, 99

intellect, debate question about, 75

intellectual culture, in annual oration, 134

intellectual excellence, debate question about, 74, 75

intemperance, debate question about, 34

interlineations, indications of, xli

intestine commotions, debate question about, 93

inventor praise, debate question about, 52–53

Irish treatment, debate question about, 36

Jacobs, Harriet, xv

Japan, 115n21

Jenkins, Earnestine, xxix, xxx

Johnson, J., 10

Josephus, Flavius, xxvi, 126, 127n3

Junto club, xvi

justice, debate question about, 48

just side in war, debate question about, 18, 19, 20

Kett, Joseph F, xxxiiin13

knowledge, in annual oration, 66. See also education

Koger, Larry, xviii

Kohne, Eliza Neufville, 44n13

Lafayette, debate question about, 108, 114n13

land-based machines, debate question about, 15

laws, debate question about, 102–4

learning, as debate question theme, xxii. See also education

Lee, Arthur Bonneau, 122, 123, 125

Legare, R. F., 12, 14, 15–16

"let your light so shine" phrase, 112, 115n19

library collection: overview, xxv–xxvii, xxx, xxxviin70, 149–51; archival purpose, xxvii–xxviii, 26; displays, 47, 116; purchases, 52, 58, 63, 82–83; rules motions, 28, 36, 37

library collection, donations: at the 1849 meetings, 24, 25, 26, 43, 44n2; at the 1850 meetings, 47, 48, 52, 53, 58; at the 1851 meetings, 69, 74, 78; at the 1853–1855 meetings, 114n15, 119, 122, 126

life imprisonment, debate question about, 33, 34, 44n11

Lindsay, J. F., 88–89, 91, 97n4, 114n18

liquor laws, debate question about, 109, 114n16

literacy. See education; library collection; reading

literary box, 6

literary glory, debate question about, xxii, 5, 8

Index

literature, debate questions about, 10–11, 79, 80. *See also* education; reading
Long, Florian H., 8, 13
Lopez de Santa Anna, Antonio (debate question about), 76, 79, 84n10
Lord, W. S., 93, 94, 96, 104, 117, 123, 131
Ludeke, Ada L., 136n
Ludeke, Conrad D.: biographical highlights, xxx–xxxi, 136n; committee appointments, 96, 109, 135; death, 136n; debater appointments, 103, 113, 131; membership admission, 86, 90–91, 92–93; office positions, 100, 119, 126; participation summarized, xx
Ludeke, Elizabeth Chloe Sparrow Wrigley Esmond, 136n
Ludeke, Julia Brennan, 136n
Luther, Martin (debate question about), 51, 64n4
lyceums, xvi
Lycurgus, debate question about, 58–59, 65n16

Macaulay, Thomas Babington, xxvi, 41, 45n16
machines, debate question about, 15
Maine, debate question about, 109, 114n16
Marks, John Garrison, xi–xii, xix, xxxixn92
married life, debate question about, 75, 76
Marshall, William E.: membership admission, 5; in membership list, 9n13; membership problem, 43, 45n20, 47, 79; office positions, 16, 19, 51, 135; request for debate presentation, xxvii, 11; as semiannual orator, 93, 103, 105
Marshall, William E. (debater appointments): at the 1848–1849 meetings, 11, 36, 39; at the 1850–1851 meetings, 48, 57, 61, 71, 79; at the 1852–1856 meetings, 90, 106, 118, 132
Maxwell, Stephen J.: committee appointments, 68, 81, 94, 96; in founding members list, 8n2; in membership list, 9n13; office positions, 3, 16, 19, 58,

59, 60, 87; as quarterly orator, xxx, 59, 70
Maxwell, Stephen J. (debater appointments): at the 1847–1849 meetings, 4, 18, 36, 38; at the 1850 meetings, 48, 54, 61; at the 1851–1852 meetings, 69, 79, 89; at the 1853–1856 meetings, 104, 117, 131
McElligott, James N., xxi
McHenry, Elizabeth, xvi
McKinlay, William, xviii, 21
McKinney, William, 105
Meagher, Thomas Francis (debate question about), 118, 119, 123n3
mechanical employment, debate question about, 83, 86
mechanical pursuit, debate question about, 37, 38
meet, the term, 60, 65n20
members, regular, listed, 139–40
membership application clause, constitution proposal, 15, 16
membership decisions: at the 1847–1849 meetings, 5, 12, 19–20, 26, 28, 40; at the 1851 meetings, 72–73, 75, 76, 77, 78; at the 1852 meetings, 86, 88–89, 90–91, 94, 96; at the 1853 meetings, 101, 104, 106, 110; at the 1854–1855 meetings, 122, 123, 125
mental culture, in semiannual oration, 92
Mexican Cession, 97n5
Mexico, debate questions about: at the 1847–1848 meetings, 4, 5, 8n8, 18, 19, 20; at the 1851 meetings, 76, 84n10
Miles, James Warley, xxvi, 74, 84n9
military careers, as debate question theme, xxii
military glory, debate question about, xxii, 5, 8
military protection, debate question about, 38, 39
minutes disputes, xix, 11–12, 13, 15, 48–49
Mishaw, John, xviii, 8, 89–90, 97n2
Mitchell, Nelson, 53, 64n10
modern history, debate question about, xxii, 40, 42

166   *Index*

modern literature, debate question about, 10–11

monarchical government, debate question about, 8, 10

The Monuments of Egypt (Hawks), xxvi, 63, 65n23

Mood, Francis Asbury, xviii, xxi, xxxvn27, 6, 9n12, 11, 41, 42

Mood, Henry, xxxvn27

Mood, John Amos, xviii, xxxvn27, 6, 9n12, 10, 11

Mood, John (father), xxxvn27

Mood, William, xviii, xxxvn27, 6, 9n12

Moore, Charles H., xxxviin70

Moore, Thomas, xxvi, 68, 84n3

moral culture, in annual oration, 134

moral excellence, debate questions about, 74, 75, 119, 121–22

moral purity, debate question about, 52

Morley, Charles, xxi

mother or wife prayer question, 32, 33

mottos, 39–40, 41

multum in parvo, 11, 22n2

Myers, Amrita Chakrabarti, xviii

Napoleon, debate questions about: as persistent topic, xxii; at the 1848–1849 meetings, 14, 15, 16, 17, 18, 23n10, 29, 44n5; at the 1851–1852 meetings, 67, 69, 83n2, 90, 93, 97n3

naval protection, debate question about, 38, 39

neglected genius, in annual oration, 32–33

New and Old Book Shops, xii

Newton, Isaac (in annual oration), 125, 127n1

Noble Deeds of Woman (Starling), xxvi, 63, 65n23

"no man liveth to himself" phrase, 99, 113n2

O'Brien, Michael, xiv

O'Brien, William Smith (debate question about), 118, 119, 123n3

office positions, elections: at the 1847–1849 meetings, 3, 16, 19, 20, 28–29, 35, 42; at the 1850 meetings, 48, 49–50, 55, 56, 62, 63; at the 1851 meetings, 68, 73, 81; at the 1852 meetings, 87, 90, 91, 93; at the 1853 meetings, 102, 103, 108, 111; at the 1854–1856 meetings, 119, 127, 131. *See also* president; reader; reporter; secretary; treasurer; vice president

office positions, installations: overview, xxiv; at the 1850 meetings, 49–50, 56–57, 63; at the 1851 meetings, 69, 73, 81, 82; at the 1852 meetings, 87–88, 91, 92, 94; at the 1853 meetings, 102, 103, 108–9, 111–12; at the 1854–1856 meetings, 122–23, 125, 131–32

office positions, temporary appointments: at the 1848–1849 meetings, 12, 13, 14, 33; at the 1850 meetings, 51, 58, 59, 60, 61, 62; at the 1851 meetings, 67, 70–71, 72, 73, 75, 80; at the 1852 meetings, 85, 86, 87, 89, 91, 92, 93, 94; at the 1853 meetings, 100, 101, 106, 113; at the 1854–1855 meetings, 117, 121, 126

Oliver, F. H., 3, 5, 8, 8n2, 9n13, 11, 13, 14

oracles, debate question about, 109–10, 111

orations, overview, xxiv–xxv, 147. *See also* annual orator; quarterly orator; semiannual orator

Oregon Country, 97n5

pamphlets of speeches, xxvi, 52, 64nn5–6, n8, n10, 74, 84nn8–9

paper donation, 6

Parker, John S., 8, 18, 20, 21

patriotism, debate questions about, 61, 111, 113, 131

Paul, Christian scripture, 23n14, 65n20

Paulding, James Kirke, xxvi, 43, 45n19

Payne, Daniel A.: biographical highlights, xvii, xviii, xxxvn28, 9n15, 97n2; honorary membership admission, 8; letters, 31, 54, 58; photograph of, 7

penalties clause, constitution proposal, 15

Penny Post, 95, 98n8

Perry, Matthew, 115n21

perseverance: debate question about, xxii, 80, 82, 83; in quarterly orations, xxiv, 43, 58

Index

philosophy, debate question about, 67

Pius IX, 44n7, n12

Plato, 127n7

poetry, debate question about, 67

Pompey, debate question about, xxiii, 89, 90, 97n1

pope banishment, debate question about, 30, 31, 44n7

Porter, Dorothy B., xvi

Porter, William Dennison, 74, 84n8

Powers, Bernard E., Jr., xiv

president position, changes in constitution, 15, 18, 104, 105, 110

president position, temporary appointments: at the 1851 meetings, 68, 73, 82, 83; at the 1854–1855 meetings, 119, 121, 126; at the 1856–1858 meetings, 130–31, 134, 135. *See also* office positions, elections

"President's hat" action, xxix, 104, 106, 107, 109, 111, 113n6, 117, 119

press restraint, debate question about, 11

primitive society, debate questions about, 111, 113, 131

principle, in annual oration, 85

professional pursuit, debate question about, 37, 38

progress, debate question about, 102–4

progressive spirit, debate question about, 126, 127

"The Progress of Poesy" (Gray), 114n15

prosperity, debate question about, 93, 102–4

Protagoras of Abdera, xvi

pro tempore, meaning in minutes, 8n5

protested minutes, xix, 11–12, 13, 15, 48–49

Psalm 68:31, xxv, 127n2

publications. *See* library collection

public opinion, debate question about, 117–18

publisher responsibility, debate question about, 72, 73

punishment, debate question about, 39

quarterly orations: characterized, xxiv; listed, 147; resolutions/motions about, 15, 36, 58, 59

quarterly orations, deliveries: at the 1848–1849 meetings, 14, 22, 42–43; at the 1850–1851 meetings, 50, 58, 70. *See also* semiannual orations, deliveries

quarterly orator, elections: at the 1848–1849 meetings, 14, 15, 21, 22, 29, 32, 42; at the 1850 meetings, 51, 59. *See also* semiannual orator, elections

quire, defined, 9n11

quorum, proposed changes, xxii, 15, 133

quorum clause, constitution proposal, 15

Rare Book Shop, xii

reader position, 3, 8, 72, 79, 81

reading: debate question about, 11, 12, 22n3; in semiannual oration, xxiv, 120. *See also* education; library collection

Regulus, debate question about, 62, 65n22

religious toleration, debate question about, 119, 121–22

rental committee, 111, 112, 114n18

reporter position, 3, 12, 16, 19, 100, 101, 126

republican government, debate question about, 8, 10

revenge, debate question about, 42

Revision of Rules Committee, 105, 120

revolutions, debate questions about: at the 1851 meetings, 69, 76, 84n4, n10; at the 1853 meetings, 108, 114n13

rewards: debate question about, 39, 40; in annual oration, xxiv–xxv, 116

riches, debate question about, 29, 30

Roberts, Benjamain L.: as annual orator, xxv, 121, 122, 125, 127n1; biographical highlights, xxxviin61; committee appointment, 123; debater appointments, 118, 132; membership admission, 110; office position, 121

Roberts, Catherine Dereef, xxxviin61

Roberts, E. Rainey, xxxviin61

Rollin, Charles, 47, 63n1

romance reading, debate question about, 11, 12, 22n3

Romans 14:7, 113n2

Romans, debate question about, 54, 55

Rome, debate question about, 38, 44n12. *See also* Caesar; Regulus

168   *Index*

Rowton, Frederic, xxi

Rubicon, debate question about, 61, 62, 65n21

rude society, debate questions about, 111, 113, 131

rule book change, 19, 23n16

Russia, debate question about, xxii, 118, 119

Sanders, Robert: committee appointments, 96, 102, 104; debater appointments, 80, 90, 106, 118; membership admission, 78; office positions, 85, 87, 93; as semiannual orator, 119, 122, 126

Santa Anna, Antonio Lopez de (debate question about), 76, 79, 84n10

savage life, debate question about, 10

Scenes in Spain, 43, 45n19

schooling restrictions, free Blacks, xiii, xviii, 9n12

Schweninger, Loren, xviii

sciences, debate question about, xxii, 80, 82, 83

Scott, Winfield, 8n8

scripture, xxv, 23n14, 65n20, 113n2, 114n12, 115n19, 127n2

secretary position, temporary appointments: at the 1848 meetings, 12, 13, 14; at the 1851–1853 meetings, 70–71, 106; at the 1854–1855 meetings, 119, 121, 127. *See also* office positions, elections

Select Convivial Society, 43, 45n21

Self-Cultivation (Porter), 84n8

self-governance principle, xvi–xvii, xix–xx

semiannual orations, deliveries, 92, 103, 105, 111, 112, 147

semiannual orator, elections: proposed timing change, 79; at the 1851 meetings, 71, 78, 80, 81, 83; at the 1852 meetings, 88, 89, 93; at the 1853 meetings, 107, 112–13; at the 1854–1855 meetings, 118, 119, 122, 126

Seminole, debate question about, 106, 107–8, 113n9

Senate speeches, xxvii, xxx, 52, 64n5

Seymour, William W., 8, 97n2

Shakespearean phrases, 108, 114n12, n14

single life, debate question about, 75, 76

Sketch of the Seminole War, 43, 45n19

slander, debate question about, 117, 118

slavery, xv, xviii, xxii–xxiii, xxvi

society, debate question about, xxii, 132

Society of United Irishmen, 113n6

Socrates, debate questions about: at the 1849 meetings, 33, 44n10; at the 1850 meetings, 48, 63n2; at the 1854–1855 meetings, 122, 126, 127n7

soldier, debate question about, 61

solitude, debate question about, xxii, 132

Solon, debate question about, 58–59, 65n16

Souls of Black Folk (Du Bois), xxix–xxx

Spartans, debate question about, 89

spelling differences, treatment of, xli

sperm candles donation, 12, 23n5

Spy Club (Harvard), xvi

Squires, Catherine R., xix

Starling, Elizabeth, xxvi, 63, 65n23

State Military Academies (Capers), 64n6

statesman, debate question about, 61

steam power, debate questions about, 13, 16, 36

Stent, Marion L., 88–89, 91, 97n4, 114n18

success, debate question about, 127, 131

supporters, listed, 140. *See also* donations

sword's value, debate question about, 87, 88

taxes, 44n13, 114n10, 136n

telegraph, debate question about, 36

territory increase, debate question about, 94, 97n5, 131

Texas annexation, 97n5

thank you actions: at the 1849 meetings, 39, 40, 41, 42, 43; at the 1850 meetings, 47, 48, 52, 53, 57, 58, 60–61; at the 1851–1854 meetings, 68, 70, 78, 81, 103, 122

Themistocles, debate question about, 57, 65n14

2 Thessalonians, 65n20

Index

169

"thrice welcomed" phrase, 108, 114n14
1 and 2 Timothy, 23n14
trade, debate question about, 113, 117
transcription process, xli–xliii
treasurer position, temporary appointments, 12, 13, 14, 16, 19. *See also*
finances; office positions, elections; secretary position, temporary
appointments
Treaty of Guadalupe Hidalgo, 8n8
"trumpet tongues must cease" phrase,
108, 114n12
Turkey, debate question about, xxii, 118,
119

University of North Carolina, xvi
Utopian Debating Society: at anniversary celebrations, 46, 66, 85; as
concurrent debating society, xvii;
donation, 26; invitations, 39, 43, 63,
78, 83, 96

Van Diemen's Land, 123n3
vice president position, temporary appointments: at the 1848–1849 meetings, 14, 33; at the 1850 meetings, 51,
58, 59, 60, 61, 62; at the 1851 meetings,
67, 70–71, 72, 73, 75, 80; at the 1852
meetings, 85, 86, 87, 89, 91, 92, 93, 94;
at the 1853 meetings, 100, 101, 106, 113;
at the 1854–1855 meetings, 117, 121,
126. *See also* office positions, elections
vote by president clause, constitution
proposal, 15

war, debate questions about, 42, 61, 113.
See also Mexico; military *entries*
Washington, George (debate questions
about), 14, 23n8, 51
Washington, Sarah E., 132n2
water-based machines, debate question
about, 15
Waterloo, debate question about, xxii,
90, 93, 97n3
Watt, James (in annual oration), 125,
127n1
Webster's Dictionary, 43, 45n18

Wellington, debate question about, xxii,
90, 93, 97n3
Weston, Hannah Clark, 97n7, 136n
Weston, Jacob, xviii, 8, 9n15, 85, 99,
113n1, 134
Weston, Lydia, 137n
Weston, Monimia, 136n
Weston, Samuel (honorary member): at
anniversary celebrations, 24, 116, 129;
biographical highlights, xviii, 9n15,
136n; honorary membership admission, 8
Weston, Samuel W. (regular member):
debater appointments, 5, 10, 12; family relationships, 9n15; in founding
members list, 8n2; in membership list,
9n13; motions by, 5, 6, 8, 11, 12, 14; as
quarterly orator, 5, 14; resignation, 14
Weston, William O.: as annual orator, xxiv, 67, 68, 86, 95, 96, 99–100;
biographical highlights, xviii, 136n;
Clio appreciation, 44n4; donation,
52; donor's gift presentation, 47; family relationships, 9n15, 97n7, 113n1;
in founding members list, 8n2; letter
presentation, 26; on member resigna-
tions, 15–16; membership discussions,
28; in membership list, 9n13; minutes
disputes, 49, 96; mother's death,
97n7; office positions, 12, 13, 14, 16,
48, 71, 93, 134; as quarterly orator,
xxiv, xxv, xxvii, 29, 37
Weston, William O. (committee appointments): at the 1847–1849
meetings, 3, 19, 26, 39–40, 43; at the
1850 meetings, 47, 51, 56, 58, 63; at the
1851–1852 meetings, 69, 81, 96; at the
1853–1858 meetings, 102, 105, 135
Weston, William O. (debater appointments): at the 1848–1849 meetings,
10, 12, 15, 36, 39; at the 1850 meetings,
51, 57, 61; at the 1851–1852 meetings,
71, 80, 93; at the 1853–1854 meetings,
108, 118
Weston, William O. (motions/proposals):
bylaws changes, 40; committee formations, 19, 105; constitution changes, 6,

14–15, 16, 28, 40–41; debate deferrals, 28, 54; debate question, 20; honorary members, 21; invitation to Utopian Debating Society, 96; meeting dates, 20, 29, 56; oration copy requests, 25, 50–51, 58, 105, 121; reading of Bass and Payne letters, 54; seconds by, 20, 21, 22, 25, 41, 50, 52, 53, 55; thank you actions, 53, 60–61

What to Read . . . (C. Moore), xxxviin70

wife or mother prayer question, 32, 33

Wikramanayake, Marina, xx

Wilson, Kirt H., xxx

women: at anniversary celebrations, 116, 123n1, 125, 133–34; donations from, xxvi, 39, 47, 58, 68; in free Black community, xvii

World's Fair, debate question about, 71, 72, 84n7

yellow fever, 124n6

youth discipline, debate question about, 89